From Lancaster, Berks, Chester, Dauphin, Lebanon and York Counties

GOD STORIES
THREE

The Regional Church of Lancaster County
www.theregionalchurch.com

Photo by Mim Hurst

God Stories 3

ISBN: 978-0-9760387-3-3

Printed in the United States of America

Dedication

This book is dedicated to the people of
South Central Pennsylvania.

Photo by Sylvan Ressler

Acknowledgments

Thank you to the many contributing authors who made this book possible.

Edited by Karen Boyd, Stephanie Eshleman, Sharon Neal, Cindy Riker, Tracy Stoltzfus, Kim Wittel and Keith Yoder.

House To House Publications Team: Brenda Boll, Karen Ruiz, and Sarah Sauder.

Proofreaders: Kathy Nolt, Denise Sensenig and Carolyn Sprague.

Cover photos by Mark Van Scyoc and Kristi Sommers

Introduction

One of the most powerful witnesses of God's love is the relational biblical unity of His people. God Stories 3 is one such witness. In the pages that follow, you will meet followers of Christ from many communities, walks of life, and ages.

Their stories honor the way God provides direction, steps in to protect, and does things that are humanly impossible. They note the way He has shown Himself in the words of a child, ordinary circumstances, and difficult situations. These stories are cause for worship!

The story tellers are neighbors throughout the region of south central Pennsylvania. When God looks upon His Church across our several counties, He sees more than our separate camps, communions, confessions and councils. He sees a "regional church," made up of believers in every community, congregation, and walk of life. He acknowledges our individual forms of church, but He knows us in a much larger and more fully relational context. He sees His children—His family.

As we draw encouragement from these stories daily, let us also pray for others in our region according to the message of the day. We may know of one who would be helped by the story of the day—share it with them. We may be prompted by the Holy Spirit to lay aside an attitude of pride or separation concerning those who follow Christ from a different perspective.

Day by day our region will be less conformed to the mold of the world system and more transformed unto the Kingdom of God. One by one we will more fully show the world the relational biblical unity for which Christ prayed and died. Increasingly, the world will know the Father has sent His Son. Jesus Christ, the Lord, is the way that the world will see and know our Father.

To this end, *God Stories 3* is dedicated on behalf of the partnership of the networks throughout the region as described at the back of this book, beginning on page 383.

—Keith Yoder

January

Open Eyes And Open Doors

"...open your eyes and look at the fields! They are ripe for harvest!"
John 4:35

"And pray for us...that God may open a door for our message..."
Colossians 4:3

I wasn't feeling very evangelistic that morning. I just wanted to fill my car with gas and keep moving. After I had figured out the computerized pump, I overheard a man across from me expressing his frustration with the system.

"Can I give you a hand?" I said as I stepped across the island.

"Sure!" He growled in irritation.

Yet, as my eyes fell on his, a sudden spark of compassion ignited my heart. It was as if I could feel the sadness and loneliness of this man's heart.

After connecting his car to the pump, I turned to him and said, "Has anyone prayed for you today?"

With a puzzled look, he asked, "Do you work here?" (He may have thought that prayer was part of the "Full Serve" treatment!)

"No, I just felt like God wanted me to pray for you."

Hanging his head, he said, "I don't think anyone's prayed for me in a long time."

His name was Harry. He explained to me that he had gone to church with his grandmother as a boy. During that time he had given his heart to Jesus. "But, I took it back again...and did some pretty bad things with it," he mumbled.

"Harry," I said, putting my hand on his shoulder, "why don't you give it back to Him?"

Without hesitating, Harry prayed one of the most sincere, "non-Christian" prayers of surrender to Jesus.

He told me that his favorite childhood song was "What A Friend We Have In Jesus." We sang it together like drunken sailors. There we stood, two total strangers, with our arms around each other, touched by the presence of the Lord. Open your eyes. The fields are ripe.

Father, open my eyes to see the doors that You are opening around me.

Dave Hess pastors Christ Community Church in Camp Hill.

The Power Of "Not Quitting"

"Then Jesus told his disciples a parable to show them that they should always pray and not give up." *Luke 18:1*

Have you ever felt like quitting? I think most of us have. At the end of 2005, I was feeling overwhelmed with the number of things that seemed to be going wrong around me. It was everything from sickness in our household to financial needs to major breaks in relationships among leaders I was involved with. Finally out of frustration, I sat down and wrote all the things I wanted to see changed. It was a total of seventeen things that I wrote down. I started to pray over these things on a regular basis.

By the end of a few weeks of prayer, five or six of them had changed and I was pretty pumped up. I continued in prayer. By the end of 2006, eleven of the seventeen had changed. Now at the time of this writing, fourteen of the seventeen things have changed. Guess what? I am going to keep praying until I see all of these things change!

This quote by E.M. Bounds has helped me: "An answer to prayer is conditional to the amount of faith that goes with the petition. To test this, He delays the answer. The superficial prayer subsides into silence when the answer is delayed. But the man of prayer hangs on and on. The Lord recognizes and honors his faith, and gives him a rich and abundant answer to his faith-evidencing importunate prayer."

There is an undefeatable power in "not quitting." In order to push through the opposition that we face, we need to first pray through it. Don't be overcome with discouragement. When climbing a mountain, the steepest part is almost always near the top. Jesus' ultimate victory (His resurrection) came out of what looked like a dismal defeat to many who were watching (His death on the cross).

Father, many of us have felt like quitting and some of us feel like quitting right now. But there is a huge difference between feeling like quitting and actually quitting. I pray that faith will rise up on our hearts right now.

Brian Sauder is the director of DCFI's Church Planting and Leadership Training School.

Prayer Cover

"In the same way, the Spirit helps us in our weakness. We do not know what we ought to pray, but the Spirit himself intercedes for us with groans that words cannot express. And he who searches our hearts knows the mind of the Spirit, because the Spirit intercedes for the saints in accordance with God's will." *Romans 8:26-27*

While on a medical mission trip to Kenya, we had the opportunity to pray with a young man who was suffering the effects of cerebral malaria. Unknown to us, the guard translating for us was a Muslim.

Afterward, we learned we should not have asked him to translate during our prayer.

Later in the week, the boy's father approached our guard asking him to find us so that he could report how his son is doing. With the Muslim guard again translating, this man testified how his son is no longer suffering from his previous symptoms! The father was overjoyed and grateful. The Muslim guard kept repeating, "Remember this man, you prayed for his son...you prayed with him."

It's awesome how God covers over our ignorance and weaknesses and uses them for His Glory.

Father, thank you for seeing our hearts and covering over our inadequacies for Your glory! It is not Your desire to see us struggle and fail nor is it Your desire to see others die in sin. We praise You for Your constant faithfulness and presence in our lives.

Loren and Melissa Kreider attend Oasis Fellowship, Ephrata.

Best Laid Plans

"Delight yourself in the Lord and he will give you the desires of your heart." Psalm 37:4

While seeking God's direction in my life, I desired to be married. At the age of 25, I was engaged to a Christian young man. As we started to plan for the wedding day, I didn't have peace in my heart. I was questioning why one evening while praying and the Lord spoke these words, "You may marry him if you would like, but he is not my best for you." Immediately, I knew we needed to part ways and wait for God's best.

Little did I know at that time God would have me wait nine years. During these years, I was involved in a singles' ministry, volunteered at a prison, worked as a secretary with several ministries and found contentment in serving God knowing He had someone special for me in His time.

Yes, I am so glad I waited! This year my husband, Scott, and I will celebrate our 20th wedding anniversary. It has been the best 20 years of my life. God is faithful as we walk in His plan for our lives. I encourage those who desire to have the right partner in marriage to be willing to seek God and wait on Him for His perfect timing. As the Scripture says, "But seek first his Kingdom and his righteousness, and all these things will be given to you as well (Matthew 6:33)."

Thank you, Father, for Your marvelous provision. Help us to always be faithful to Your plan for our lives.

Karen Jackson serves on the eldership team at Oasis Fellowship, Akron.

Long Term Commitment

"Honor your father and mother—which is the first commandment with a promise—that it may go well with you and that you may enjoy long life on the earth." *Ephesians 6:2-3*

I t takes only one mouse to start me and an elephant on a stampede. A rat might cause us both to collapse. Apparently that was not the case with an elderly woman from a suburban Los Angeles home. She had 120 rats, called pets, in her house. She also had 25 bunnies, three parakeets, a dog, a quail and a cockatiel—a virtual animal house.

If that isn't shocking enough, her comment concerning where the rats came from belies her 81 years on this earth. To the city's Animal Service Department, she stated how overwhelmed she was by how quickly the rats reproduced.

Despite the humor, there's definitely a flip side. This woman had no food in her house for herself. She seemed disoriented and had open wounds from bite marks covering her arms. If it were not for someone notifying authorities about "unkempt conditions at the house," she probably would have died an awful death.

Where was her family? It's difficult enough having to get old with all the aches and pains and problems the elderly face. But it's tragic when there's no one to accompany them on the journey, or, at the very least, make sure they are still on the journey.

The Scriptures are crystal clear—we are to honor our parents. This is stated to the Israelites and reiterated in the New Testament several times (*Exodus 20:12; Deuteronomy 5:16; Matthew 15:4; Ephesians 6:2*). Nowhere is the thought conveyed that when they get to a certain age we can ignore them.

The bumper sticker "Be nice to your children. They'll decide your nursing home" has some truth to it. One would hope, however, the entire family unit would stay together out of love, respect and honor, or, at the least, be in contact with one another before the rats take control of the house.

Father, help us honor our parents with love and care, even as You bless us with love and care.

Dr. Dan Allen, pastor, writer, radio commentator and director of Pinebrook Bible Conference, East Stroudsburg.

Integrity

"Furthermore, you shall select out of all the people able men who fear God, men of truth, those who hate dishonest gain…."
Exodus 18:21 (New American Standard)

During the 1930's Depression, my father moved to a cheap one-room apartment in Chicago in the hopes of finding work. He spent most of his days on his feet, walking from business to business, applying at every place he could find. In order to look presentable for job interviews, he purchased "cardboard" shoes—shoes that were very inexpensive, but had a nice-looking black polish. The only problem was that they had cardboard soles and would fall apart if they became wet.

Across the hall from dad's room was a man named Al. Al seemed to always be throwing parties. He took a liking to my father and offered my dad a high paying job—to stand on a certain street corner at a certain time, passing on a package to one of Al's customers.

My dad thought about it for a long time and decided that he did not want to get involved. He was not sure why—he just did not have a good feeling about it. Al tried to convince my dad to take it. He put his arm on my dad's shoulder and said, "C'mon Vernie, it's good money, and I know you won't find such an easy job like this anywhere else! Besides, I know you are hungry and could use a good job."

My dad thanked Al, but told him that it just did not seem right to accept it. Al gave an "okay, no hard feelings" kind of a response, and they went their separate ways. Eventually, dad did get a job in which he could support himself and forgot about the incident. Years later, as he picked up a copy of a newspaper with a picture of his friend, Al, and the headlines "Al Capone, Gangster, Dead," he was especially glad that he did not take the job that "good 'ol Al" offered him.

Sometimes, it is the little decisions we make that prevent us from making big mistakes. I am thankful for the example of integrity that my dad showed me! My dad has since passed on to a better life, but I often remember his stories.

Lord, thank you for those who are an example to us. Help us to be more like You because of their example.

Jim Schneck is a free-lance interpreter for the deaf.

Forgiveness In Rwanda

"Forgive, and you will be forgiven." *Luke 6:38*

A few months ago, I flew with two friends into the nation of Rwanda to speak at a Christian Leadership Convention. We were greeted by church leaders at the airport who took us to the Genocide Museum in Kigali. Even though I had seen the movie "Hotel Rwanda," and had known about the terrible genocide in their nation, I was unprepared to come face to face with one of the worst tragedies in all of history. Over one million people from the Tutsi tribe were slaughtered by their Hutu tribe neighbors within three months. At the Kigali Center alone, there are 256,000 body remains. There are many other memorials throughout the nation, and they are still finding bodies. Many were lured into church buildings by unscrupulous religious leaders who told them they would be safe. The doors would then be locked, the killers called, and every person in the building murdered. Five hundred thousand women were raped, with many infected with HIV—a part of the killers' plan.

My African friends who invited me to Rwanda had been in exile in neighboring Congo during the killings. They came home after the genocide to find their family members murdered and hundreds of thousands of orphans in the land. Most Christian families in Rwanda today have taken orphans into their homes. But they had to face the hard question, could they forgive those who had so ruthlessly murdered their loved ones? God gave them grace to forgive.

Today, in the midst of all of the pain and bad memories, the nation of Rwanda is peaceful. Rwandan Christians are now going into the prisons and sharing the gospel and forgiveness of God through Jesus Christ with those who have murdered their families. After Rwanda, my problems seemed so small. If our brothers and sisters in Africa can forgive and trust God to go on, so can we.

Lord, I forgive every person who has sinned against me, in Jesus' name, and I ask You to bless them for Jesus' sake.

Larry Kreider serves on the executive team of the Regional Church of Lancaster County and as the International Director of DOVE Christian Fellowship International.

God's Faithfulness

"But God chose the foolish things of the world to shame the wise;
God chose the weak things of the world to shame the strong."
1 Corinthians 1:27

As I am writing this, my husband and I are eagerly awaiting our first baby. It is an exciting time and at the same time very nerve-wracking. First of all, the chances of me getting pregnant were slim according to medical standards. And once I did get pregnant, the doctors thought the baby might be small like me. And because of Shawn's heart condition, they thought the baby might have a heart defect. As of this point, God has proven the doctors wrong. The baby is perfectly normal and healthy.

Isn't it great when God shows His power and awesomeness and confounds the wise? I love when He shows His greatness and goes beyond human reasoning. We serve such a faithful and loving God. Why not take some time today and thank Him for the many times He has shown Himself faithful in your life? You will be blessed for it.

Lord, thank you for Your loving-kindness and for showing Yourself faithful. Forgive us for the times we doubt You and, in our minds, limit how powerful You are. We give You all the praise and glory. Amen

Jennifer Paules-Kanode is a DJ for WJTL Radio.

Twenty-Four/Seven

"Therefore be careful how you walk, not as unwise men but as wise, making the most of your time, because the days are evil."
Ephesians 5:15-16 (New American Standard Bible)

As a young boy, I had plenty of time to play ball with the neighbor boys and to ride bike and camp out on islands in the middle of the Susquehanna River. That was then; now time slips through my fingers. The other day I was in a meeting and, almost as if on cue, two of us looked at our watches. Why? We didn't know; it was just a habit. We were more time conscious than people conscious.

Gerhard Geschwandtner writes, "In primitive societies, no one has a watch, but everyone has time. In advanced societies, everyone has a watch, but no one has any time."

In 1994, Fran and I were ministering in Calcutta, India, with our missionaries, Mike and Lora Bordon. Mike suggested we visit Mother Teresa. We said, "Of course!" So without making any phone calls to secure an appointment, we simply went to the place where she stayed, knocked on this small nondescript door, and asked if we could meet with her. In a short time, Mother Teresa came into the room and we had about a ten-minute conversation with her. No appointment, no schedule, no "take a number," and in fact they didn't even ask who we were. We just walked in! I was impressed that her life was more about meeting with people than following a tight time schedule. To this day I doubt very seriously that she ever remembered the day she met Richard and Fran, but we remember the day she met with us!

Lesson learned! People are more important than schedules. I want to be more attuned to understanding the will of the Lord, slowing down, and having meaningful conversations with those in need.

Lord, help us to be mindful of devoting the time needed to strengthen others in need of our words of encouragement. Amen

Richard Armstrong serves as Assistant Director of Worship Center Global Ministries in Lancaster.

Spiritual Alignment

"Do two walk together unless they have agreed to do so?" *Amos 3:3*

I n the early 1970's I found myself in military boot camp. As a teenage Lancaster County boy whose mother made his bed everyday, boot camp was a rude awakening. There were days that the physical and mental pain were so great that I wanted to quit. Everything in me cried out, "**enough!**" As I watched young men break down around me and listened to the drill sergeants scream orders, I came to a very important realization, I could begin to agree with (align myself with) the process or resist the process. Those who kept resisting would one day disappear from our unit, never to be seen again.

To "align" oneself means *to bring into cooperation with a particular group* and to "agree" means *to come to one opinion or mind and to have the same view.* Agreement with the process of making me into a soldier was essential to not just survive in the environment, but to thrive. The military was not changing their procedures to accommodate me.

There is a similar correlation as I see it in the Kingdom of God. Agreement is a critical component. If you agree with what God says you can do, then you can do what He says. Each time that I resist God and do not agree with Him and His Word, I am aligning myself with someone or something else. If I agree with Satan, I empower Satan in my life. If you are a young person and you align yourself with the wrong crowd, you will empower the influence of that crowd in your own life.

Like a car needs an alignment at times, it is appropriate to assess your alignment with God and His Word. 1 Corinthians 2:16 tells us that we have the mind of Christ and the mind of Christ is always in agreement with the Father.

Jesus, help us to fix our thoughts on You today so that we are in spiritual alignment with You.

Steve Prokopchak serves on the apostolic council of DOVE Christian Fellowship International.

Going Long

"...being strengthened with all power according to his glorious might so that you may have great endurance and patience, and joyfully giving thanks to the Father..." *Colossians 1:11-12*

One of my main personality faults is a lack of patience. Ask my wife or any of the staff here at Habitat for Humanity of Chester County. However, over the years I have been reminded on a number of occasions that good things really are meant for those who are patient and enduring.

Five years ago, I came to Habitat for Humanity as the executive director. One of the first things I did was to meet with the mayor of a town to discuss opportunities to work in his community. Habitat had built a couple of homes there a few years ago, but we were overdue for a return. I thought that it was just an opportunity to meet and exchange ideas. The mayor called a few weeks later to tell me that he had a long-time friend of his who was in the market to sell some parcels of land and that he thought Habitat would be the right group to buy them. It only took about two months for us to strike a deal.

Sounds great, right? Well, then came the fun part: environmental testing, subdivision approval, zoning, planning, sewer and water approvals, finding house sponsors, and finally Borough Council approval and building permits. In all it has taken us nearly four and a half years of work just to break ground on five new homes.

So we praise God for giving us the endurance and patience to work through all of the obstacles in order to build for His people in need in Chester County. On a personal level, I *know* that without Him we would not have made it this far.

Father, thank you for providing for the needs of Your people in Your timing, not necessarily in ours.

Chip Huston is the executive director of Habitat for Humanity of Chester County in Coatesville and an elder at Paoli Presbyterian Church.

Broken Heart Healed

"Love never gives up…Love cares more for others than for
self…Love doesn't want what it doesn't have…Doesn't force itself
on others…Isn't always "me first"…Doesn't keep score of the sins of
others…Takes pleasure in the flowering of truth…Puts up with
anything…Trusts God always…Always looks for the best…Never
looks back…But keeps going to the end."
Paraphrase of 1 Corinthians 13:4-7

From the time I was a little girl, I always desired a relationship
with my father, but he was "not available." He had no time for
me. My heart gave up. And he never noticed. He moved away
and didn't bother to leave me a forwarding address.

This year on Father's Day, when I was reading my Bible, I had a
strange prompting to call my Dad who now lives in Florida. I hadn't
spoken to him in years! On the third prompting, I believed it was really
God so I telephoned my Dad to wish him a Happy Father's Day. It was
the usual response. He was cold, indifferent, and full of pride. I ignored
his response and continued in conversation. He began to tell me that he
was scheduled for a major surgical procedure and he may not make it
through. I told him that I would pray for him. He abruptly handed the
phone to my step-Mom. She informed me of the plans if something
should go wrong. My Dad did it again! He rejected me and he rejected
my God! But something was different *inside* of me this time.

I immediately went to prayer on behalf of my Dad. I began to petition the Lord that my Dad would live. Then something swept over me
and I think it was love…suddenly, my Dad's response really didn't
matter. I was free to love him just as he is without expecting to receive
anything in return.

A few days later, I did receive a phone call! My Dad came through
surgery and he is doing well. God answered my prayer. In moments
like this, I stand amazed at the power of God to heal a broken heart and
to set a captive free.

*Father, the spiritual walk of many of Your children is hindered
because they are broken and wounded. Come and heal the
brokenhearted and set the captives free!*

Sharon Weaver serves with Reading DOVE Ministry Center.

To See God's Glory

"...Jesus said, 'If you hold to my teaching, you are really my disciples. Then you will know the truth, and the truth will set you free.'"
John 8:31-32

D id you ever wonder what God looks like? I know that I have often pondered this question. I am intrigued by the glorious mystery that surrounds the omnipotence and awesomeness of God. Even Moses, who spoke with God as a friend does face to face, requested to see God's glory. In Exodus 33, we read that he was covered by God's hand in the cleft of the rock and could only see God's back as His glory passed by Moses.

While we may never fully know the physical appearance of God until we stand before Him, we do know and can claim His characteristics and promises that beautifully define Him. Scripture clearly defines these characteristics. This was fully manifest as the "Word became flesh" in the person of Jesus Christ and is, now, fully available to us through the Holy Spirit. What an awesome plan!

I often ask persons seeking pastoral care what their image of God is or how they envision Jesus. Their answers are as varied as the situations and crises represented. Their answer often reveals how the enemy has effectively distorted the truth and filled their minds with lies and images totally contrary to Scripture. These lies become powerful, consuming, and effective. This only further distances them from truth and experiencing freedom in Christ.

God was concerned about His people and used Moses to lead the Israelites from physical bondage to freedom. He is equally concerned that each of us experience His glory and live in the full freedom we can have in Jesus Christ. He wants His children to be free! The truth of the Word will set us free.

Jesus, anoint me afresh with Your glory today and may I claim my full identity and the freedom I have in being Your child.

Brian E. Martin serves as lead pastor at Weaverland Mennonite Church in East Earl. He and his wife, Shirley, have four children.

Challenging The Hills

"Oh, the depth of the riches and wisdom and knowledge of God!
How unsearchable are his judgments and how inscrutable his ways!"
Romans 11:33 (English Standard Version)

I was flying into Denver, Colorado from Pennsylvania, and in the last 45 minutes of the flight I was mesmerized by the flat farmland that sprawled to the horizon. Green and brown squares, circles, and rectangles were all neatly platted out like a giant quilt before me. It was a serene view and a marvel to behold.

About 30 minutes before touchdown, I saw non-geometric areas among the other shapes beginning to appear. In them ran pencil-thin doodles, like the tiny wrinkles you smooth out in the sheets before the bed is made. I was surprised that such hard-working, resourceful people would allow these areas to go unplowed and fallow. The final approach to Denver showed even more of these messy, blank areas which disturbed the symmetry of the scene. It was only then I realized that the "wrinkles" I was viewing were actually hills and hill formations that must have been large enough and steep enough to the farmers on the ground that their time was better spent working on the flat land.

I smiled to myself as I thought about how God must view the hills in my own life that loom so large to me. His wisdom sees so much in one glance that I could not ever comprehend what that entire glance holds. Yet, even though I instantly judged the farmers for what I thought was an unintelligible decision, His Word tells me there is no condemnation for me when He sees me. That's because He knows the whole picture of my life and dearly loves walking me through what He has created my life to be.

Father, You alone know the big picture of my life today. I pray that when things seem like looming hills to me You would help me, in that moment, to see how You are viewing that instance, my day, my week, and my life. Help me to trust Your wisdom over my own, God. Oh yeah—and God, help me not to judge others so quickly about their hills, too!

Carolyn Schlicher is a homeschooling mother of 5 children in Elizabethtown. Together with her husband, Darryl, they own and operate LiquidWholeFood.com, a nutrition and homeopathy business.

Like A Mighty Wind

"...God sent the Spirit of His Son into our hearts...." Galatians 4:6

"Lord, where is the power that I see when I read the scriptures? Who is living like the early church? I'm not and I don't see anyone else who is." Many times as a teenager and a young mother, I lamented these sentiments and questions to God. I was so hungry for more of Him, but I did not know how to receive.

My sister-in-law, being quite a reader herself, often gave me books to read. In this particular stack was one titled, *Like a Mighty Wind*. It told the story of the Indonesian revival. Drinking in every word of this story, I couldn't put the book down. All of the time my heart was saying, "This is what I need! This is what I want!" Even though I still didn't know how to receive, I constantly asked God for help; I asked Him to show me.

One glorious day, my friend asked me to go along to a Bible study. She said that she had been filled with the Holy Spirit the night before. I answered, "Yes," but the enemy was immediately telling me all the reasons why I shouldn't go. I went, sat on the "hot seat," and they said I spoke in tongues.

In the weeks following, my mind kept saying, "That's you speaking baby talk; that's not the Holy Spirit." One night before bedtime, I told the Lord I was tired of myself, tired of struggling, and I was turning it all over to Him. The next morning I awoke to the air being full of seeming electricity. Later that day, something like a power drill entered my head and exited my feet. I was full of the Holy Ghost and spoke with other tongues. Believe me, I was NEVER THE SAME AGAIN!

Lord, fill me anew daily. I desire to walk in the Spirit.

Sharon Eberly serves with her husband, Lester, at DOVE Westgate Celebration. She co-ordinates an intercessors' team for Sunday mornings.

Contend

"Dear friends, although I was very eager to write to you about the salvation we share, I felt I had to write and urge you to contend for the faith that was once for all entrusted to the saints." *Jude 1:3*

It started one day last spring. A tiny bird landed on the handle of our back door. He began to peck as if he wanted to come in—peck, peck, tap, tap. click, click. After several minutes, he flew away only to return the next morning.

This was so cute, in the beginning. He would stand on the handle of our French doors, knocking. After a few days, we rattled the handle to scare him. He would fly away and then return. This little bird would not give up. In fact, he began to return a few times daily, pecking and pecking at the brass plate surrounding the door handle.

I sensed that this was an illustration of something that the Lord wanted to show us. I asked, "Lord, what are You trying to tell us by this bird?" No answer. After a few weeks, my husband wanted to see him gone! I continued to be amused and to seek the Lord for what He was trying to show us.

Then one day the answer finally came—**contend**! Contend for righteousness, peace, and joy in the Holy Spirit. Contend for those who are lost and without hope. Contend for those who are bound by deceptions and despair. Contend and never give up. It is never too late for God and nothing is too hard for Him, so contend.

Immediately upon hearing "contend" from God, the bird was gone. No more pecking, tapping, or clicking. The message was delivered. The messenger vanished. God is amazing!

Lord, help us to stand firm in united spirit and purpose, striving side by side and contending with a single mind for the faith of the Gospel.

Debra Benedict is a member of Christ Community Church in Camp Hill, serves in the missions ministry, and is a board member of Strategic Global Services Network.

Idols

"... how you turned to God from idols to serve the living and true God who is alive and true and genuine." *1 Thessalonians 1:9b*

As a young boy and then later as a man, I had one goal in mind - to excel in sports. My every waking moment was consumed by baseball, softball, ice hockey, or football. You name it—I loved it! Most of the time, watching others compete was my joy; however, I became actively involved in fast pitch softball and ice hockey. Tripping others, slamming them against the boards, and high sticking in the ribs was normal activity in every hockey game. As the catcher in softball, taunting others at the plate and taking them out just before they reached the plate was pure ecstasy. And jawing at them, face to face, with steam coming out my ears - well, there was nothing better that I could be doing!!

Truly, an idol had taken over my life.

In 1968 and 1969, our team won the State A Soft Ball Championship. We were each given a huge, red, silver and white, gorgeous trophy. By that time, I had received Jesus Christ into my life and my idol was being replaced. Still, there was pride in receiving that beautiful trophy. A shelf was erected in the basement to display IT plus many others, including an MVP award.

But when that trophy was placed on the shelf, it came crashing down; broken. Both my trophy and my pride.

Today, Jesus Christ has totally replaced the idol of sports in my life. Sure, I'm still very knowledgeable in the sports field. I enjoy all kinds of sports, but Jesus is the One I live, breathe and exist for. He consumes me, for HE IS LORD.

Father, thank You for helping us put aside every idol and serve You alone. You are worthy of our lives. Amen

Lester Eberly serves on the leadership team at DOVE Westgate Celebration, working closely with small group leaders, the Young At Heart group, and visiting the sick or those in prison.

The Wounded Travelers...

"Enter in at the narrow gate; for wide is the gate, and broad is the way, that leads to destruction...."
Matthew 7:13 (New King James Version)

The onset of winter was a magical time in my childhood. Along with my four brothers, we could count on endless hours of sledding, ice hockey, and on cold, snowy days, the entertainment of the crash-em-up derby outside our home. That's right, a crash-em-up derby. The poor, unsuspecting victims would drive down our hill and we could expect anywhere from 5 to 10 spin-outs or wrecks during every big storm, throughout the winter.

As a child, I had no perception of the great difficulties and trials that these victims experienced as they ran the Conestoga Road gauntlet. There was one occasion, however, that startled me into reality. Normally, the boom and crash of metal on metal never led to anything serious. One evening, however, that changed significantly. A man was carried into our home, bleeding from the head, and was laid carefully on the floor. *So much for entertainment.* I looked wonderingly at this man and it dawned on me that he was *actually* injured...and suddenly all of my childish illusions disappeared.

The Lord reminded me of this experience and made me aware of what is happening in our current culture. All around us are those who are running the gauntlet of life. They have made choices that have placed themselves on a road to destruction. The moral bankruptcy of me-first narcissism, conscience-numbing sexual license, and life without boundaries and restraint, are leading people to untold heartache and ultimate spiritual peril. And the question is, have I allowed myself to become calloused to both sin and its horrific effect upon these human travelers?

Oh God, keep us from our childish illusions, or from running away from the wounded. May we see the wounds of the broken, and bring them the balm of Gilead. And may their hearts be open to receive the healing mercy that only You can bring.

Scott Lanser is Pastor of New Hope Bible Fellowship in East Hempfield and Director of Associates for Biblical Research.

God's Power

"No temptation has seized you except what is common to man. God is faithful and He will not let you be tempted beyond what you can bear but with the temptation He will also provide a way of escape, so that you are able to bear it." *1 Corinthians 10:13*

I was watching Charles Stanley on TV and he was doing a teaching on prayer. He was saying we spend too much time talking and not enough time listening so we can hear God's voice. That was typical for me, so I thought I would try it.

Alone in my room, I told God that I was ready. What I heard next was something I didn't want to hear. He spoke to me about my 27-year-old habit of smoking. He matter-of-factly told me this was His temple, not mine (1 Corinthians 6:19).

I fell to the floor in despair, for I have tried to quit several times before with no success. The next morning, one cigarette remained in my pack and as if in an out-of-body experience, I smoked it! I couldn't believe it. Though, when I was done, I packed up all my paraphernalia, put it in a trash bag and knew I would never smoke again. I believe He allowed it to make my testimony even greater because you don't start out your day with a cigarette and then quit, especially after 27 years. January 19, 2008, marks five glorious years without smoking. God's grace allowed minimal withdrawal and great success. He's the best antidote on the face of this earth. No pill, patch or any other concoction the world comes up with could ever match His power!

Thank you, Father, for Your power, mercy and grace. I pray that we would all come to see that You are the ultimate Healer and that we would spend more quiet time with You.

Eileen Christiansen, serves as a leader and youth leader for Celebrate Recovery, a Christ-centered 12 Step Recovery program at Kingsway Church in Sadsburryville.

The Value Of Human Life

"So God created man in his own image, in the image of God he created him; male and female he created them." *Genesis 1:27*

Shortly after I was elected to the public school board, I was given an orientation on Special Services or as it used to be called *Special Education*. This is one of the fastest growing areas of expense in our public schools today. Large amounts of money are spent to educate children with special needs and challenges.

As I was interacting with the director of our Special Services, she kept apologizing to me for how much her department was costing the school district and how much the costs were rising each year. As this conversation continued, it seemed like the Lord gave me a download about the value of human life. That is the reason that School Districts spend the amount of money they do on special education each year. In the Western world we have a high value for human life, because we still largely have a Judeo Christian world view.

I shared my revelation with her that money spent on special education is actually a "pro-life" statement. Judging by her response, I don't think it meant as much to her as it did to me, however the point remains that from the first days of Christianity, Christians protected and honored human life regardless of its form or quality.

Early Christians opposed the depravity of the Greeco-Roman society and its infanticide, child abandonment, abortion, human sacrifices and suicide. Widespread slavery in the Greeco-Roman world was also opposed by Christians as well as in England and in America in the 1800's. God loves all the same. All people are His creation.

God...we ask today that You give us a renewed appreciation for the people around us. Some might have physical, mental or emotional challenges, but also some are just different than us one way or another that we might not appreciate. We recognize that all people are Your creation. We want to love all people as You love them.

Brian Sauder is the President of the Manheim Central School Board.

God's Grace Is Sufficient

"Grace, mercy, and peace, which come from God our Father and from Jesus Christ his Son, will be with those who live in truth and love." *2 John 1:3*

In early June 2006 my mother, Doris Groff, was diagnosed with cancer. The doctors gave her three to six months to live. She ended up passing into Heaven *only* a month later on July 5th.

Mom went through her life always loving God, always having an abundance of compassion for others, and always showing an excitement about Heaven as she encouraged other people to come with her. When Mom became ill, she immediately started believing God for her healing and was first in line to let the doctors and nurses know that. Even in her last days, with inadequate strength, she would raise her hands in worship and prayer, never once asking "Why me?" but just completely keeping her heart devoted to God.

God's hand was evident throughout the entire situation. Everything happened quickly, meaning the season of illness was short and she had almost no suffering; yet, God provided just enough time for all of us to say our good-byes. Also, it happened in the beginning of summer before most of my siblings, their spouses, and I had taken our vacation time from work; therefore, we were all readily available to care for Mom.

I share all this to say that though it was tremendously hard for my family and me to lose Mom, afterward we realized that God's grace was sufficient enough to take her in the best way possible - peacefully and without suffering.

God's grace is, and always will be, sufficient for *all* who love Him. We also can *peacefully* enter *the all-perfect* Heaven for all of eternity, and it is through Christ alone we can be sure of this. He is *truly* our provider wherever we have need, and therefore He *is* all we need.

Lord, may Your grace and mercy abound throughout my life, for it is You alone I serve.

Jamie Groff is worship and youth leader at D.O.V.E. Christian Fellowship, Westgate Celebration, Ephrata.

Build My Faith

"We live by faith, not by sight." *1 Corinthians 5:7*

I t was my seventeenth birthday and I had been ministering in Mexico for almost a month. Sitting in a hammock overlooking the Pacific Ocean at the mission base, I prayed a simple prayer: "Lord, please build my faith."

I had no idea that He would answer my cry so soon. That evening, my team was driving an old van back from town which was about forty minutes away from the mission base. All of a sudden the van started sputtering and stalled. It was night and the roads were not safe for us to be parked along. So we started praising the Lord and asking Him to get us home safely. As soon as we started singing praises to Jesus, the van started to work again and whenever we would stop singing the van would stop working. There were times that the van kept going up a hill but the engine had no power. We finally got to the base and pulling into the driveway the van shut off and did not start again. *Thank you,Jesus, for providing.*

God pays attention to every part of our lives. It matters to Him if our car works or does not work. He cares if you have money for the groceries or not. He cares. Many times we just have faith that God can do big things like healings and miracles but we miss out on the everyday things that He cares about, too. Jesus has many great plans for our lives and what better way to live it but by having faith that He will provide for every detail.

Jesus, help me to realize that You care about every part of my life and that You want to be involved in it. Come and build my faith that You can do the little things and also the impossible.

Angela Hoover, intern at Gateway House of Prayer, Ephrata.

Never Give Up

"Now to him who is able to do immeasurably more than all we ask or imagine...to him be glory in the church and in Christ Jesus throughout all generations, for ever and ever! Amen." *Ephesians 3:20-21*

I have to admit that I had given up on my friend Shawn. After prodigal wandering, Shawn had come to faith in Christ at age twenty-four, was full of enthusiasm for the work of Christ, and sensed God's call to vocational ministry. As he pursued his biblical education, he drifted from his evangelical faith and became enamored with liberal theology. In one of our conversations, he talked at length about his enthusiasm for his liberal ideas, unencumbered by any belief in the Trinity or the deity of Christ. I was saddened by his departure from evangelical faith, and because he was so convinced of his new beliefs, sad to say, I gave up on him.

Then as part of his field service for theological education, working at a hospital under the supervision of a Lutheran pastor, Shawn met with frequent situations of emergency, trauma, and death. In this confrontation with reality, he realized that he had no word of hope for grieving people, and, still more seriously, if he did not have Jesus Christ and His gospel at the center of his world, he himself had no place to stand. So, with humility before God he returned to a Christ-centered evangelical faith.

Soon after this, Shawn came to my office to tell me of his re-conversion and to request mentoring in practical ministry. Shawn now has a passion to take the whole gospel of Christ to our world.

We are both rejoicing because of God's grace and mercy at work in Shawn's life.

God, we thank You for Your ongoing redemptive work, bringing people back to You and the truth of Your Word. Help us not to give up hope on any person.

John Hawbaker is senior pastor of Manor Church (Brethren in Christ) located south of Mountville in Manor Township.

Open Wide

"...I came so they can have real and eternal life, more and better life than they ever dreamed of." *John 10:10 (The Message)*

After signing in and finding a seat in the waiting room, I began remembering all the days I had gone without flossing. There were countless other places I would have rather been than in a dentist's office. With my head preoccupied with fears of drills, these words quickly raced across my mind: right big toe, lower back. It was the Holy Spirit! I felt that God wanted me to pray for the people who had these pains.

"Brandon," the assistant said, calling me back.

Sitting down in the chair, I "stepped out of the boat" and said, "I have a random question for you. Do you have any pain in your lower back or your right big toe?"

Wide-eyed and amazed she said, "My back has been killing me today. How did you know that?"

I explained that God loves her so much and cares about her back. As we prayed, I watched the Lord touch her, quickly relieving her pain.

"I think I know who has the right big toe pain!" She said jumping up from her chair.

She was hooked, too! We were both excited to see what else the Lord would do!

Soon she brought another assistant into our little cubicle who had broken her right big toe. We prayed that God would simply do what He said He would do. Within moments, the Lord had healed both of these dear ladies! This was the best trip to the dentist I have ever had!

I am convinced that God wants to turn the most boring places we enter into the most exciting places on the planet. Even if you have never prayed for someone outside of church, today will be your day! Get ready for an adventure with Jesus. There are doors of supernatural excitement waiting for you.

Lord, open my eyes to see what You are doing so that I can flow with Your Spirit today!

Brandon Hess is a student at Penn State, Harrisburg.

It All Belongs To God

"Life does not consist in the abundance of... possessions."
Luke 12:15

During my nine years as a Marine officer, Sharon and I packed up our house eight times. It became a powerful antidote for materialism. We soon learned the futility in the labor of packing and unpacking what we would not use anyway. So we began filling the van with things we had not used since our last move and with things we knew we wouldn't need once we arrived at our new destination.

Though first it was tough letting go, it soon became liberating. Instead of mourning the loss of "our" stuff, it became cathartic to unload our unneeded excess. Even more, it reminded us that all we call ours really belongs to God, and He is the one we should be striving to possess more than mere property. As we learned to give, we discovered the blessing therein, taking joy knowing that someone else would benefit from our surrender.

Now settled in prosperous Lancaster County, I struggle to keep this perspective and teach it to my children. Our society of "militant consumerism" is inculcated with an insatiable lust for the passing material, whose attitude is summed up in the popular Christmas song, *Here Comes Santa Claus*. The chorus rings, "Let's give thanks to the Lord above 'cause Santa Claus comes tonight." It is not Christ, the Lord of the Universe, that enthralls us the most, but the transitory junk we'll get on His birthday. Sadly, we cannot remember what so enamored us last Christmas, and we'll soon forget what it was that we so eagerly anticipated this time around.

The words, "To whom much is given, much will be required" cause me great fear, for few have ever been given more than we.

Lord, You made us to find ultimate satisfaction in Thee; may we not waste our lives pursuing transitory junk, no matter how appealing.

Gibson C. Armstrong is vice president at American PowerNet, an energy management company; a member of Calvary Church; and a former member of the PA House of Representatives.

Faith That Won't Fail

"...Satan has asked to sift you as wheat. But I have prayed for you, Simon, that your faith will not fail. And when you have turned back, strengthen your brothers." *Luke 22:31-32*

This morning (May 28, 2007), I read the story of a young woman who struggled with what she had believed about God. She said that she had family members who prayed that her faith would not fail in an extended time of grief.

All of a sudden, tears grew in my eyes as I realized that God, by his Spirit, was giving me a fresh awareness of how to pray for those I love. I'm referring to those who once accepted Jesus as Savior and believed that there is a God to whom we will give an account of how we have lived. For various reasons these beliefs became hard to live with.

And so I remember the words above of Jesus to Peter in Luke 22. Satan tries to separate us from God in places of hardship, trials, or grief. How many times has my faith been tested, but Jesus and other people have prayed that my faith would not fail?

God has been faithful. I will pray the same for those I love. If these words connect with you, take heart and don't give up praying. Remember the words of Jesus in Mark 11:22: "Have faith in God."

Father our faith is in You who sustains us and helps us to pray by Your Spirit.

Kathleen Hollinger leads the prayer ministry for Acts Fellowship, Lancaster.

A Willing Offering

"When the princes in Israel take the lead, when the people willingly offer themselves—praise the Lord!" *Judges 5:2*

I felt the gentle nudging of the Holy Spirit, "Ask her to come to Mom's group." "Oh, she wouldn't want to come. She doesn't like church, remember?" I countered. Again, "Ask her." I had been praying for this neighbor for a long time and did not seem to get very far. For the last three months, I had been praying with a greater passion and frequency. Now it was time to put my prayers into action. I picked up my courage and headed off to the bus stop where we chatted each morning before sending our children off to school.

I took a deep breath and blurted out the question before I could change my mind. To my astonishment, but probably not God's, she said, "Yes." Immediately! Praise the Lord! I just kept smiling. Since then our relationship has blossomed. I continue to pray intensely that she will come to trust the Jesus I love. Each step of obedience to the Holy Spirit's nudging has added depth to my prayer and courage to my actions. God continues to work in the lives around me as I willingly offer myself to Him.

Lord, the desire of my heart is to be a willing volunteer in the work of Your Kingdom. May Your Kingdom come and Your will be done on earth as it is in heaven. Praise the Lord! Amen

Audrey Kanagy is the wife of and co-laborer with Pastor Robert Kanagy. She and her husband serve Masonville Mennonite Church in Washington Boro.

Greatest And Most Excellent Way

"...Love the Lord your God with all your heart and...love your neighbor as yourself." *Matthew 22:37-39*

An expert of the law, who probably had the first five books of the Bible memorized, asked Jesus a very good question: "Teacher, which is the greatest commandment of the law?" Jesus' answer was to love the Lord with all your heart, and others as yourself, as all the law and the prophets hang on these two.

When I personally realized this is not just a good idea or a suggestion, but a command and choice I needed to make as a way of life, I began to see and experience the love of God as never before. As I began to experience God's love in this way, I also realized I had a much greater love for others than ever before. I truly realized God is not interested in my giftings, giving, and service if not ministered in love.

I agree with Romans 8:35-39 that asks who or what shall separate us from the love of God. Nothing. Because we know and experience this love of God that surpasses knowledge, we are filled with all the fullness of God, and that is a lot of love.

Communion has become a time when I experience this love of God as never before, in brokenness for Christ's awesome love for me personally in dying on that cruel cross. At the same time, I experience joy unspeakable because He arose from the grave, and we serve a living God.

I experience personal freedom because the blood of Jesus Christ cleansed me from all sin, and He sees me as holy, righteous, and pure because I repented of my sins and have by faith received this wonderful gift of forgiveness and eternal life with Him forever. That is good news and a privilege to share it with all.

Thank you Lord for revealing to me, "Love Never Fails."

Ray Deiter serves as a pastor at Living Stones Fellowship and Operation Transformation in southern Lancaster County.

Spiritual Warfare

"For our struggle is not against flesh and blood, but against the rulers, against the authorities, against the world forces of this darkness, against the spiritual forces of wickedness in the heavenly places." *Ephesians 6:12*

I f only we could see behind the scenes when we pray, we'd realize how powerful our prayers are. This reminds me of a time toward the end of my marriage when things between my husband and me were really bad. Being unequally yoked, our relationship was mirroring friction in the heavenly realm.

One night my husband wasn't home, the children were in bed, and I was watching TV in the living room. Suddenly I felt this presence watching me from the dining room. When I looked around, I couldn't see anything, but I felt it. The hairs on the back of my neck stood straight up and there were goose bumps on my arms. My prayers must have been stirring something to cause this demonic visit.

My first reaction was to pray. I demanded that the enemy leave in Jesus' name, and I pleaded the blood of Christ over the whole property, to cleanse it. The enemy had to leave. It cannot stand up against Jesus' name or His shed blood. After having prayed these two things, I felt a peace come over the room.

Jesus' name and His blood are two powerful weapons we have when battling the enemy. We must not forget to use them when doing battle. The unsaved around us need us to battle for their souls. The enemy has won for too long. It is time to take back what has been stolen. So let's all join in and fight the good fight.

Jesus, thank you so much for dying on the cross and shedding Your blood for us. Give us the strength and the prayers to fight the good fight, so we can take back what has been stolen.

Julie Gehman serves on the Prayer and Ministry teams at Ephrata Community Church.

Love One Another

"Dear Friends, let us love one another, for love comes from God. Everyone who loves has been born of God and knows God." *1 John 4:7*

Recently we were invited to an Amish wedding in Ohio. On the wedding day, I picked up a sister and her family early and took her to the bride's home where the activity was under way. We got out of the car and saw the ladies already frying the chicken (all 320 pounds).

As I hurried back to my car, it was parked where, within hours, dozens of buggies and vans would be unloading hundreds of wedding guests, I gasped! The car was locked and all the keys, even the spare, were inside. I hurried back to the three "English" ladies, who were frying chicken, and announced, "I'm locked out of my car, and it's parked in the wrong place!"

We soon realized the gravity of the situation. Because there were no phones in the Amish home and cell phones had poor reception, one of the ladies offered to drive me the half mile to our daughter's house to call AAA. Our son-in-law had difficulty explaining that the address he was calling from was in Tuscarawas County and the car was just across the line in Holmes County. Finally, he directed the locksmith to the car. People were already arriving for the wedding. Shortly, the locksmith arrived and resolved the situation.

For the next three days, every time I transported the bride's grandmother or sisters, they reminded me, "Do you have the keys?" and "Is the door locked?" I began to feel very cared for and loved, so that I would not repeat that mistake. God in His Word has reminded us many times to "Love one another." Sometimes we either forget or don't know how to love as God loves. Let's be reminders to others to love as God loves.

Lord, give me reminders when I fail to love as You love and make me Your loving servant. Amen

Miriam Witmer lives at Landis Homes Retirement Community. She enjoys quilting, visitation, and praying.

Don't Go Looking For A Fight

"Refuse to get involved in inane discussions; they always end up in fights." *2 Timothy 2:22 (The Message)*

D o you know someone who *loves to argue?* If you haven't, turn on ESPN about 5:00 p.m. and you can listen to four sports writers and an emcee debating some aspect of the sports world. They like to give their opinions on the latest "controversy" or hot topic. I have yet to hear the five of them agree on anything, except perhaps how disagreeable they consider one another. My long-suffering wife, Dianne, absolutely detests this show, because it simply sounds like "inane discussions" and the truth is, a whole lot of what is said is intended to be more argumentative than instructive.

I have sat in Sunday School classes with people who seem to delight in being "the devil's advocate," but sometimes their disregard for the faith development of the people in the room or their willingness to twist Scripture to "have a good discussion" probably makes them more the devil's *advocate* than they would like to admit.

The desire to be argumentative simply because you love a good argument is rarely helpful. This is especially so as we deal with our witness in the world. More and more I am discovering that the general combativeness of some Christians tends to annoy people more than transform them. The purpose of our speech is to share the gospel of Christ—to help them know the Word of God so that they might consider its truth for their lives.

So much of the world is in partisan combat—verbally or literally. We must ask ourselves, "Do I want to win an argument over a small matter or help win someone's heart to the deep life-changing truth of God?"

Lord, help me love the Good News more than a good argument.

Dr. Stephen Dunn is the lead pastor for the Church of God of Landisville and evangelism trainer for the Eastern Region of the Churches of God.

February

The King Of Hearts

"Then Samson said, 'With a donkey's jawbone I have made donkeys of them. With a donkey's jawbone I have killed a thousand men.'"
Judges 15:16

I love games. Almost every Sunday was spent at my grandparents' house playing card games—mostly Pinochle or Haus with an occasional Hearts or Rook. I always felt so special that my grandpa picked me over any of my relatives to be his partner. When he passed away in 1998, we even buried him with a perfect Haus hand in his coat pocket—two right bauers, two lefts, and a few aces and kings.

My love of games has developed over the years to include planning and leading activities for bridal showers, baby showers and birthday parties. I always thought how cool it would be to have a full-time job just doing games, but easily dismissed the idea.

Then my husband and I heeded a call to come to Fortaleza, Brazil to work in the ministry here—a largely youth ministry. I realized that this love of games had actually come from God and that He had been cultivating this in me for years. Then I read the story about Samson and how he killed a thousand men with a simple donkey's jawbone. A jawbone! I was utterly amazed at how God could use just a simple thing to do something so great.

Then I remembered my deck of cards. Wow. God has been using a simple deck of cards to help me form relationships, learn Portuguese, make friendships, have fun, etc. Thank you, Lord! You are the King of my Heart!

Thank You, Lord, for using the small things in our lives to do great things to further Your Kingdom. Help us not to overlook the small things, but in all we do, may it be to glorify You.

Lyndell Thiessen serves with her husband, Bruce, in Fortaleza, Brazil. Before moving to Brazil, they attended DOVE Westgate. Lyndell currently is involved in teaching English, leading groups of teenage girls and leading game nights!

Edge Of The City

"Now the Lord said to Abram, 'Go forth from your country...To the land which I will show you....'"
Genesis 12:1 (New American Standard Bible)

Have you ever heard of a "land" called Reading? My heart began to be burdened for this "land" in 1998. I wasn't living there at the time but joined intercessors and prayed for the city. My wife and I talked occasionally of how inexpensive some houses were. We understood the area was experiencing some hard times thus bringing down the value of real estate. Perhaps we could invest in properties there in the future.

One day God dropped a challenge into my spirit: "I'm going to move you to the edge of the city." I knew this meant Reading and I was sure that this was for the future. After all, I was a farm boy who loved the country and was taking a big step living in a town.

In a matter of weeks, I was conversing with a friend who lived in Reading and was preparing to minister in Israel. She informed me that she wanted to sell her house; I said I would keep my ears open. I asked where the house was located. She replied, "I live right on the edge of the city."

That wasn't too hard to figure out. How often I had asked the Lord to speak more clearly to me—this was pretty clear! Within a few months, the move was made. The ensuing years have been anything but normal and the fruit will be just as unusual. Interestingly, I found a number of people who have been called to this same "land." Do you suppose God has some special plans in store?

Thank you, God, that You move Your servants to the lands that You have called them to. You have wonderful destinies to fulfill in this process.

Daniel Symonds is an elder at Hope of the Nations Christian Center in Reading's inner city. He is a teacher and mentor of the prophetic in the Reading School of Transformation.

Fire Walk

"...when you walk through the fire, you will not be burned...."
Isaiah 43:2

An ordinary June morning dawned filled with errands and packing for our much anticipated New England trip of visiting family and awaiting the arrival of our newest grandbaby. Mid-afternoon found me rushing back from Roots Market amidst light rain. Before the storm broke loose in earnest, I had arrived home and unloaded my precious purchases of our grandson's favorite cinnamon bread, Tastykakes and other Lancaster County love-gifts for our children.

A thunderbolt struck in the back cornfield filling me with the fear of having lost one of our few trees. Racing onto the porch, I was greatly relieved to find all trees intact. Returning to the kitchen for supper preparation, a strange sound of running water caught my attention. However, as my eyes began to sting and my nostrils filled with the stench of smoke, the realization came that it was the sound of fire, not of water!

Calmly dialing 911, I wondered if I was over-reacting, until the fire alarms on all three floors sounded. Almost immediately, three local fire companies arrived with nine emergency vehicles and thirty firemen. I was rushed to my neighbor's front yard as the firefighters descended on our home to search for the fire's source. With axes poised to chop through the roof, the call came from the basement crew to halt all other activity, for flames had broken through the ceiling and the first floor. With hoses in hand, the blaze was soon under control. Although inwardly I remained calm, outwardly my body trembled.

With flames extinguished, the fire chief reviewed the chain of events. Apparently, after the lightning bolt struck the ground, it traveled forty feet and latched onto our gas line, igniting a fire around the gas pipe running the full length of our townhouse. What he didn't understand was why the line had not exploded. My explanation was God's intervention. The fire lay smoldering beneath my feet. God had truly caused Romans 16:20 to live in my life—"The God of peace will soon crush Satan underneath your feet."

Dear God, thank you for Your divine protection and causing Your Word to literally live in my life. Amen

Susan Kulka is a wife, mother and grandmother and attends DOVE Westgate with her husband, Michael.

Words Of Life

"Have not I commanded thee? Be strong and of a good courage; be not afraid, neither be thou dismayed: for the Lord thy God is with thee whithersoever thou goest." *Joshua 1:9 (King James Version)*

The day was hot and the sun was bright as we stood outside the shelter where we were staying. I was one of a small group carrying the Bible in the language of our sisters and brothers who were restricted from praising the Lord freely. Their faith was growing and they hungered for the Word. I was about to learn some things about my own faith.

At church on Sunday evening before departing, the words of a young man struck fear in my heart. His words were, "God said go, He didn't say He would bring you back." I was the mother of two young children and wrestled with obeying the call or staying in a place of comfort with my children.

I struggled with the temptation not to go. A sister in the faith, whose language I did not understand, came to pray for me. As she prayed, my ears heard unfamiliar words, but my heart knew and understood her prayer. She prayed for me to trust the Lord with this day as I had trusted him for my salvation.

As the heat of the sun touched my skin, I looked across the cloudless sky and saw the most beautiful rainbow. In my heart I knew *all is well*. He spoke through the words of a woman I did not understand. He painted the sky with a rainbow; I knew the Lord was near. The word of the praise song, "He Touched Me," rang through my heart. We serve a mighty God who cares about our weakness and our dreams.

Thank You, Lord, that Your love is unconditional; that You reach out to us when we are weak and shepherd us through the struggles and storms of life. Amen

Diana M. Watt is Director of Development, Water Street Rescue Mission.

Change Of Heart

"On hearing this, Jesus said, 'It is not the healthy who need a doctor, but the sick. But go and learn what this means: 'I desire mercy, not sacrifice.' For I have not come to call the righteous, but sinners.'"
Matthew 9:12-13

Before I joined the staff of the church, I was leaving the parking lot one Sunday. I looked at the pickup truck that was in front of me and noticed a sticker on the back window. When I read it, I realized that the message was sexually inappropriate. My first thought as I saw it was, "I'm glad he was in church today."

I then smiled as it hit me that something had changed in me. It would not have been too long ago that I would have been offended that someone had the nerve to have a sticker like that on his truck and park it in a church parking lot.

Somehow, in a way imperceptible to me, the Holy Spirit had moved me from a position of judgment to mercy. I never asked God to do this in me, but He did it anyway. I don't think it was right for this young man to flaunt his sexual desires by having this sticker on his truck, but I realized that he wasn't going to decide to remove that sticker by sleeping in on Sunday morning or staying home to watch TV. If Jesus could go to a party with "notorious sinners," can't I go to church with them?

I don't know his name or anything about his life, but I have noticed that the sticker is no longer on his truck. Maybe the Holy Spirit changed him just like he had changed me.

Lord, thank You for making me more like Jesus even in ways I do not realize. I pray for this young man I don't even know, that You would work in his life, too.

Jim Whiteman is the Spiritual Formation Pastor at LCBC - Lancaster.

Loving The Lost

"Three things will last forever—faith, hope, and love—and the greatest of these is love. " *1 Corinthians 13:13 (New Living Translation)*

Marty Reddig was a vital part of Reading DOVE Christian Ministry Center for many years. A tall man with a gray beard, he was a spiritual father to many. Marty was diagnosed with lymphoma in February 2005. Though Marty always loved the body of Christ and had a heart for the lost, something changed drastically inside of him when he heard this diagnosis. His focus became the lost. He talked to everyone about Jesus and His plan of salvation. Marty had a special audience with anyone who had cancer; as they listened intently to each word he spoke.

Even though Marty was not well, he went to the Midnight Ministries Outreach. Fearlessly, he spoke to drug dealers face-to-face. He spoke to alcoholics even prostitutes on the streets. Elderly Spanish ladies would run and bring him chocolate cake and insisted that he eat it!

One evening on outreach, Marty met a young man covered with tattoos and a fierce countenance to match it all. This man was even taller than Marty and outweighed him, too. As Marty spoke to him about Jesus, this tough guy laid his head on Marty's shoulder and began to weep, saying, "All I want is a Daddy."

Marty's eyes and heart were always in search of the lost. On Sunday mornings, he would stand outside the church and invite folks just walking by to come in. On one occasion while on outreach Marty felt compelled to leave the church and just walk down a street. He came upon a drunken man who had fallen into the gutter, and his beer cans went rolling down the street. Marty gathered the beer cans and handed them to the man. Their eyes locked. Marty said, he just couldn't explain it, but when he looked into the eyes of this man, he just *loved* him.

Marty went to be with the Lord he served so faithfully on March 25, 2006. At Marty's funeral, people stood one-after-the-other and gave testimony to this man and the God he served. Marty touched many lives. The funeral director said he had never seen anything like it.

Lord, may our hearts be so turned to the lost. May our compassion be like Yours—a true reflection of Your love.

Sharon Weaver, Reading DOVE Christian Ministry Center

God Stories 3

The Doughnut Temptation

"No temptation has seized you except what is common to man."
1 Corinthians 10:13

God uses many different ways to get our attention. I was watching "Veggie Tales" with our friends' little boy the other evening, and the theme was temptation. The next day my devotional was…you guessed it—temptation.

Recently my husband and I changed our eating habits to be healthier. My greatest "temptation" has been pastries, and I had been very good in resisting them. The day after watching "Veggie Tales" and reading the devotional someone brought donuts to work. Now that may seem like a little thing, but to me it was a very big temptation. It was because of the Lord's gentle reminder that I was able to resist. I never cease to be amazed how He cares about every little detail in our lives. Nothing is too insignificant for our Father.

No doubt the temptations in your life are greater than resisting junk food, and I have certainly had bigger challenges than just donuts; however, no matter how big or small, I have found that God is there for us in every one.

Father, I love You and thank You for caring so much about us and knowing us so well. I am amazed at Your love and concern for us. Help me to be obedient when I hear Your voice.

Jean M. Henry, serves with The Net and is a servant of Jesus Christ along with her husband, Darryl.

Harvest

"Then He said to his disciples, 'The harvest is plentiful but the workers are few. Ask the Lord of the harvest, therefore, to send out workers into his harvest field.'" *Matthew 9:37-38*

The mission in Haiti was changing hands after nine years of solid ministry directorship. A series of events recently led to the missionary couple who had served faithfully returning home, and shifting the children's school and child sponsorship to our ministry partners in Missouri. My wife and I along with the couple recently traveled to Haiti for a three day whirlwind trek to sell one of the vehicles, to secure some of the assets for liquidation, and perhaps most importantly to "let go" of the whole thing, allowing God to do as He desires.

As we traveled along the only highway from Port-au-Prince to Mont-Rouis, I thought about the years of annual visits to the island. While exiting the airport, the "sea of humanity" had closed in around us. We experienced pushing and shoving as many desperate Haitians tried to compete for a few American dollars. I thought about all the needs imposed because of incredible poverty. I continued to sense how that poverty carried over from the physical to the spiritual.

I wondered what positive changes occurred for the Kingdom of God during those years, but I was reassured seeing a thriving elementary school and many new homes. Most importantly, we heard from many with tear filled-eyes, gratefully thanking the missionary for many acts of charity done in the name of Jesus. Many asked me if the medical teams will continue. I was reminded of a plaque seen at the Baptist mission in Port-au-Prince, "To the world you might be one person, but to one person you might be the world."

I am challenged that God calls us all to become workers in the harvest field.

Father, I am reminded that You call us all to serve as workers in the harvest field. Move me to total surrender.

Dr. T. Scott Jackson serves on the eldership team and in worship at Oasis Fellowship in Akron.

Welcome Home

"His lord said unto him, Well done, good and faithful servant; thou hast been faithful over a few things, I will make thee ruler over many things: enter thou into the joy of thy lord."
Matthew 25:23 (American Standard Version)

Several weeks ago, I was traveling oversees. I had been in several countries and some of the places where I had been were a bit tense. Upon my return home, my flight arrived at an airport on the East Coast. When I arrived at the passport control, the agent looked at my passport and then I heard these words with a smile, "Welcome home."

Those were special words to hear since I had been gone for more than two weeks. I was looking forward to seeing my wife and my family. I was also looking forward to seeing my church family. On the day I arrived, I had flown for just about 16 hours and hearing those words was very special.

I can hear the Lord saying one day, "Well done, good and faithful servant; ...welcome home." These are the words we all desire to hear. We read them in scripture. Matthew 1:13 says, "...they will call him Immanuel which means, 'God with us.'" In chapter 28, verse 20 the Lord says, "I am with you always, even unto the end of the world." And He says in John, "...that where I am, there ye may be also." His desire is to be with us forever, therefore the words, "Welcome home."

Heavenly Father, I ask You to give us the spirit of wisdom and revelation so that we might know Him better in order that we might be ready to meet You on that special day and hear those special words, "Welcome home." Continue to call us to a Holy way of living and give us cleans hands and a pure heart. In the name of Jesus, Amen

Dick Landis is an associate pastor of the Living Hope Community Church. He also gives leadership to The Friends of The Uzbeks, a ministry to the Uzbek people in Central Asia.

When God Calls

"The One who calls you is faithful and He will do it."
1 Thessalonians 5:24

"Is that you God?" "But what if...?" "What about my plans to...?" "Are you sure God?" This is just some of my conversation with God when He began calling me back to teaching. Unfortunately, I cannot say that I answered God with the faith of young Samuel: "Speak, for your servant is listening." Nor did I answer with the willingness of Isaiah: "Here am I. Send me." No, my initial response was more like Moses or Jonah, with lots of reasons why I could not do this and the desire to run in the opposite direction. After all, I had "resigned" from teaching 17 years ago when my husband and I were blessed with our first child. I had enjoyed teaching, but so much had changed: DVDs, computers, internet, and PowerPoint presentations.

Yes, technology has changed, but the need to share the love of Christ with young people has not, so I said "Yes" to the Lord. I trusted His promise that, "The One who calls you is faithful and He will do it." God made it clear that this was an opportunity to reflect His Son and to share the love of worship and prayer that He has given to me.

I worked very hard and put in many hours to prepare for my classes, and God was faithful. He guided my plans and gave me creative ways to encourage learning. Among the greatest gifts He gave me were acceptance from my students and a love for them that I could not have imagined. What a privilege it has been to get to know and learn along with this fine group of young people. A year ago, I could not have imagined teaching again and now I cannot imagine how much I would have missed if I had not said "Yes" to the Lord and followed Him.

Father, Thank you for Your faithfulness.

Cheri Miller, wife, mother, teacher at Lancaster Mennonite Schools, intercessor for SVPS, member of Middle Creek Church of the Brethren

The Knife

"For He has rescued us from the dominion of darkness and brought us into the Kingdom of the Son He loves." *Colossians 1:13*

I t was a cold, winter night in a gypsy village in Romania when I was reminded of God's transforming grace. This story begins in a standing-room-only, crowded, little church building filled with gypsies. They were eager to experience the three-hour worship service of heartfelt music and testimonies given by each American team member. Through an interpreter, the Word of God was powerfully presented. An invitation was given by the Romanian pastor. Many people responded by slowly moving forward through the packed crowd. Prayer was offered for the respondents. Little did I know (until returning to America) that the man standing next to me in the service had a concealed twelve inch knife up his shirt sleeve. He had brought it into the sanctuary to murder another man in attendance. God opened this man's heart to His amazing grace and saved him. Later that year he was baptized in the Danube River, and he continues to follow his Savior Jesus Christ.

The story does not end there. This past May another team returned to Romania. Some of the members were building a swing set, and others were completing some grounds-keeping chores for the "House of Joy," a home for orphan children. A tool was needed to trim the grass along a fence. The Romanian pastor had the perfect tool. As he walked outside he announced "this is THE KNIFE!" We all rejoiced as we reflected on the interrupted intended use of this knife four years ago by a gracious Heavenly Father. How amazing! How astonishing! My eyes were filled with tears as I remembered a murderer's heart, by God's grace, was changed and now that knife was being used to beautify the grounds of an orphanage. From hatred to love. From darkness to light. From bondage to freedom. That is what God's transforming and redeeming grace is all about.

Sovereign Lord, my Redeemer, help me to boast in Your grace alone. Thank you for Your transforming power that delivers sinners from the domain of darkness and brings them into the Kingdom of light, and all for Your glory. Amen

Pastor Leon R. Shirk is senior shepherd to the body of Christ at Bethany Grace Fellowship, East Earl.

Release Your Burden

"Come to me, all you who are weary and burdened, and I will give you rest. Take my yoke upon you…and you will find rest for your souls. For my yoke is easy and my burden is light." *Matthew 11:28-30*

One of the most significant aspects of taking Christ's yoke upon us is learning how to yield to His accomplishment of forgiveness (Hebrews 10). Forgiveness is a familiar word, but probably one of the most misunderstood. The "burden" of the forgiveness process lies with *Christ*. The benefits are to be experienced by *us*. Christ sowed through death and reaped through resurrection life. So we sow by dying to ourselves and reaping the freedom from the crippling effects of bitterness and resentment.

My wife of 27 years is the person who has taught me the most about forgiveness because I do many things for which I need her forgiveness. We need to forgive because we need to be forgiven (Matthew 18). Our closest relationships are the ones most prone to suffering the consequences of unforgiveness. Recognizing our propensity to offend others creates the greatest reason to be "quick to listen, slow to speak and slow to become angry" (James 1:19). Pointing out another's faults means you'd better be ready to take responsibility for offenses you caused other people.

Forgiveness allows us to escape the battle of trying to hold everything together by ourselves, and it relieves the stress of trying to hide the inconsistencies in our lives. When we trust the Lord, we give everything over to Him and come into a blessedness of rest.

Lord, help me to forgive my debtors more often, sooner than later, and at a deeper level than I have before. For the person I think I have forgiven, but really haven't (at least to the degree You desire me to), help me to acknowledge my need for Your help in forgiving, see my anger, separate the fact from fiction and allow You to begin the healing process in my heart.

Dr. Edward Hersh, provides counseling and healing prayer ministry to individuals and families, trains lay counselors here and abroad and helps leaders receive spiritual renewal.

Whose Report Do You Believe?

"Now faith is the assurance of things hoped for, the conviction of things not seen." *Hebrews 11:1 (New American Standard Bible)*

On May 17, 1987, our son was born. Within the first hours of his life a mortal battle took place. He stopped breathing twice and resuscitation was needed to bring him back. A few years later, testing revealed that the battle would continue. A specialist stated that his early life struggle had contributed to developmental problems and that a diagnosis of mild cerebral palsy was evident.

Special education resources were needed throughout his elementary education. Often he would say, "I can't do it!" Our response was always, "Try your best and God will take care of the rest." We always challenged and encouraged him to strive and meet his potential.

When our son was about ten years old, a counselor approached me and suggested that I needed to help my wife with the denial she had about the degree of our son's condition. This counselor felt that both of our behaviors were in denial of our son's challenges. The counselor also stated that our son would probably never advance beyond fourth or fifth grade academically. I never shared this with my wife until our son was about to enter high school.

As our son was "mainstreamed" into regular high school classes, we continued to pray God's guidance and strength into his life. God continued to move mightily and faithfully. Each semester our son attained scholastic honors and graduated with honors and awards.

Today, he is a student at Millersville University and continues to acquire A's and B's in all his studies. His vision is to serve the Lord in foreign missions.

Faith very seldom aligns with what we initially see, hear or feel. It is a stand that can move the hand of God.

Lord, may our faith in You sustain us through all life's challenges.

Norm Fennimore is director of The Jeremiah Project, a ministry to individuals struggling with addiction, their affected family members, and the training of the church.

Love Is Patient

"Love is patient, love is kind,…it always hopes, always perseveres."
1 Corinthians 13:4,7

The attractive young woman always crossed her legs and bounced her foot as she sat in the counseling room. We had many visits together. It started with a series of pregnancy tests over a number of months that indicated a dangerous desire to become pregnant without the benefit of any semblance of a healthy relationship. Raised in a religious home, she also knew sexual abuse and abandonment by her father. She eventually became pregnant, and we walked through those months together. Two years later, we repeated the process, this time with a different boyfriend.

We talked about the Lord many times, and reviewed God's plan of salvation. Susan was always open to prayer, and sometimes prayed with me. Her "colorful" language began to modulate, and she made an earnest effort to improve her situation and provide for her children. Still, she could not seem to turn from her pursuit of unhealthy men and turn to Christ.

One day she sat with her car keys in hand while we talked. The keys bounced along with her knee, jingling rhythmically. "Susan," I said, "when are you going to turn the keys of your life over to the Lord?" The nervous jingling stopped abruptly.

After years of connection and many intermittent visits, an image captured her attention in a new way. Her prayer that day went to a much deeper level, as she opened her heart to Jesus.

Lord, give us patience to walk the long, slow road with someone in need of Your love.

Joan Boydell serves as Senior Director of Amnion Crisis Pregnancy Centers, as a consultant with Care Net, and with her husband, Bruce, in Lifespan.

God Provides

"...for your Father knows what you need before you ask him!"
Matthew 6:8 (New Living Translation)

"And if God cares so wonderfully for wildflowers that are here today and thrown into the fire tomorrow, he will certainly care for you."
Matthew 6:30 (New Living Translation)

As the air ambulance Lear Jet landed at Lancaster Airport, a Manheim Township ambulance was waiting to take my husband to Lancaster General Hospital.

I had no idea where I would live until a friend, Carol, invited my 1½ year-old-son, Brian, and me to move in with her. I anticipated a temporary living arrangement, so living with her and her teenager would be fine. I was so grateful! Three weeks later when our daughter, Beth, was born, five of us called her two bedroom apartment home.

A month earlier, our family left Belize abruptly and arrived in Miami, Florida, for my husband, Duane, to receive medical attention. Instead of recovering, he became comatose due to a medical accident. With many around the world interceding, we thought our miracle-working God would answer our prayers for divine healing. However, some plans do not go as we anticipate. Duane never awakened; we didn't return to the mission work in Belize.

After 15 months of sharing Carol's apartment, I was eagerly anticipating living on my own with my children. Diligently, I looked for a house...and God provided beyond what I could imagine. The seller left the furniture we needed, custom made furnishings in each room, plus garage items and tools that were such a blessing.

God directed our steps and provided wonderfully more than 20 years ago and He continues to do so. Praise Him!

God, my Provider, blessed be Your name. Before I ask, You know my need. You are a Father who takes care of Your children. Thank you for being attentive to our prayer for help, even when things don't go according to our plan. May Your will be done!

Nancy Leatherman, an administrative assistant at Teaching The Word Ministries, resides in Manheim Township where she exercises hospitality.

I Will Exalt

"Yet I will rejoice in the Lord, I will joy in the God of my salvation."
Habakkuk 3:18 (King James Version)

When I was a student in college, I wrote a song called "Haze."
It opened:

Been down this road so many times before
Don't know where I'm going or where You are
I thought the road would be much straighter than this
But life is teaching me to watch for unexpected turns

At 19, I was not a particularly world-wise individual. These are the words of a confused teenager going through typical teenage problems: relationship woes, deciding whether my faith was my own or my parents', and trying to figure out my future. I was crying out to God for understanding: *Please clear my vision, or O Lord, please make me blind.*

Sometime after I wrote this song, someone pointed me to the book of Habakkuk (I can't pronounce it either). I was struck by the fact that the Bible includes this story of someone questioning God so bluntly: *"How long, O Lord, will I call for help, and You will not hear?"* And that is when I realized that questions, doubts, and not knowing how things will turn out are all part of the journey.

I cannot tell you that things suddenly became easier or that I never struggled through questions, doubts, and disappointments since then. Because things actually got worse before they got better. But I can tell you that looking back now, I can see how God was faithful and led me to where I am today through those difficult experiences.

So today as I sit here having recently gone through health issues, experienced my dad suffering from a mini-stroke, struggling with unexpected expenses—and still wading through all of the other junk in life, yet I will exult in the Lord, because He is with me and will grant me understanding somewhere down this road.

Great is Your faithfulness, O Lord.

Ryan Geesaman, producer and musician, is the Video Production Director and member of the Worship Team at LCBC Lancaster.

In Everything By Prayer

"...in everything, by prayer and supplication, with thanksgiving, let your requests be made known to God."
Philippians 4:6 (New King James Version)

Several years ago we visited our daughter, son-in-law, and grandchildren in France. (They have been serving there for thirty years in church planting.) One morning I gave a ten-franc French coin to each of our three grandchildren, and they were delighted to receive it.

Shortly thereafter, our older granddaughter, Sarah, went out to play in the area just beyond their garden. Apparently, Sarah took her ten-franc coin with her and somehow lost it while playing. This of course caused some tears.

It occurred to me that here was an opportunity to teach the children a lesson about the place and importance of prayer. Therefore, I suggested that we pray and ask the Lord if it would be His will that we would find the lost coin. So we prayed and then went to search for it. We had searched for some time and were just about to give up, when suddenly I found the coin in the grass. This gave us cause for joy and thanksgiving. However, finding the coin presented another opportunity to teach the children that we should give thanks to the Lord for answering our prayer. So we prayed again and thanked the Lord for His goodness in answering our prayer. As the Word of God instructs us, "in everything, by prayer and supplication, with thanksgiving, let your requests be made known to God."

Dear Lord, thank You that we may bring to You even the little things of life and that You are so gracious to undertake and to meet us in our need. We give You praise in Your precious Name, Amen

Eric G. Crichton serves as Pastor Emeritus, Calvary Church, Lancaster.

Single But Not Alone

"'You are the God who sees me,' for she said, 'I have now seen the One who sees me.'" Genesis 16:13

Single parents have the toughest job in the world, and, like the Energizer bunny, they keep going and going: working 24/7 earning a living, fixing meals, caring for kids, helping with homework, doing household repairs, cleaning house, paying bills, repairing the car, handling medical needs and insurance, doing the finances, shopping for groceries, being involved in children's activities, needing child care, dealing with visitation schedules, and on and on.

As a single parent myself, I know that it sometimes feels like you are all alone. But God loves and cares about you and always has. Single parents are near and dear to His heart. So much so, that we have to go back to the first book of the Bible to take a peek at the first single parent. In Genesis 16, Hagar fled to the wilderness to grieve the loss of her relationship with Abram. The Lord speaks to her and gives her hope and direction for her future. From then on, Hagar called the Lord, the God Who sees me. He saw where she was, knew her need, and promised to meet those needs.

Where do you find the time and energy to meet your spiritual, emotional, and social needs? I found that God and His people are a great source of power. It is vital to connect with Him through the Word, prayer, and fellowship with followers of Christ. Therein lies all that we need to be the parent the Lord has called us to be. You may be single, as in not married, but you are not alone in raising your children. God sees you, loves you, cares for you, and is mindful of what you are going through as a single parent!

Father, I am so grateful that You see me, love me, and care for both me and my child.

Sharon Blantz is the proud mother of Lauren and serves as regional pastor of support and care ministries at the Worship Center.

We Carry One Every Day

"… I have come that they may have life, and that they may have it more abundantly." *John 10:10*

I recently asked some Senior High students if they would describe the picture that came to mind when I said the word "God." After tossing around some theologically correct, but descriptively weak answers, I asked them to describe the picture of another word: "Pencil" I said.

Quickly, each student gave very specific words and images describing this common object. "Why was that so easy?" I asked. Without fail, each student responded by saying, "Because we carry one with us every day." A somewhat sober atmosphere took over our group as they realized what they had just confessed.

The purpose in asking those questions wasn't to come up with the most accurate pictorial description of God—it was to consider if we were as aware of His constant presence with us, as we are with a pencil.

Jesus said His purpose in coming was to bring us life—abundant life—life to it's fullest! Life that is filled with God moments, with God stories! Each student in the discussion agreed they believed Jesus' statement was true, that He was the way to have the fullest life. But in stating their belief, an awesome and terrifying reality broke in—were their lives reflecting a life full of God? Is my life reflecting a life full of God? Is God's presence as real to me as the pen in my pocket, the car in front of me, or the barking dog outside my home? Am I living with an awareness of Him in the extraordinary as well as the ordinary of my day? If not—is it possible my life is not "full?"

Jesus, friend of sinners, help us know Your nearness today. Help us live in the fullness of knowing You, and in the fullness of friendship with You.

Josh VanderPlate serves as Worship & Youth Director at Living Hope Community Church. He and his wife, Yolanda live in Lancaster with their children, Levi & Abigail.

Remembering God's Word

"But the Comforter, even the Holy Spirit, whom the Father will send in my name, he shall teach you all things, and bring to your remembrance all that I said unto you." *John 14:26*

"I feel the Lord wants me to give you this word." It was several years ago, while my son was taking his swimming lessons with other homeschoolers, that a sister in Christ shared this verse with me: "Peace I leave with you; my peace I give unto you...Let not your heart be troubled, neither let it be afraid" (John 14:27).

I didn't know how much I would need this verse in the coming days, weeks, and years, but God did. And indeed He kept bringing it back to me. For a season, we were intensely involved in walking alongside our loved ones as they went through deep waters.

Like Mary in Luke 1:38, my heart received and lived in the reality of verse 37: "For no word from God shall be void of power."

An invitation came to attend a "Women of Faith" conference that required staying overnight and leaving behind a fragile situation. I received the affirmation to go, and as we got ready to depart, our host asked one of the women to give a short devotional. You guessed the text: "Peace I leave with you; my peace I give unto you...Let not your heart be troubled, neither let it be afraid" (John 14:27).

Father, let me never forget that no word from You is without the power to accomplish that for which it is sent. Thank you for the Holy Spirit that comforts and reminds us of what You have said. Be it unto me according to Your word!

Betty Eberly is a homemaker and grandmother, serving in Behold Your God Ministries and on the leadership team with Hampden Mennonite alongside husband Ken (eighteen years).

Life Lessons From A Marathon

"And he knows everything, inside and out. He energizes those who get tired, gives fresh strength to dropouts."
Isaiah 40:31 (The Message)

I set three major goals for myself running the Harrisburg Y2K Marathon: 1) Physical - Complete the race in less than four hours; 2) Financial - Raise $50,000 for the Camper Endowment Fund; 3) Spiritual - Pray during training that each camper would begin a vital lifelong relationship with Jesus Christ at Summer Camp.

Somewhat depressed in only meeting the third goal, missing the physical goal by one minute and five seconds, and the financial goal by $7,000, I prayed. "Lord, I confess my pride in setting the physical goal to prove that I'm still a runner not a jogger; if it is pride to continue asking others for more funding so that I can meet my financial goal, I'll not ask another person." It wasn't ten minutes later that I received a phone call: "My wife and I have been praying and we believe that we should send you $10,000." It was as if God was saying; "Bob, it isn't about you; it is all about Me. Without Me you can do nothing."

Key Lessons: 1) God permitted me to run with a partially torn Achilles tendon *without* pain; 2) I learned how encouragement from family and friends helps lift you mentally and physically to persevere right through to not give up; 3) Raising funds beyond my wildest dreams— "with God all things are possible," "He energizes those who get tired"; and 4) God was preparing us for something even greater. The Black Rock Bike-a-thon was born from this event and has raised hundreds of thousands of dollars.

Lord, help me to always remember that whatever situation I find myself, You are providing me with the opportunity to learn another lesson about Your great love and care.

Bob Bender is the former Administrator of Black Rock Retreat and is now on the Administrative team at Teaching The Word Ministries. He and his wife Sue live in Southern Lancaster County.

The Love Of God's People

"Dear friends, let us love one another, for love comes from God...."
1 John 4:7

Have you ever wondered how you would get through a situation that seemed overwhelming? Would there be something—or someone—that would sustain you through the darkest nights? I've asked myself these questions so many times.

On June 8, 2006, I lost my husband of almost thirty years. There are no perfect marriages, yet we never doubted that our love would keep us together until God called one or both of us home. When God called my husband home, I began the journey of experiencing God in a new way. Through our years together, I saw firsthand how God used His people to minister to others. As a pastor's wife I was accustomed to meeting people's needs in service. However, I'm not sure I understood how much I needed others to extend God's love to me through word and deed.

This past year God has given me a fresh appreciation for family and friends. Through the support of loving family members, kindnesses of friends, and care from a wonderful church family, I've learned to see God in a whole new way. He's present in their actions, deeds, thoughts, conversations, and prayers (mowing my lawn, flowers delivered, special days celebrated, and sending cards and notes). So many have made God's love real to me that I can begin to feel undeserving, and then I remember, I am undeserving. No one deserves God's love, but that's what makes God's grace so amazing. He lavishes us with His love and longs for us to receive it through others. I praise Him for His people who radiate and demonstrate His love.

Father, let me never stop thanking You for family and friends and the love they give because of You and Your grace to us. Amen

Mona Engle served alongside her husband Dale in the Brethren in Christ Church for almost thirty years. Presently employed as a Practice Administrator for Drs. May Grant (Lancaster), she continues to serve in the church.

Finish Well

"Even to your old age and gray hairs I am he, I am he who will sustain you. I have made you and I will carry you; I will sustain you...." *Isaiah 46:4*

I would like to introduce you to a friend of mine. I have served as her "preacher" (that's what she calls me) for seven years. In just a week, she will turn 104 years old. Her name is Alice and she lives in a nursing home.

One part of my job that I enjoy is spending time visiting with Alice every other week or so. Even at her age, she spends most of her days crocheting hot pads. She is able to complete between three and four each day. Her mind is still sharp and I love getting her to talk about what life was like when she was growing up or when she was a young wife and her children were little or when she was ministering to children in our church. Even now, her days are filled with family and friends who stop by to visit regularly. Yet what amazes me most about Alice is when we talk about Jesus.

Alice grew up in the Reformed Church outside Bowmansville. She married her husband and joined my church in 1921. We often talk about what life was like in church back then and how life in the church has changed over the years. However, Alice is not one to sit on her accomplishments for Jesus. Each day, she is up before dawn and spends the better part of an hour in prayer and reading her Bible and a devotional book. She is one of my most consistent prayer warriors.

Many senior citizens and those with disabilities may be wondering how they can be effective for the family of God when they are in nursing homes or confined to wheel chairs. Let me encourage you to become prayer warriors for your pastor and home churches. Your prayers are valuable and though your hair might be gray, God is able to sustain you, and you can continue to minister to others.

Lord, thank you for those prayer warriors, like Alice, who consistently hold up the many ministries in our communities in prayer.

Kevin Kirkpatrick is the "preacher" at Berean Bible Fellowship Church in Terre Hill. He is blessed to have other home bound prayer warriors as well.

God's Perfect Timing

"...According to your faith will it be done to you." Matthew 9:29

Recently, I was busily preparing to leave on an overseas trip. My wife and I had been waiting for a package to be delivered. It would have been so convenient and helpful if we had received it before we left at around 3 PM. that day! A timely delivery would mean there was no need to arrange for someone to collect the package, no phone calls from overseas to sort out some of the related business. So I prayed that it would arrive before we left...but thought, "I have no idea whether it will come or not, whether God really wants to do that for me or to do something else." I was at peace, but not necessarily expecting too much.

Later in the day, while packing for our trip, something welled up inside me that compelled me to pray again – only this time I had a strong sense that God really *did* want the delivery to arrive, for whatever reason, before we left for the airport. With the time of 2:30 PM. in my mind, I prayed for a delivery by that time, knowing deep inside that God was now working. At 2:30 PM. exactly, the UPS man came to the door with my package! God answered my prayer to the exact minute!

On reflecting on this incident, I realized that God did not expect me somehow to whip up faith or stir myself up. It was all initiated by Him. I needed to respond in faith, but really He nudged me in that direction. It was the Lord who told me how to pray and who gave me the faith in the first place. I merely needed to receive it and act upon it.

Thank you, God, that You are interested in the details of our life, and that, in all things, we can rest in You, simply responding to Your nudges to pray, act and serve, as You build Your Kingdom.

Peter Bunton serves as the Director of DOVE Mission International, the missions wing of DOVE Christian Fellowship International.

Gold Lettering

"… Blessed is he who trusts in the Lord." *Proverbs 16:20*

The ministry sign by the highway was looking shabby. Paint was peeling and colors were dull. I thought, "We can't afford it, but we *must* get a new sign. We'll just have to trust the Lord to supply the finances."

I asked Sharon to accompany me as we drove around looking at business signs, discussing the type we thought would work well. We particularly admired the elegant, ornate ones with carved gold lettering. They were eye-catching and beautiful. But we were certain such a sign would be way out of our price range.

A couple days later, I received a call from an old friend with whom I had not spoken in years. He said, "John, my wife and I drove past your place recently. I said to her, 'It looks as though Abundant Living is ready for a new sign! So, I've informed the fellow who makes signs for me that you will be stopping by to order whatever you need. I'll cover the expense.'"

I was thrilled and explained how timely his offer was…definitely more than a coincidence. Even as I spoke, I was already struggling with the thought, "But I can't take advantage of his kindness by ordering one of those more expensive signs."

My friend continued to say, "You may order any sign you want, but my wife and I were also commenting on how nice it would look on that property to use one of the more elegant, ornate signs with the carved gold lettering!"

By this point in my Christian life, you'd think I shouldn't be surprised, but such unexpected blessings never cease to amaze me! If salvation were God's only gift, that would be all I would ever need. But He gives in so many more ways, big and small. Do you have a need today? Dare to *trust* your heavenly Father. He may use unexpected ways to give you what you need, but *He will provide!* And for icing on the cake, He may even throw in some gold lettering!

Father, I am asking You to provide for my needs today. Thank you for surprising me over and over again with Your goodness!

John Charles is director of Abundant Living Ministries, near Lititz.

Who?

"And the things which you have heard from me in the presence of many witnesses, entrust these to faithful men...." *2 Timothy 2:2*

Having spent the better part of the last two decades immersed in ministry leadership posts, I have seen the best and worst of it surrounding the question, "Who are the future leaders?" One answer goes like this — God will bring them to us. Well, He might. He certainly can. And, you get points for answering spiritually. But, if we take the model Paul suggests, the answer may well be no one, if we don't identify, encourage, and invest into the next generation of leaders.

The Armed Forces seems to get the message; they need to recruit and train. Corporate cultures that are successful over a significant period of time recruit employees and invest into their lives to retain them. They have a talent pool who knows their culture and can be tapped for future initiatives and opportunities. So, what's up with the Church?

Do we have an intentional activity of identifying talent to develop Kingdom players for the future beyond recruiting for our elder boards? If so, kudos, and recognize that we will need to give God the freedom to develop that talent in the same manner as He did ours, as He is doing with me - Patiently. If not, then it's time for leadership development to show up on our radar, in our calendars, and in our budgets.

Father, help us as the Church to take time and have eyes to see the people You have to lead Your work this side of heaven. Thank you for Your patience in developing Your people. May we exhibit the same. Help us in the midst of our busyness. And thank you for Gil Peterson who took a chance on me.

John Zeswitz currently serves as Executive Director of Ministries for LCBC's Lancaster campus. Prior to that, he served 15 years at Lancaster Bible College and Graduate School in a variety of senior leadership capacities. He and his family reside in Lititz.

Nothing To Do With Me

"...Even so, come, Lord Jesus." *Revelation 22:20*

The hours ticked off as we slowly bumped along on the horrendous and twisty roads in southern Romania. The vehicle was hot and stuffy and the travel was making me ill. We were enroute to encourage new believers and emerging churches in various villages. I knew there was a full church waiting with a lengthy service planned, in which I was scheduled to preach. In my heart I did not have the energy or the passion to minister because of my weariness and fatigue. When we arrived it was just as I imagined - people everywhere. The church was packed with standing room only. I began to imagine how Jesus must have felt when He was weary in ministry with the crowds pressing around Him.

As the service began, I was wondering how I was ever going to get through it without becoming sick. While I don't recall what I spoke about, I do remember how I felt. When I finished, I felt the sermon came across flat and uninspired. Feelings of failure and disconnectedness only added to my already nauseated feeling. The interpreter surprised me as he motioned to me that he was going to follow through with an invitation. In my heart I wondered, "Why bother?" The service felt like an absolute failure.

As an invitation was extended for people to accept Jesus as their personal Savior or to recommit their life to Christ, the Holy Spirit fell on that packed church. I began to weep as I witnessed afresh that it has nothing to do with me. It is all about Jesus.

Our feelings, abilities, opinions—or the lack, thereof does not inhibit or dictate the full work of the Spirit of God and what He desires to accomplish in our midst.

Lord, use even me for Your Kingdom service today. May I be a faithful vessel and dwelling place of Your Holy Spirit.

Brian E. Martin serves as lead pastor at Weaverland Mennonite Church in East Earl. He and his wife, Shirley, are the parents of four children.

When The Gate Blows Shut!

"What He opens no man can shut, and what He shuts no one can open." *Revelation 3:7*

It was planned that morning that we would head to a higher elevation. It was a day to claim territory for the Lord at the top of a Rocky Mountain peak and romp and play as little children exploring. As we turned off the main road and headed up, suddenly we came to a gate across the road—it read "Road Closed." Dejected and disappointed, we sat in the Explorer and pondered, how can this be? This road is normally not closed unless there is snow, not a likely prospect on July 2. Without any hesitation, my son got out of the vehicle and approached the gate. With one little push, the gate swung wide open. The gate was just blown shut because it was not chained properly to the post.

How many times do we turn back, I thought, supposing the road is blocked? Supposing our plans cannot be accomplished, we give up much too soon. We at least need to test the gate. Perhaps the wind has just blown it shut. With a little more effort, we can be on our way.

Perhaps we need the younger generation to do that for us when we're too stuck in our ways. Perhaps we need to help them when they don't have the experience to know that with a little more effort they can push open a way.

Here I am now one month later and another gate has blown shut. I thought I was to go to Africa but missed the deadline for plane arrangements. I know I need to get to Uganda. My heart is already there, just as it was already at the top of the mountain peak that day in Colorado. How to test the gate and push it open?

P. U. S. H. Pray Until Something Happens!

Lord, teach us to pray, to push through obstacles, to reach new heights and new places with You.

Nancy Clegg is a worshiper and Kingdom mobilizer in Chester County and the nations.

Photo by Nancy Clegg

March

Lessons From My Daughter's Field Trip

"…it is the gift of God." *Ephesians 2:8*

It's every father's dream. The 6th grade field trip to our nation's capitol! It's a year-end educational field trip, they say. As we toured the various memorials, a lump grew in my throat, and it wasn't my street vendor lunch fare!

I was humbled by the hundreds of thousands who did what God never asked me to do - serve Him by fighting for freedom, by dying for freedom. As we rounded the flowing trees dotted with late spring foliage, we came upon the Korean War memorial. The words "Freedom Is Not Free" were emblazoned upon the polished grey stone. What a powerful reminder that the freedom to live our lives, say what we want, worship as we do, all was purchased with someone else's blood.

Sounds familiar, I thought. We speak so often of the free gift of salvation and at times lose the realization of the great price that was paid. A perfect and Holy Father, who loved His son very much, was exceedingly proud of Him, reveled in the perfection of His attributes, watched that very son die at the hands of misguided men, like me. My freedom was purchased by Jesus. I didn't do it. I couldn't do it. Jesus did it. And, it wasn't free—not to Him or His Father. That grace realization helps to set life and relationships in perspective.

Father, forgive me by taking so much of my relationship with You for granted. Help me not to run by the huge price You paid with Your son. Thank you seems so inadequate yet it's the best response we have. Here's my life. Thanks for using it, and loving me.

John Zeswitz currently serves as Executive Director of Ministries for LCBC's Lancaster campus. Prior to that, he served 15 years at Lancaster Bible College and Graduate School in a variety of senior leadership capacities. He and his family reside in Lititz.

God Defines Us

"Do not conform any longer to the pattern of this world, but be transformed by the renewing of your mind..." *Romans 12:2*

D rug addict, alcoholic, promiscuous, workaholic. These are words that once defined me. For a time each gave me a sense of being loved, belonging and significance but then one by one each led to feelings of rejection, isolation and emptiness.

What I did defined who I was and the sad thing was that even when those were no longer things I did, they were still the definitions I lived by. My past was defining my present and in my mind would also define my future. I learned how to appear confident yet always had a sense of shame as I thought, "If only you knew who I really am." In my mind I hadn't just done bad things, I was bad.

The truth is, the moment I put my trust in Jesus Christ at age 25, I was instantly redefined by God (2 Corinthians 5:17), but I have had to undergo the process of replacing faulty definitions with His truth to experience the freedom of walking in His new definition. I am loved, I am forgiven, I am cleansed, I belong and I have purpose. What I do now is determined by who I am in Christ and what I did in the past has no power in the present or the future.

God defines us on the basis of who He is, not what we have done. If you are presently defining yourself by your past, be set free by God's truth: He knows your past and He made a way for you to be redefined because in His love He canceled the record of the charges against you and took it away by nailing it to the cross (Colossians 2:14 NLT).

Father, thank you for the cross. Thank you that we are not defined by our past. Help us continually walk in the freedom of that truth.

Chris McNamara is the Director/Mentor Coordinator of New Mornings Reentry Services, an initiative of Life Transforming Ministries in Coatesville.

Remember Those In Prison

"Remember those in prison...and those who are mistreated as if you yourselves were suffering." *Hebrews 13:3*

A few years ago, I traveled to China to minister to eighty of the key leaders of the underground church movement. There are presently over 100 million believers in the nation of China, with an estimated 25,000 becoming Christians every day through house church movements. Ninety-five percent of these leaders, many of whom had traveled four days by train to get to the secluded leadership training seminar, had been imprisoned for their faith.

I met a group of women who oversee hundreds of thousands of believers. They told stories of being raped in prison, yet they stayed true to the Lord and continued to start new house churches.

I was asked to teach on the biblical truth of becoming spiritual fathers and mothers. After the sessions, these men and women stood, prayed and repented. It was such a humbling experience. They repented because they felt they were so caught up in the work of God, but they were not focusing enough on the workers of God. This is a great lesson for all of us to learn. We can become so caught up in our work, including God's work, that we lose sight of our call to train the next generation by mentoring spiritual sons and daughters.

Lord, we pray for our brothers and sisters in Christ who are in prison for their faith. Grant them strength and may they be released soon to serve You in freedom.

Larry Kreider serves on the executive team of the Regional Church of Lancaster County and as the International Director of DOVE Christian Fellowship International.

Horses And Trucks

"...Horsepower is not the answer; no one gets by on muscle alone. Watch this: God's eye is on those who respect him, the ones who are looking for his love. He's ready to come to their rescue in bad times; in lean times he keeps body and soul together."
Psalm 33: 17-19 (The Message)

March is known for winds, but the storm my husband drove home through in 2001 was especially memorable. Navigating the wet, windswept streets, he noticed the wires up ahead were swaying treacherously. They stretched across the road and he watched as they whipped back and forth, each time gaining power. He knew that the force of the wind on the wires could gain momentum and snap the pole. The Lord must have been heightening his awareness of this situation because sure enough, he watched and it happened. He knew his truck was fast and he hoped that if he could floor the gas pedal, he might make it safely.

In those split seconds, he could see the snapped pole coming toward his windshield. As he got closer and closer the tension of the wires snapped the pole up in the air like a yoyo as he floored it. When he looked in his rear view mirror, he saw the opposite reaction of the pole shooting to the ground and impaling itself into the road right behind his truck.

In my devotion time the next morning, God confirmed what He had done. It wasn't the speed or power of the truck or my husband's fast thinking, although they were God-given. It was God Himself, His eyes were on those He loved, and His unfailing love delivered my husband from certain death.

The enemy roams about like a roaring lion but You, O Lord, are mighty to save us physically and spiritually. You, O Lord, are our hope. You, O Lord, are our Mighty Rescuer. Thank You, Lord.

Christina Ricker, wife of Glenn, mother, grandmother. We attend Petra Christian Fellowship.

Transcendental Trepidation

"Serve the Lord…with trembling…." *Psalm 2:11*

Port Authority, Manhattan. Should I talk to somebody about Jesus while waiting for my bus?

The old lady giving away Jehovah's Witness material? *No.*

That guy eating lunch? *No.*

The fellow hawking Transcendental Meditation albums featuring music from ex-Beatle George Harrison? *Yes.*

Bizarre conversation! Once the guy realized I was a Christian (and not a vegetarian or a customer), he went for the jugular vein: "You Jesus freaks drink blood and eat the Lamb of God!" A few more insults later, he aborted our "talk."

"*Don't let him get away*," the Holy Spirit nudged. Shaken by God's insistence that I pursue the man, I followed him and told him I was sincerely concerned for his soul. Shocked, he listened—but soon brushed me off again.

"*Not done yet*," the Holy Spirit said (though I was *sure* this guy was done with *me!*) I watched him corral a woman coming off an escalator. Aggressively pushing his product, he wouldn't take "no" for an answer—when God moved me to interrupt his sales pitch. "I'm sorry, ma'am, for the hard time this guy is giving you. Here…" (I handed her a Jesus street paper) "…this is *free*."

Mr. TM grabbed the paper and flung it backwards over his shoulder. "You'd better watch out!" He threatened me angrily. "You're messin' with a dangerous guru!" I said I was sorry for getting in his business, that I loved him and Jesus loved him and…suddenly he cursed me, shoved me and stalked off into the crowd.

As I turned to apologize to the wide-eyed, unwitting participant of this spiritual wrestling match, the Spirit said, "*All done.*" Dazed and trembling, I wandered toward my bus line. Once aboard, I shared my experience with a fellow seated with me. That opened a conversation which lasted all the way to our destination (and he didn't push me out of the seat even once!)

Father, please let me know—someday—how this all turned out!

Mark Ammerman, member of Regional Council for the Regional Church of Lancaster County, talks about Jesus even when he doesn't want to.

Hakuna Matata

"Out of the mouth of babes You have ordained strength, because of Your enemies, that You may silence the enemy and the avenger." *Psalm 8:2*

My wife and I and our two toddler boys just returned from the mission field in Peru. We were supposed to serve there two to three years, but through a series of difficult events we were back in the US in six months.

Because of the suddenness of the transition, we were without a job, without a home, and most of all, depleted of faith. Graciously, my in-laws took us in but the pressure to provide for my family and to get God's direction loomed daily over me.

I remember in particular one night as we drove up into my in-laws driveway, my wife and I both were facing what felt like one of the darkest of nights. Usually as husband and wife we have the ability to pull each other out of this pit of despair, but this time we both were in it together and we felt very alone, even wondering where God was in all of this. We sold most of our belongings, we followed God's call to Peru, and now here we were back in the US in the front seat of our car literally sobbing because of the sense of failure and hurt that plagued our hearts. But then came this little voice from the back seat- it wasn't God's or was it?

It was our three year old son saying, "Dad— Mom... Why are you crying? Hakuna matata!" For those of you who are Lion King Lovers, you know that "hakuna matata" is a famous song in the movie and it is Swahili for "no worries—no problems." When our son spoke these words, God's Spirit came with them and my wife and I went from total brokenness to belly laughter.

With those simple words from our child's mouth, it was as if God lifted this mountain of care and we were able to see again, hope again, and laugh again. God used our child to remind us that He was still there.

Father, continue to use the faith of a child to soften our hearts to believe again, to hope again, to trust You again. Amen

Craig Nanna lives in Reading with his amazing wife and three kids, and together they serve as Sr. pastors of Reading DOVE Christian Ministry Center. Craig also serves as the director of the Reading Regional Transformation Network.

Keep Praying

"You need to persevere so that when you have done the will of God, you will receive what he has promised." *Hebrews 10:36*

Wow! We finally arrived in Scotland to begin our service in mission work. We had prayed so long for this day to come. The vision to be on the mission field somewhere was a prayer point for us even before we were married. It had been over 15 years of bringing that request before the Lord. In those years we took every opportunity to be involved with missions in one form or another. Supporting missionaries, sending boxes, picking up or taking people to the airport, you name it we did it. Year after year we would pray for the day when it would be our time to go. We knew the Lord had put a desire in our heart and we were determined to see it through.

As the time grew closer and closer for us to leave for the field life became nothing short of an adventure. Situations that seemed like mountains fall away to mole hills before our eyes. We watched as God moved so sovereignly on our behalf. It became extremely humbling. There were times that we just sat and wept and were left speechless at his grace and love for us!

If you have a need or request DO NOT give up praying about it. It could be a call to the mission field, salvation for a family member or healing from an illness, KEEP PRAYING!

I once heard a story about two farmers. Both needed rain and prayed. Only one of the farmers went then and prepared his fields for the rain. Which do you think received it?

Pray but then ready yourself for the answer. Even if it takes 15 or more years to see it. Don't give up!

Heavenly Father, give me the strength to persevere in prayer for the requests of my heart. Teach me how to ready myself in time for the answers You will send. Help me never to back up, back down or quit! I want to persevere no matter how long it takes. I want to grab hold of what You have promised. Amen

Beth Miller and her husband Rob are formerly from Lititz. They are presently serving Living Waters Community Church, a DOVE Christian Fellowship partner church, in Peterhead, Scotland. They have been married 15 years and have three sons.

Sentiment Or Substance?

"...the substance of things hoped for..."
Hebrews 11:1 (King James Version)

One of the biggest misconceptions about faith assumes it is a feeling or positive mental energy that we have to drum up. If we "drum it up" enough, we'll get what we ask for, but if we don't, we won't. Not a scriptural perspective.

I had been visiting my daughter and planned to take the metro from where she lived in Fairfax, Virginia, to Union Station, and there catch an Amtrak home. My ticket was reserved for 5:30 PM, so we left in plenty of time to catch the train. Well, something happened on the way to DC. The metro stopped. I mean a total halt. All you could see out the window was a mass of *immoveable* concrete block. I kept looking at my watch and as the time ticked away, it became clear that I would likely miss my connection. So, I started to pray, but must admit, at the same time was wondering where I might spend the night. *Lincoln bedroom maybe?* Finally, the metro started moving; it was 5:30. My mind told me it was now impossible to make the train. But undaunted, as soon as the metro pulled in, I dashed off, running as fast as possible through a crowded menagerie of people, all the while searching for Amtrak signs. After finally making it to the ticket counter, I hastily got through the line and was directed where to go. I reached the train, still running full bore. The door had already closed but the conductor motioned me on, and in a second, we were off.

What had caused me to run like a madman even though I *felt* all hope was gone? Faith was activated when I prayed. My spirit responded to a very real substance that went beyond feeling.

Lord, help us not to confuse faith with feeling. May we realize we might have more faith than we think.

Becky Toews leads the women's ministry at New Covenant Christian Church and is an adjunct professor at Lancaster Bible College.

How Can They Believe?

"...How can they believe in the one of whom they have not heard?"
Romans 10:14

His clothes were tattered and dirty. His hair was unkempt and knotted. He seemed to be in his own world, talking to himself or an imaginary person. His constant scratching made my skin feel like it was crawling.

Should I approach him with a bag lunch or should I walk on by him, my mind raced with the question. I wasn't exactly afraid of him, but somehow I figured he wouldn't be interested.

As I drew near, our eyes met. I smiled while holding the bag lunch up with a gesture to offer it to him. Without a moment's hesitation he turned and quickly walked away. I was disappointed he refused the lunch.

As I continued walking, I whispered a short prayer that our paths would cross again. A few days later, my prayer was answered. Again he refused the lunch, this time not even waiting for me to get close.

In the days and weeks that followed this same scenario happened many times. Not wanting to give up, when I would see him I would smile and offer him the lunch.

One day to my surprise he took the lunch. I felt like I hit a grand slam home run in the bottom of the ninth inning scoring the winning run. However, I knew this was just the beginning of what God wanted to do.

As time passed, our chats turned into long discussions about the Bible and a personal relationship with Jesus Christ. The other day at the close of our conversation he said, "I used to run away from you but now I enjoy talking to you. I know God is speaking to me and I'm listening."

Lord, help us to have the courage to share YOU with those in our lives today whom appear to be uninterested.

Joetta Keefer from DOVE ELANCO serves with Hands of Hope, a ministry to the homeless in Philadelphia, meeting physical, emotional, and spiritual needs in a practical way.

Now I Lay Me Down To Sleep

"...He giveth his beloved sleep." *Psalm 127:2*

I had just returned from a quiet weekend at St. Joseph's House of Prayer, a Franciscan retreat house in a small town in New York State. While there, I'd read through a brief book on healing prayer, and my "faith level" for miracles was pumped. I came home to find my wife suffering from a torturous migraine headache—so bad that she was sick to her stomach. At bedtime, the throbbing pain would not allow her to lay her head down on the pillow. So she sat up in bed in the dark as I laid my hands on her in silent prayer.

A picture formed clearly in my mind of an overheated electronics control room (Terri's brain) where severed power cables spewed hissing sparks, and electric charges arced with one another like clashing light-sabers in a Star Wars film. As I prayed, I saw myself in that power room, grappling with the cables, connecting them one to another in an attempt to avert disaster. Finally, the cables were whole, the danger had passed, and the room was filled with a quiet, peaceful hum. The picture faded, and I became aware that Terri was suddenly sound asleep.

A strange story, and a rare thing to happen to me. But I'm convinced it is a God story, and that the picture that played in my head as I prayed for my wife was a picture that God put there as His own hands reached into my wife's aching head to bring order, peace, healing and a deep, sweet night's sleep.

My mom taught me to pray this bedtime prayer: "Now I lay me down to sleep, I pray the Lord my soul to keep. Watch over me throughout the night, and wake me in the morning light. Amen"

Mark Ammerman, author, artist and member of Regional Council of the Regional Church of Lancaster County, serves on the leadership staff of In The Light Ministries in Lancaster City.

Sowing Seeds

"A farmer went out to sow." *Matthew 13:3*

I n my time serving with Youth with Mission (YWAM) in Maui Hawaii I found that playing basketball was not just one of my escapes from daily routine but one of my greatest ministries.

A local guy by the name of Kupono Franco became a friend of mine as we played ball together. I soon found out that he was a ringleader in the town doing and selling drugs. As I began to pray for Kupono opportunities arose to share my love for Jesus with him, he would also allow me to pray over him concerning the issues he was dealing with.

Almost a full year went by without seeing Kupono; people in town would tell me things they heard about him being in jail: one rumor said that he was dead! My heart was burdened for this friend I could not find, and then one day on the beach I saw a familiar figure in the distance....

Sure enough it was Kupono! He was standing on the shore with his body board looking at the surf. As I approached him I could tell there was a peace I had never seen inside him before. When he heard me call his name he turned to greet me with a smile. I said, "Kupono, where have you been?" He pointed up and said, "Corey, I took your advice, I'm following the LORD." I gave him a hug and we talked a bit about what all he'd been through since we last saw each other.

As we parted that late afternoon and I watched Kupono run toward the ocean to catch the evening surf, my heart was filled with joy to have been a simple farmer, a friend sowing seed in Kupono's life.

Father, grant us eyes to see the opportunities around us to sow seed into people's lives. Grant us perseverance to pray over those seeds of salvation to see them spring up in due time producing a bountiful crop.

Corey Martin, son, brother, friend, husband and soon to be father!

A Living Sacrifice

"… present your bodies a living sacrifice, holy, acceptable to God, which is your reasonable service."
Romans 12:1 (New King James Version)

I stood in the back of the room with tears streaming down my face. I had just made the decision of selling my life's dream. Every dream I ever had in farming had become a reality, but I had just decided to sell the farm and become supported full time to lead the church that I helped plant earlier that year in 1987.

As I talked to the Lord, I said, "Lord, it is so hard realizing all of the close family times I am giving up—the times of taking my wife and children with me on the tractor, the times of working together as a family. This is who I am; this is what is familiar; this is what is secure. It is too big a sacrifice."

The Lord said, "Open your eyes and look up." I opened my eyes, and on the wall was a large world map that we used for the purpose of praying for nations. The Lord continued to speak, "You are concerned about spending time with your children in tractors and pick-up trucks, but if you follow Me, I will take you and your children to the nations!"

As I write this, I am on a plane returning from a two week trip to Scotland, Holland, Bulgaria, and an overnight in Germany, with our sixth and youngest child. Over the past years, when each of our children turned 14, I took them with me somewhere in the world to give them a broader world view. The Lord is indeed faithful, and if we follow Him, He will be faithful to complete all that He said that He would do.

I thought I was making a sacrifice for Him, but in reality I have gotten back far more than I have ever given to Him.

Father, I pray for every person today who is sensing a call from You for something new and is struggling with giving up that which is secure, safe and familiar. Give them the courage to follow Your call wherever it may take them.

Ron Myer serves as assistant international director of DOVE Christian Fellowship International.

Essence Of Life

"But his delight is in the law of the Lord, and in his law he meditates day and night." *Psalm 1:2*

The Psalmist challenges us in this verse to meditate, to delight in the "law of the Lord," which is the Word of God. Did you ever think about meditating upon the law? We do not meditate when we see a speed limit sign that says 65 M.P.H.: we just try to obey such laws. But the Psalmist tells us to meditate upon the law of the Lord.

This tells me that God's law is more than just a law that is to be obeyed, but that there is the essence of life wrapped up in the "law of the Lord."

First of all, these are the words of God; God gave His beloved creation His Word to live by so that our lives may be honoring and glorifying to Him.

Secondly, we must realize that in obedience to His Word, life will go well with us. We have libraries full of laws and codes and ordinances, but in God's Word we have the fortress that has been given by God to guard our lives eternally.

A third thought is that His Word teaches us of the perfect plan of God for His creation. It allows us to know when we have fallen short of that plan in our lives. We are to seek God's grace and mercy in forgiveness through the precious blood of Jesus Christ. The laws are beneficial to sustain our lives. Verse three of Psalm 1 says we become like a tree firmly planted, with refreshing water to sustain our existence, and we bear much fruit and are prosperous. To meditate on these laws is a move that brings us into an ever closer walk with the heavenly Father—what a glorious place to be!

Lord, the very essence of life is wrapped up in Your Word. Help us to delight in Your Word today.

Tom Weber is the pastor of Akron Church of the Brethren.

A Word Of Advice From God

"He who belongs to God hears what God says." *John 8:47*

A few years ago, my wife and I were wrestling over a major decision which would mean that we would move to another country and take on new ministry responsibilities. It felt major in every way. What about our children? What about our house? There was a lot to decide.

We would fast and pray, but did not seem to get clarity or direct answers, certainly not in the usual ways we were expecting. I knew about hearing God; I had even taught on it—but God did not seem to have heard my teaching!

After a period of time, some things began to happen. For example, we met a businessman and told him about our deliberation concerning our house. He instantly spoke a simple and clear word of advice—but it felt that it cut straight to our hearts and spirits - so much so that it did not seem just a human voice. We knew this was a direct word of guidance from the Lord. We do not know whether the man was even a Christian—yet his word proved true and helpful to us as we made our major decisions and plans.

The scriptures tell us that the Lord Jesus is the Good Shepherd and that we are His sheep. As one of His sheep, each of us has the capacity to hear His voice. He longs to speak to us, and we are capable of hearing Him. It just might not be the way we expect, or it might come through an unusual instrument—God is God!

Lord, I thank You that we can hear You speak to us. Help us to be open to Your words in whatever way they come.

Peter Bunton serves as the Director of DOVE Mission International, the missions' wing of DOVE Christian Fellowship International.

Savor Life

"You have made known to me the path of life; you will fill me with joy in your presence, with eternal pleasures at your right hand."
Psalm 16:11

To know that I am on the right path fulfilling the purpose for which I was created is important to me. When I am busy doing things and my schedule is full, I rarely take the time to question whether I'm fulfilling my purpose. When my schedule is less hectic and my pace has slowed down, I feel guilty because I'm actually enjoying some free time.

On one of these "free time days," I was with my grandson. Watching him through my kitchen window, I saw him talking and laughing as if someone were with him, but there was no one around. He was happy and free enjoying the outdoors, driving his trucks in the sandbox. The scene was peaceful, happy, and enjoyable, and I watched him for quite some time soaking in the moment.

God whispered to me, "Just as you love watching your grandson play and love life, I too love watching you enjoy life." At that moment, I was overwhelmed with the thought that God wants us to enjoy this life.

To be good stewards of what God has entrusted us with can be all-consuming and at times we may lose our joy.

Plan times of rest with your spouse, family, and friends so that you can be renewed in spirit and have great joy in this life, for this is the Father's good pleasure.

In our work and in our play, may we be people of purpose, and may the path we are on bring us great joy and eternal pleasures.

Anne Beiler is the founder of Auntie Anne's Soft Pretzels. Her passion is family, grandchildren, motorcycle riding, music, reading, speaking, and giving.

In His Hands

"He will call upon me, and I will answer him; I will be with him in trouble, I will deliver him and honor him." *Psalm 91:15*

The numbers on the clock seemed to move slowly from 2:20 to 3:00 to 3:15 in stark contrast to the constant rush of thoughts in my mind. After over twenty years of suffering with hepatitis C, my husband Domenic's liver was failing. Having researched his condition, I knew that this could indicate liver cancer. The prognosis for those with liver cancer is not usually good. Memories of family and friends who lost their fights with cancer filled my head. I tried to pray. I tried to meditate. Nothing helped. The endless swirling of negative, fearful thoughts continued. I wanted to scream!

I got out of bed, went into the bathroom, and turned on the fan. Certain that Dom couldn't hear me, I cried out to the Lord. "Lord, I don't know what's going on. I have no answers from the doctors yet. In the meantime, I have to be able to function in faith." Nothing.

I kept praying. "Lord, I need your peace. I need a word." Nothing. I can't remember ever having demanded anything from the Lord, but all of a sudden from somewhere deep within me, I cried out, "Lord, I need something right now!" At that very moment, a quiet word came to me. "His life is in My hands." No specific promises, no guarantees, just the plain truth that Dom's life was held in His heavenly Father's loving hands. That was all I needed. I had immediate peace, knowing that God had heard me and was with us in this trial. This assurance carried us through the difficult days that followed and keeps us trusting our Lord today, four years later.

Lord, I thank you that Your ears hear the words of our mouths.

Peachy Colleluori and her husband Domenic have served as staff members at the National Christian Conference Center in Valley Forge, for over twenty years.

New Life

"Create in me a clean heart, O God; and renew a right spirit within me." *Psalm 51:10*

The call came late on a Saturday evening. As my wife was awakening me, the questions came: "Did we fully discuss this? Is this what we decided to do?" We made our way to the hospital as quickly as possible, all the while offering many prayers for God's protection, His grace, His peace, but most of all for the family of the organ donor. He had the foresight to think of others should the unthinkable happen. In his death, an opportunity for new life was presented to me. At the hospital, things were being prepared for the surgery.

After five hours of testing and waiting, all was ready. I was wheeled into the operating room. Despite all the prayers, I was still frightened. The last thing I remember hearing was the tinkling of instruments.

I opened my eyes after what seemed like a short time. The operation had, in fact, taken over eight hours. I was thankful to be alive. God had answered our prayers. As I lay on that bed and thanked Him, I also asked Him to renew my heart. I knew this operation was not only for me. I was sure He had other plans for my life, and I wanted my spiritual heart as healthy as the new liver I received. The transplant surgery took a relatively short time compared to the renewal process for my heart. My salvation twenty-three years before put me on the road to redemption. The surgery gave me new life to press on. God's renewal is a lifelong process. I pray God never stops operating on my heart, renewing me daily.

Lord, I pray that my life will always be a reflection of Your grace and mercy. May others see Your Holy Spirit and its saving grace, and may they look to renew themselves daily in You.

Domenic Colleluori has served as a staff member at the National Christian Conference Center in Valley Forge for over twenty years.

Touched By God

"People brought all their sick to him and begged him to let the sick touch the edge of his cloak, and all who touched him were healed."
Matthew 14:36

For many years, I had been suffering from an uncontrolled seizure disorder that stemmed from a vaccination that I had received while serving in the United States Air Force. On one occasion when I had a seizure, I had fallen down a flight of stairs and tore my rotator cuff. For the next five years, I suffered through doing daily tasks that required the lifting of my arm. Throwing a baseball with any velocity was impossible. God has touched me regarding my seizure disorder. I went from having six a week to perhaps one or two a month. I've been really thankful for God's hand upon my life, but I still suffered from having little strength in my right shoulder (I'm right-handed).

One day while in Reading after a day of prayer and fasting, I was loading up my wife's vehicle and a gentleman approached me. He was heading to a church to do a healing service and asked me if I was experiencing pain in my right shoulder. I told him yes. He asked me if I believed that God would heal me, and I told him yes. As this gentleman laid his hand on me and prayed, I felt the fire of God's Spirit in my shoulder. I felt great! I had not felt so good in my shoulder in five years. The next day I went outside with my brother-in-law and threw a baseball. Not only was there no pain, but I had enough velocity behind my throws to hurt his hand. God is good and faithful.

Dear Lord, I pray that You just reach out and touch those who need a miracle in their life today. Whether it is physical, emotional or financial, Lord, be sovereign in our lives. Lord, as dawn breaks, come in and transform us!

Aaron J. Durso is the Pastor of LOVE Christian Fellowship in Birdsboro, Pennsylvania. He is also the vice-president of the Birdsboro Borough Council.

A Truly Grateful Spirit

"Loving-kindness and truth have met together; righteousness and truth have met together; righteousness and peace have kissed each other. Truth rises ... and righteousness smiles down from heaven."
Psalm 85:10

My seven children were wound up tight and it was raining! I was in no mood for arguments, sibling rivalry and complaints. I called them for lunch. They came running, bumping into each other and continuing their various exchanges.

I prayed, "God, we hate this day, why did You have to make it rain today? We really don't like this food, and we are so bored. There is never anything exciting around here. We are angry at each other and You."

Was this giving them a wrong concept of God? Could I even talk to God like this? My religious mind almost went into shock. I finally finished, "In Jesus' name, Amen."

When I looked up, I saw seven pairs of eyes glaring at me in disbelief. Our oldest began, "Mom, you don't talk to God like that!" By this time, my heart had been emptied of anger and frustration. I replied, "But why not? God knows what is in our hearts right now. We would not be able to pretend as we pray. He is not shocked when we are honest before Him. He is more than willing to forgive us and free us from our bondage in trying to be good without His power and grace to help us. Let's talk to Him again so He can help us think and talk differently."

By this time, we were all subdued and in a much better frame of mind to humbly pray: "Dear Jesus, You are our Helper, please forgive us for our attitudes and selfishness today. We do need You, and even though it is raining, You are watering the earth for us. We give praise to You for Your many blessings and thank You for helping us learn an important lesson today in Jesus' name, Amen."

Thank you, Lord, that we can be honest with You and share how we really feel. Thank you that You love us no matter what.

Naomi Sensenig and her husband, LaMarr, attend and serve at Lancaster Evangelical Free Church in Lititz.

God In The Ordinary

"He [God] gives strength to the weary and increases the power of the weak." *Isaiah 40:29*

Does God know technology? The sound and video pro was having difficulty showing the PowerPoint slides with the borrowed projector being used one Sunday morning. I started to walk away from our tech coordinator but felt a nudge in my spirit to go back and pray with him about the problem. I prayed over him and the equipment, and he later shared publicly that God answered. He had discovered a way to display the slides. It was a lesson for me that God works in the ordinary. I had felt self-conscious praying for the "technology problem."

There had been some "big things" we as a congregation had prayed for. We pleaded for God to answer in miraculous ways. The miracles didn't happen. We saw God at work, yes, but not in the ways we had hoped for. Had we not prayed right? Was there more we should have done? We felt like the Emmaus disciples who replied to Jesus, "But we had hoped."

We didn't lose faith in God. We experienced God's grace. We acknowledged Him as sovereign. But we pondered; we wondered. Together we grieved. We affirmed our hope in God for now and eternity. We experienced God's drawing us closer to one another.

We are primed in our world, and in the church at large, to look for the spectacular, the dramatic, the extraordinary. When God does great things, we celebrate. How do we respond when the faucet leaks, the baby keeps crying, or the car doesn't start?

Is not God's grace miraculous when it sustains us in the ordinariness of life? Is not God still great when our prayers are not answered in the way we had hoped? Does it not take as much faith to trust God when the healing doesn't come, as when it does?

O God, whether we see You in the extraordinary, or the ordinary, we worship You!

Jim Leaman, husband, father, and grandfather, pastors Groffdale Mennonite Church, Leola.

Cleaning Out The Closets

"Purify me from my sins, and I will be clean; wash me, and I will be whiter than snow. Create in me a clean heart, O God. Renew a loyal spirit within me." *Psalm 51:7;10 (New Living Translation)*

The beginning of the spring and fall seasons are reminders to organize and clean out closets. I would imagine that this chore is a Pennsylvania Dutch tradition because I believe it was passed down from my grandmother to my mother and then to me.

You probably know the drill. Clothes that haven't been worn in more than 12 months probably are not going to see the light of day in the near future. Some excuses I have used are weight-loss, weight-gain, out-of style patterns, lengths, colors, trims, etc. If you are organizing office closets and encounter college assignments or paid bills from 1987, it is most likely time to purge the papers into the shredder and trash container. I believe that when the closet light turns off, they procreate until the next time I open the door.

It is difficult to let go of these possessions; there are always lingering thoughts: "maybe I could use this some day, or better yet, maybe my friends will use it in the future," so I must keep it!

Much energy is needed to clean out the stuff I don't need! It is not only physically, but also mentally tiring. On the other side, or the brighter side of this chore, there is an incredible sense of accomplishment and in the space I have cleared, everything is "right with the world."

Cleaning out closets is much like my relationship with Christ. I believe that Christ has "cleaned" me one time (when I accepted Christ as my Lord and Savior), which spans my past, present and future. However, when I feel the junk of the "world" or "my possessions" of sinfulness piling up into spaces which should only be overflowing with God's goodness, I need to surrender those things to Christ and accept His wholeness and the transparency of His ever lasting love.

Dear Father, thank you for Your never-ending faithfulness and love in spite of my 'junk.' I am always amazed when You, in Your magnificence, remind me of Your unconditional love and that You are in complete control of my life! I humbly serve You. Amen

Jane Keller, Human Resources Director at Water Street Rescue Mission, Lancaster; Lancaster County Bible Church partner; breast cancer survivor.

A Quiet Peaceful Place

"As the deer pants for streams of water, so my soul pants for you, O God." *Psalm 42:1*

One day on my early morning meeting with God, I was reminded again of His faithfulness. I stood on a hill looking down into the Buffalo River in Moran, WY, with the skyline of the Grand Tetons hovering behind as a picture framing the landscape. I again was mesmerized by the greatness of God, the Creator/Artist who hand-made the entire earth for humans to enjoy.

Just as I was praising Him, I looked down into the river valley only to notice a clump of yellow daisies blooming on a cleft of the hill on an island of dirt. They were leaning alone, looking upward into the heavens at their Creator as if they were praising Him for giving them life abundantly!

As I was meditating quietly in my solitude, a mother deer came out of the willow bushes seeking a drink of water. "Oh Master," I cried, "just like you to show me a picture of myself. Many times I can feel like being on an island, needing a fresh anointing to encourage my soul and to be renewed by Your Spirit of love as I come to drink from Your very being, desiring to be filled by Your presence."

God created the Garden of Eden as the first home on earth. He fellowshipped with the first humans He created in the cool of the day. Jesus also went to the garden to talk with His Father and pray often. God delights in us and enjoys the quiet moments we spend with Him.

Oh God, I praise You as You lead me beside quiet waters and I worship You in Your spirit of holiness, You restore my soul to a place of quiet peace and rest. Amen

Dona L. Fisher is Chairman of the local National Day of Prayer, director of Change of Pace Bible Studies and is a free-lance writer for Lancaster Sunday News.

God's Law Of Sowing And Reaping

"For I know the plans I have for you…to give you hope and a future." *Jeremiah 29:11*

Dialogue with the Lord during this past year of workplace transition.

"Son, I want you to work at a place that will bring you joy, for you will bring the best service there."

"But which one, Lord? None of the open doors seems to bring joy—or all of them could. The doors look ominous and like hard work."

"You must fight and win the battle in your mind. You can't do everything and you must commit to something. All paths will have struggles and obstacles. But these will not seem terrible when you are focused and committed to the goals and purposes I have for you."

"Father, which path should I choose? The one that looks easy or the one that seems more difficult? What are the benefits of choosing more difficulty that I need to stay in for a longer time? I would normally choose the easiest and shortest route. But, does the longer and harder path result in more lasting lessons? My fear is the path is just longer and harder with no additional benefits."

"Son, that cannot be, because of the laws of faith and My law of sowing and reaping. The law of delayed gratification says that no effort goes unrewarded. My law of sowing and reaping says you *will* reap WHAT you sow, LATER than you sow and MORE than you sow. Are you planting vegetables for a season or fruit trees for the next generations? When there's a delay in receiving your investment, yields are larger and result in multiplied dividends and compounded interest."

Lord, help my brothers and sisters in transition, just as You are leading and guiding me. Thank You for Your plans, Your destiny for each one of us. Help us to build and to occupy until You come—for the praise of Your glory. Amen

Bill Goodberlet is a member of the convening council for "York Coalition for Transformation" and an elder at Emmanuel Christian Fellowship. He has recently acquired his health insurance license.

Expectancy

"In the morning, O Lord, you hear my voice; in the morning I lay my requests before you and wait in expectation." *Psalm 5:3*

The sun was just starting to rise above the hill line, thin beams of light creating halos as it filtered through the leaves on the trees. It was going to be another beautiful day.

I threw my arms wide as I marveled at the sight, thanking the Lord for the opportunity to experience what He would provide that day.

It had been a struggle for the past several months, with family and job issues; but as I had found answers in His Word and through the support of others, I had come to see Him work more and more in all types of situations. It wasn't that He hadn't been there before; it was that I now was able to experience His blessings more and more as my walk with Him deepened.

I now had reached a point of expectancy, seeking throughout each day to see where the Lord was working, being prepared to enjoy new experiences He might bless me with even when, at the time, they might seem a bit hectic or traumatic. Whom might He put in my path who would provide a bit of inspiration or with whom could I share an encouraging word or prayer?

Yes, it was going to be a beautiful day.

Lord, help me today and each day to be focused on You and Your goodness. Help me to truly see and experience the work You are doing all around me and help me to fully appreciate how You are the center of it all. Please help me to live each day in a state of expectancy. Amen

Casey Jones, an organization management and grants advisor, resides in Parkesburg. He also focuses on family ministries and those that come alongside the hurting.

Learning Mercy

"Speak and act as those who are going to be judged by the law that gives freedom, because judgment without mercy will be shown to anyone who has not been merciful. Mercy triumphs over judgment." *James 2:12–13*

I walked into class, toting two of the special bluebooks we needed for essay exams. "Oh, no," I heard, "I forgot my bluebook." I sat smugly, proud of being a responsible student who would never make such a gross error. I had one extra bluebook but thought, "I might need it. Besides, it looks like more than one person forgot, so I don't have enough for everyone."

I heard another voice, "Oh, don't worry. I brought extra bluebooks in case people forgot theirs." I watched as she pulled out a thick stack and graciously passed them out. Shame welled up inside of me and for the first time, I understood the meaning of "mercy."

The incident began a deconstruction of the harshness with which I'd judged both myself and others. On inducing humility, God showed me that my intellect is genetic, my wise decisions are based on a secure childhood, and I basically have no bragging rights upon which to base my self-esteem. He showed me the fallibility of assessing my righteousness by comparing myself to "all of those other people who do really horrible sins." He helped me fight the ubiquitous lies that "acceptance of others may be misconstrued as approving what they do" and "reasons are just excuses." Those are the messages that had grown inside my self-righteous, little heart while squeezing out the truth of God's grace and mercy. Since then, I've learned the joy that comes from assuming the best of others and giving them space to be human.

Additionally, through teaching me how to extend grace and mercy to others, God has helped me to accept the unconditional mercy He lavishes on me.

Dear Jesus, Please keep my heart warm and open so that I can pass on the mercy You've shown to me.

Tricia Groff, M.S. is a counselor at Crossroads Counseling Center, Lancaster.

Strength In The Heat Of The Day

"But the Lord stood at my side and gave me strength, so that through me the message might be fully proclaimed..." *2 Timothy 4:17*

The hot sand sifts into my shoes as I struggle to adjust my long skirt. The heat lingers beneath my head covering creating tiny beads of sweat. *So this is Africa.*

Our *School of Global Transformation* team had joined a medical team from Pennsylvania, and together we traveled to a Muslim community in Kenya called Garissa. Unlike Kenya's modern, lush capital, Garissa's streets were filled with women in long head coverings, piles of burning trash and wandering cows. Our week in Garissa was spent assisting the medical team as they treated more than 700 people and cleaned up from the recent floods. Between the heat, work and oppressive surroundings I thankfully collapsed into my bed each night.

Crouched in the sand one afternoon, with a dozen small black hands waving in my face with fingers caked in paint, I felt a strange overwhelming feeling of fulfillment. It was one of those moments where you know you are exactly where God wants you to be, doing just what He desires, and suddenly nothing else holds appeal.

I think it's safe to say that perhaps it's this kind of feeling that gives us the strength in the "heat of the day."

Sometimes we worry that if we do God's will it could take us some place we don't want to go...like a hut in the middle of Africa. But it is only when we are in God's will that we find true fulfillment and His desires become our desires. And as we walk in His will He gives us a strength that often contradicts our surroundings and circumstances.

Thank you, God, for the strength and grace that You give me to do Your will. Help me to seek Your will daily and allow Your desires to become my own.

Marisa Barnett is a recent graduate of the School of Global Transformation and is a youth leader at DOVE Christian Fellowship Elizabethtown.

Finishing The Work

"I don't know what awaits me… but my life is worth nothing to me unless I use it for finishing the work assigned me by the Lord Jesus – the work of telling others the Good News." *Acts 20:23-24*

I thought my life was about operating a third generation hardware store, so I could provide for my family and give to ministries, support my wife, and explore the Canadian tundra each winter on snowmobile.

That thinking changed on May 6, 2007, while traveling on Route 81 in New York State. I fell asleep at the wheel and was awakened by my wife screaming my name. The first thing I saw was trees coming at me at precisely the same speed I'd set my cruise control to – 70 miles an hour. I wrenched the steering wheel away from the trees and heard my wife yell, "Jesus!" I had no control over the vehicle. We became airborne and rolled three times.

I wasn't a stranger to accidents. As a teenager, I had a serious motorcycle wreck and ten years ago I had a cheating-death-experience while snowmobiling. Both times I escaped unscathed and deep down inside took credit for skillful maneuvering.

But this time, I couldn't take credit. I believe Jesus' response to my wife's cry was the reason we walked away from the accident unharmed. And it was probably His intervention that saved my life the other times as well.

As we looked at our totaled vehicle with the rescue team, knowing we escaped without bloodshed or broken bones, no one doubted it was a miracle.

I realize I could have died, and God could have easily found someone else to run the hardware store. So he must have other assignments for me. Like Paul, "I don't know what awaits me…but my life is worth nothing to me unless I use it for finishing the work assigned me by the Lord Jesus."

Father, thank You for extending our lives. Help all of us to use our time for You.

Ron Hosler operates Hosler's Hardware & Tire Center.

This Far And No Farther

"The boundary lines have fallen for me in pleasant places."
Psalm 16:6

After crying "Jesus" at the top of my lungs before Ron and I swirled through the air in our truck, tumbled through a swamp, and then climbed out virtually uninjured, I asked God to show me specifically how He'd protected us.

Bit by bit, He revealed His hand.

The first thing we realized was that the swamp cushioned our impact. We shuddered to think of what could have happened if we'd hit trees or boulders or even just hard-packed ground. Instead, Jesus directed the path of our vehicle into a mud bath. We were filthy from the muck that splashed through our broken windows, but we were protected.

Next was the man who retrieved something in front of our truck that had flown out as we rolled. It was my Bible. Symbolizing the Living Word that went out in front of us, it was as though Jesus said, "This far and no farther. This accident is completely within My control and I determined that this vehicle would stop here, land upright, and not hit any trees."

The final thing was the most powerful. Eight days later as I closed my eyes to worship, I immediately saw a vision of our mangled red truck at the accident scene, with torn up ground all around it. Perched on top of the truck, presiding in pristine glory with beautiful shining white feathers, was an image of the Holy Spirit as a very large dove. His wings were spread triumphantly over the top of our vehicle, the wing span looking to be 20 feet or so.

The words of Psalm 91:4 came to mind—"He will cover you with His feathers. He will shelter you with His wings. His faithful promises are your armor and protection."

Father, thank You for preserving us for the fulfillment of Your promises and purposes in our lives.

Lisa Hosler is Ron's wife and serves as president of Susquehanna Valley Pregnancy Services and with the Regional Church of Lancaster County.

Why Me?

"He fell to the ground in worship and said: 'Naked I came from my mother's womb, and naked I will depart. The Lord gave and the Lord has taken away; may the name of the Lord be praised'…Shall we accept good from God, and not trouble?" *Job 1:20-21; 2:10*

The late Arthur Ashe, the great tennis player who contracted AIDS through a tainted blood transfusion, said, "If I were to say 'God, why me?' about the bad things, then I should have said 'God, why me?' about the good things that happened in my life." Challenging reflection, isn't it?

My family is currently experiencing a period of testing regarding God's timing. I've asked the Lord, "Why are you not answering my prayers?" Maybe you are asking God the same question. Or perhaps you have thought, "Why am I the one who had to lose my job? My coworker got to keep hers, and I work twice as hard as she does!" Others have asked, "Why did my spouse leave me? I was faithful to her and to You, God!" Or why you can't seem to make ends meet even though you work two jobs, while your neighbor always has enough.

Every one of us has at least one "Why?" for God. Very rarely are these questions trivial. The Bible is full of men and women of faith who questioned God's will for their lives. But instead of trying to reason with God about why He hasn't given us what we think is best, consider asking another series of "Why" questions. How about asking, "God, why have You allowed me to have a house with electricity and plumbing? Millions around the world do not have either one!" Ever wonder why you have access to hundreds of versions of the Bible while others wait for the first Bible to be translated into their language? Or why you can own this devotional book with no thought of a threat to your life because of it? Let's not forget the most important question, "Why have You allowed me to be ransomed through Christ's death and resurrection and given me the hope of being with You forever?"

God, help me to trust in Your perfect plans for my life. May I, like Job, praise Your name in times of triumph and times of heartache. When I ask, "Why me?" may it be out of a thankful heart for Your goodness and faithfulness in all things. Amen

Maria Buck is the wife of Petra's Worship Pastor, Gary Buck.

God Stories 3

His Plans

"'For I know the plans I have for you,' declares the Lord, 'plans to prosper you and not to harm you, plans to give you a hope and a future.'" *Jeremiah 29:11*

I n January 2006, I turned 13. Thirteen was a difficult year for me, although when I look back I would not necessarily consider it a bad year. It was a year that, through the start of an eating disorder, God made me stronger. Actually, I really hadn't been eating enough for a full year. After trying their best to help me, my parents decided to take me to a therapist to get help.

In therapy, we discovered that I had a "bully" living inside my head. This "bully" worked to get some control and once it did, it took more and more control until I became its robot. I was in therapy fall of 2006 through spring of 2007 and over that time I and learned how to fight my bully. It was a verbal, mental and physical fight.

Using my mouth to counter a lie with the truth, trusting even when the "bully" yelled lies and eating even when I "wasn't hungry." This past year I've watched myself grow two inches and have enough energy to do things that I enjoy doing because I'm eating again! Don't get me wrong, I still have my struggles day to day and week to week but, looking back, I see that God is always bigger than the "bully" and has made me stronger through all this and still is working. God knows the plans he has for my life. As it says in Jeremiah 29:11, "For I know the plans I have for you...." God is redeeming what the devil wanted to use to destroy me to make me stronger so that I can fulfill His plans!

Daddy God, thank you so much for all You do in my life and all that You have done. I pray that You would give strength to all of us when we can't see how a hard time can make us stronger. Please redeem all that the devil wants to destroy in our lives. Amen

Elisabeth Schlicher attends DOVE Christian Fellowship Elizabethtown and its youth group and Bible quizzes with the Highspire First Church of God Quiz team.

Provision

"And my God will meet all your needs according to his glorious riches in Christ Jesus." *Philippians 4:19*

I n July of 1994, we accepted a ministry position in Paradise, Pennsylvania. We were living in Florida and were preparing to move twelve hundred miles away to a place where we didn't know anyone. We would be leaving our church, home, family, friends and everything we had grown to love about our life in Florida. We knew that God was leading us and we were to go, but we were still anxious. The ministry position required that we raise our own support, something we knew nothing about. For us, this was the biggest step of faith we had ever taken.

One evening before we left Florida, I got out some of my craft supplies and painted a small plaque. The plaque, which read *"The will of God will never lead you where the grace of God cannot keep you,"* represented our faith and trust in God to take care of us.

I later packed it and planned to hang it up once we got settled in Pennsylvania.

When we arrived in Pennsylvania, we entered the room we were to stay in and the first thing we saw was a single little plaque hanging in the middle of the wall with these simple words on it *"The will of God will never take you where the grace of God cannot keep you."*

In the years since we came to Pennsylvania, we have taken many steps of faith, each time remembering how God saw to it that a little plaque would be waiting for us to quietly confirm His love and grace.

Lord, thank you for Your all-sufficient grace that sustains us in whatever You call us to.

Linda Bird is the Director of Beginning In the Right Direction Ministries in Lancaster.

Photo by Linda Page

April

Experience A "Jesus Clean-Up"

"There is therefore now no condemnation for those who are in Christ Jesus...." *Romans 8:1 (New King James Version)*

It was a beautiful spring afternoon and I was enjoying the companionship of another young mother as we watched our children playing. Our conversation was interrupted by our kids returning to the porch. My welcoming smile quickly turned to a frown when I noticed my daughter's shoes. She had worn her brand new white sneakers to play and they were now completely caked in thick mud. "Jennifer, what were you thinking? Just look at your new shoes!" My heart sank as I thought of another unexpected expense. Finances were tight in those days and providing shoes for our children was an on-going challenge.

"I'm sorry, Mommy," she sighed as she bent down, trying her hardest to scrub away the mud. She was truly contrite, yet my irritation persisted. Instead of accepting her apology and moving on, I brought the subject up a few more times that afternoon. Of course, that only intensified her shame as she repeatedly apologized. After the third apology, my heart was suddenly filled with grief. I realized that I had not demonstrated to my child the loving forgiveness which my Father had extended to me countless times. Now it was my turn to ask my child's forgiveness and receive her accepting hug.

How grateful I am to have a Father who forgives my sin and never reminds me of it again. I don't need to plead repeatedly to be forgiven and try my hardest to "clean myself up." I am righteous because of His finished work on the cross, and as I walk in daily repentance, He delights to forgive and restore me to relationship with Him.

Are you walking in shame for past sins and failures? Our enemy delights in keeping us bound but we have a loving Father who longs for us to experience the freedom of forgiveness.

Father, help me to receive Your forgiveness and walk in the freedom You long for me to have.

Nancy Barnett serves with her husband Tom in pastoring DOVE Christian Fellowship Elizabethtown.

Give Us Your Compassion

"When he saw the crowds, he had compassion on them, because they were harassed and helpless, like sheep without a shepherd."
Matthew 9:36

Recently, my children and I visited New York City. Like proper tourists, we gazed in wonder at the skyscrapers and jewelry stores and the limousines. But the occasion that brought the most discussion from my children was when we occasionally passed a thin, haggard person on the street or subway tunnel panhandling or begging for money. The questions began immediately: "Daddy, what's he doing? Is that how he gets money? Where does he live? Where's his family?"…and so on. The result was a long and lively discussion about how people live and that everyone (surprise!) does not live like us.

This discussion brought to mind the ministry of Jesus and how he "had compassion" on the poor. "Poor" can mean many different kinds of needs: physical, some of which we saw in New York, as well as mental, emotional, spiritual, and relational. But Jesus chose not to ignore the poor but instead ministered to the poor through the power of the Holy Spirit in His life.

What an example Jesus gives us! On the other hand, it is easy for me to forget the lessons my children are learning, that not everyone lives like us. It is tempting to ignore or overlook the poor or rationalize why I won't help the poor: they'll never get any better; they are in a hopeless situation; the government will do it; someone else will do it.

I came away from my New York trip with an unexpected benefit - a new attitude to do what I can to minister to the poor, like Jesus did.

Lord, forgive me for my excuses. Help me to see the poor through Your compassionate eyes. Please show me where I can minister in Your Name. Amen

Allen Dise serves as the senior elder of the Newport Dove Church in Elm.

Are You Growing?

"This book of the law shall not depart out of thy mouth; but thou shalt meditate therein day and night, that thou mayest observe to do according to all that is written therein: for then thou shalt make thy way prosperous, and then thou shalt have good success."
Joshua 1:8 (King James Version)

My wife and I traveled to Virginia with our four children to a Bible Conference sponsored by The Navigators on "Making your life count for God." The speaker gave an open invitation to meet personally with anyone who wanted to know more about applying what they heard.

All six of our family met with this man in his cabin that same morning. He asked us what we were doing in our Christian lives to grow. I said reading the Bible every night together as a family and going through a Christian magazine together. He complimented us for our efforts and for the amount of time we were investing in our family to walk with the Lord.

I wanted to know what else I could do in order to make my life more effective in counting for God. I knew right then that I needed to invest time in memorizing Scripture and make a commitment to do it regularly. I determined to skip lunch and go out in a row boat and not return until I memorized Joshua 1:8.

This commitment worked, and I have never forgotten the verse, nor have I given up on my commitment to memorize. Other brothers in the Lord have also held me accountable to memorize consistently, and I make it a priority and use small segments of time throughout the day to practice and review my latest verse. I've never forgotten nor regretted that commitment that I made back in 1966.

Thank you, Father, for Your Word and for the power that it works in us who believe.

Leon Faddis is a retired businessman who has been a friend and partner of many ministries. He and his wife, Giny, have been married 61 years and are committed to the Great Commission to "go and make disciples."

Pruning Promotes Growth

"He cuts off every branch in me that bears no fruit, while every branch that does bear fruit He prunes so that it will be even more fruitful." *John 15:2*

As a teacher, I enjoyed a variety of summer jobs. One summer, I was taught how to prune small trees and bushes. Even with no experience, it was easy to see and remove the dead branches. The far more difficult and time-consuming task was pruning the branches that looked healthy. This process lets in more light and air which promotes increased growth.

Several weeks after I started pruning, I happened to read John 15. It was no coincidence. I clearly saw a correlation between the pruning needed in my life and pruning all those bushes. The dead branches that bore no fruit were just like the "dead branches" in me that bore no fruit. The healthy, fruit-bearing branches in the bushes and in my life provided the biggest challenge. I began to realize that God wanted to prune good activities in my life that were no longer in His plan so that I could continue to grow and mature.

I realized it was time for some of my good branches to be cut off and one of them was for me to stop teaching after 27 very rewarding years. God was pruning me in order to bear new fruit through a ministry to help low-income people have "repaired homes and restored hope in Jesus Christ." Although this was not an easy decision for my wife and me, God brought us to a place of peace and unity. Most importantly, He has provided abundantly for our family since that time.

That summer I had a true object lesson that helped me understand what is being said in John 15.

Gracious Father, thank you for the practical and spiritual lessons that You teach us.

Jim Ford is founder and director of Good Works, Inc., headquartered in Coatesville.

Is Your Name Registered?

"If someone's name was not written in the book of life, he/she was thrown into the lake of fire." *Revelation 20:15*

I n April of 2001, I was visiting Lancaster County from Mexico. A brother drove me to the airport to return home. Once I had arrived, I went to check in and presented my ticket. After several minutes, she seemed confused and said, "Your name is not registered in the system."

I thought that perhaps she had made a mistake. I showed her my ticket again, hoping that she could understand that I was correct and that someone else had made the mistake of omitting my name from the system. She looked at the ticket carefully and said, "Your flight is out of Baltimore." I said, "Yes, I know." She then asked, "What are you doing here?" I replied, "Excuse me! Do you mind repeating that again? I believe that I am not understanding." She said to me again, "Your flight is from BWI. What are you doing here? You are in the International Airport of Philadelphia." I had my ticket, but my name was not in the system, because I was in the wrong place.

Many people think that they have the ticket to heaven, but they do not take the time to assure that their names have been written in the system of heaven, the Book of Life. Jesus says in John 14:6: "I am the way and the truth and the life. No one comes to the Father except through me."

You can be assured that your name is in the Book of Life only if you confess Jesus Christ as your Lord and live obeying and walking in His commands. That is possible if you pray this prayer:

Dear God, I confess that I am a sinner. I believe that Jesus' sacrifice is enough to forgive and clean my sin. I open my heart to Jesus and invite Him to be my Lord and Savior, and please write my name in the book of life. Amen

Mario E. Araya pastors New Holland Spanish Mennonite Church.

God's Presence

"God did this so that men would seek him and perhaps reach out for him and find him, though he is not far from each one of us."
Acts 17:27

A s I stood there that May afternoon, I felt God's presence. Where was I, you ask? Was it at a church building? Was it during a worship gathering? Was it in a bible study surrounded by other Christ-followers? That afternoon when I felt God's presence, I was standing in the Tate Modern Art Gallery in London looking at two different paintings by Salvador Dali. I was in London visiting churches, church leaders, and various places of interest, and God showed up for me almost more powerfully at an art gallery than in any worship gathering that we attended during those two weeks.

What does this say to us? God is not limited to only working where we expect Him to work. God shows up, sometimes when or where we least expect Him. Kester Brewin, founding member of Vaux (an alternative worship gathering in London), puts it like this: "There is no place where God can't be found. Even in the places that seem Godless, they are full of God for that—full of God's ache to pull people there and do something."

When I go on a mission trip with our Youth Ministry, I ask our youth at the end of each day, "Where did you see the face of Jesus today?" It gives them a lens through which to look at their world. If we pray that we will see the face of Jesus, He will show up in the world. He'll show up in the face of the poor, the elderly, in art galleries, in movies, in culture, and in creation. May we seek to find the face of Jesus in our world.

Lord Jesus, give me eyes to see Your face in the world today.

Ryan Braught serves as pastor of Youth Ministries and Nurture at Hempfield Church of the Brethren as well as leader of Veritas, an Emerging Missional Community of Faith.

Burnt Stones

"...do they actually think they can make something of stones from a rubbish heap—and charred ones at that?"
Nehemiah 4:2 (New Living Translation)

I've been "burnt" a few times, haven't you? A few years ago, we signed a contract for a company to do some work at our house. The work performed was way below the quality we expected, but we had agreed on a price, so we paid the bill.

Burnt! The phrase "I got burned on that deal" is one we use when we expect one thing but receive the opposite. My experience was minimal compared to the broken marriage vows, jobs lost, careers cut short, and expectations not met. These episodes catalog the stories of "burnt" people.

Nehemiah used the "burnt and charred stones" to fortify a city! His antagonist, Sanballat, thought burnt stones were of no value. He did not expect the burnt stones to be revived. They were!

Sanballat saw the burnt rubbish of what he assumed was unusable material; Nehemiah saw the opportunity encrusted in the burnt realities of past experiences! All that was needed were warm strong hands to guide them into place. Do we see the precious glimmer of God-given value placed in the people around us? Look for it. Nehemiah did! And in fifty-two days the rubble of chaos was replaced with order and safety. Jesus is able to take the burnt and charred realities of life and change them into usable stones that will rebuild our lives for His glory.

Lord, prepare our hands to be Your hands extended to those who are hurt and burnt in our communities. Amen

Richard Armstrong serves as Assistant Director of Worship Center Global Ministries in Lancaster.

No Strings Attached

"For great is your love reaching to the heavens! Your faithfulness reaches to the skies." *Psalm 57:10*

I always enjoy telling women in prison that they are my most "captive" audience! This particular night I decided to share with them a huge need that my husband and I had. We were full time missionaries and for many years had learned much about trusting God for our monthly financial needs. This month we received our smallest check ever, and we still needed $2,000.00 in order to pay all our bills. I shared that we trusted God to "send money from the sky." I asked the women to join me in praying for this need with us. "Next week," I told them, "I'll share with you how He answered our prayers."

Just a day or two later, I walked up to the mailbox and pulled out an envelope from a donor friend in Texas who occasionally sent some funds to our ministry account. I opened their letter and out fell a check with thread sewn across the top of the check. A note said: "Here is a gift for you with NO STRINGS ATTACHED!" I gasped and praised God when I saw it was for the amount of exactly $2,000.00! You can only imagine the rejoicing the next week at the prison when the girls heard of God's wonderful provision.

The amazing thing is that most donations go through headquarters and have taxes and other benefits deducted, but God had nudged them to send the full amount directly to us as a Love Gift.

Father, I praise You for Your never ending faithfulness! For You provide more abundantly than we could ever think or imagine. You are always faithful, even when we are not.

Jeannette Taylor has been a prison volunteer with REST Ministries for 17 years. She and her husband serve as full time missionaries with The Navigators in Coatesville.

APRIL 9

Great Grace

"For I know the plans I have for you," declares the Lord, "plans to prosper you and not to harm you, plans to give you hope and a future." *Jeremiah 29:11*

Ever since a friend shared that verse with me in middle school it has meant so much to me. It became even more meaningful when my daughter was born a year ago. Aliya was diagnosed with vacterl and spent the first 10 days of life at the Children's Hospital of Philadelphia. A year later, we continue to see her seven specialists and her pediatrician. She has had three surgeries and is anticipating four more. We have had countless procedures leading up to surgeries which often were hard experiences. This past month was different.

Aliya was scheduled for a heart cath at 10 AM. By noon she had still not been taken and I couldn't believe she wasn't complaining of hunger. She had not eaten anything in 18 hours and had only a few ounces of milk early that morning. My husband and I were dreading the IV. It would often take multiple attempts and 20-40 minutes of screaming before they could get the IV inserted. Around 12:15 the nurse came to us and said they were going to sedate Aliya before inserting the IV. By one o'clock Aliya was sleeping, her IV was inserted with her waking only briefly and she was taken for her cath.

This day was truly a miracle. When Aliya woke up, she was happy and interacting with her nurses as if nothing happened to her. She had to lay flat for four hours, and even that went smoothly.

Not all days in the hospital go this well, and I am thankful for the ones that do. I never could have imagined what I went through this past year; yet, God's hand of mercy and grace were with me all the way. I don't know what lies ahead for Aliya. We have hope that her heart will be strong. When I begin to stress, I go back to the verse in Jeremiah and remember that God knows the plans he has for Aliya. He will hold her in His hands and provide no matter what life may bring our way.

Thank you, Father for cradling us in Your arms when the storms seem to be too strong. Thanks for promising to never leave us and to provide all our needs. May we always turn to You in good times and bad.

Melodi Miller, her husband, Jonathan, and daughter, Aliya, live in Ephrata and attend DOVE Christian Fellowship Westgate Celebration.

108   *God Stories 3*

Don't Miss An Opportunity To Pray

"...Spread your protection over them, that those who love your name may rejoice in you. For surely, O Lord, you bless the righteous; you surround them with your favor as with a shield." *Psalm 5:11-12*

J ust the other day, I was listening to the radio, and the local news came on along with the traffic report. There was an accident in Ephrata, on the road our son, Steve, travels to work and around the time he would have been passing through. Steve wasn't working that day so I recall thinking, "Oh good, it's not him." Steve rides one of those fast motorcycles, and one of the prayers I always pray is for God's protection over him and that he will be careful and aware of those around him.

Within the hour, my husband called to inform me that Steve was in the ER; he had an accident on his motorcycle—not the one in Ephrata but somewhere else. He was taken to the ER the same time I heard the announcement on the radio.

How could I have missed what God was trying to tell me? Why wasn't I listening to His voice? Even though I felt so sure that Steve was not involved in that accident, I missed an opportunity to take the time to pray for him.

Nevertheless, God's faithfulness never fails, and He answered my prayers from all the other times I prayed. Steve apparently passed out, and he and the cycle flipped. The cycle was in many broken pieces, but Steve walked away in one piece with only some light brush burns and a headache. God directed Steve's bike to a narrow grassy area directly beside the road to cushion his fall. It was only by God's guiding hand that Steve landed where he did. We look back and see how much worse that accident could have been. God had spared Steve's life once again.

Thank you God for blessing us with Your favor even when we don't always listen to Your voice.

Denise Sensenig is employed by DCFI, lives in Terre Hill, with her husband, Craig, and three adult sons.

Ill-Equipped And In Survival Mode

"Though my father and mother forsake me, the Lord will receive me." *Psalm 27:10*

I did not experience any of the bonding that normally happens between parents and their children. I grew up in a home unloved and neglected by my mother and eventually abandoned by my father at the tender age of twelve. I was emotionally alone for the remainder of my childhood while making all minor and major decisions concerning myself. Bitter and confused, I began an ill-equipped, insecure, and controlling journey into adulthood. Many heartaches and disappointments naturally followed. I was unhappily married by eighteen.

Ten years later and two children didn't alter the fact that my painful childhood negatively affected every aspect of my present life on a daily basis. I was very disturbed and needed answers. Why was I even born?

It was about this same time that a friend invited me to her church.

There I heard the offer of freedom from my past and hope for my future, for the first time. I met Jesus and discovered a different plan for my life. I surrendered my attempts at survival and have walked a journey of love and acceptance ever since. I asked for and received forgiveness for my sins, which led me to forgive others and myself. I learned how to love and serve others. Giving up control of my life remains a struggle at times, but believing that Jesus will never leave me and "His" equipping will never end is my strength.

Lord, somewhere, as early as the hospital nursery ward, possibly a nurse, somewhere prayed for me. Now I pray for the ill-equipped souls that are still in need of Your touch. Draw them to Yourself, Lord, and save them as You have saved me. With an ever grateful heart, I pray in the name of Jesus Christ. Amen

Irene Briner, a wife, mother, and grandmother is self-employed, and a ministry worker at New Holland Church of the Nazarene.

Only God

"What, after all, is Apollos? And what is Paul? Only servants, through whom you came to believe—as the Lord has assigned to each his task. I planted the seed, Apollos watered it, but God made it grow. So neither he who plants nor he who waters is anything, but only God, who makes things grow." *1 Corinthians 3:5–7*

All who follow Christ are to make sure that their words and actions reflect Godly living and not become a stumbling block for others. Even when successful at doing so, we can still get frustrated by what appears to be a lack of fruit in our ministry efforts.

In 2005, my wife and I met a new family through a local service organization. We cultivated a relationship with them, invited them to church, asked them to lunch, and even clearly shared the Gospel with them. After several such opportunities, there was no fruit to be seen from our efforts.

The fact that this family did not come to know the Lord right away was discouraging. We knew that they would soon relocate because of their jobs and our involvement in their lives would be minimized. Thankfully, the visitation team at church quickly followed up on the information card the family filled out. They went over the Gospel again and the family trusted Christ that night. We were overjoyed! It brought to mind the above verses and humbled us again with the reminder that God is using us even when it isn't as anticipated.

Father, we are called to be witnesses but we will not always reap the harvest...sometimes we plant and other times we water. May knowing this keep us from feeling the "pressure" often associated with sharing our faith. Help us to be faithful and obedient. We are watching for the growth only You can bring!

Brad Hoopes, an ordained minister, has been in a variety of ministry roles over the past ten years. Most recently he has served as a fund-raiser for WJTL radio and as manager of TheCookieSale.com (an effort to feed starving people around the world).

April 13, 2007

"For our struggle is not against flesh and blood, but against...the spiritual forces of evil in the heavenly realms." *Ephesians 6:12*

As I sat in the hotel lobby in Miami on the eve of my third trip with the Cuba for Christ Ministry Team, I was amazed that as we prayed about our up-coming trip, all of us felt we had been having more than the usual hassles with our personal lives before this trip. I personally was undecided whether to go due to my Dad's poor health. We agreed that Satan didn't want this trip to happen. Maybe it was because this was our first time to teach and train 100 new Cuban pastors on Bible study with emphasis on teaching from Scriptures.

Fast forward to Tuesday morning, April 17. I was sitting in the customs office in Holguin Airport along with our interpreter, Pastor Ortiz. The customs agent had confiscated my Bible and all our biblical study guides. We felt confident that we would get our materials because we had just spent several hours at the Communist Party headquarters getting a permit from a general to pick up our materials.

We walked into the customs office and gave them our permit to pick up our materials. They promptly sat us down beside an armed guard and told us to wait. They came out in a few minutes and said we can't have the materials. It is propaganda and not allowed. We asked them to reconsider so they went back in their office again.

As Adamino and I sat there, I looked at the guard beside me and saw that he was drawing in a notebook. It appeared to be some kind of a demon. I nudged Adamino to look over at the drawing. I started praying, the first few times out loud "In the name of Jesus cast out this demon" over and over loudly and then under my breath. Suddenly another guard came over to the guard, who was still sketching this demon and took his keys and radio and told him to go take his lunch break. Right after he left, all four of the customs officers came and said if we will sign a paper we can pick up all our materials. Was that chance? I call it a miracle – a battle won against Satan.

I praise God for his help and strength as we daily battle for His glory.

Bill Wingenroth, former owner and president of Robert E. Getz, Inc. Fire Equipment; member of Mohn's Hill E.C. Church; former deacon, past president of Cocalico School Board; member of Cuba for Christ Ministry Team.

Mercy

"Let us therefore come boldly to the throne of grace that we may obtain mercy and find grace to help in time of need." *Hebrews 4:16*

So many things went wrong this year. Yes, I can honestly say, this year was the most difficult year of my life! I had watched my eldest son's marriage disintegrate into fiery rubble. My mother's heart ached, as I watched him deal with grief over his loss. How could a relationship so full of promise end in such pain?

Within a few months, our middle son was stricken with multiple sclerosis, sustaining permanent spinal cord damage. Days became months, filled with excruciating, unrelenting pain. Financial, personal and physical setbacks had us reeling. I remember saying, "Lord, how long will You see our grief and not respond?"

A final blow came early in July when my companion, my horse Ali, was stricken with laminitis. The inflammation had raged through both front legs. My beautiful spirited companion was unable to walk or stand. The prognosis was bleak.

As I waited for the vet to confirm the extent of the injury, I questioned our life choices. Was the Lord telling us to sell Rancho Milagro, to sell everything and forsake it all?

"Just tell us Lord, so that we can follow," I said. We bought the ranch for our horses, as a haven for our family, and a place of fellowship for ministry. A miracle is what we needed, an affirmation of our faith and trust in Him. I asked the unthinkable, "Lord, give us a miracle to confirm Your will for us to stand and not give up." "Let my horse Ali, be healed."

The phone rang; I gulped. It was our vet with her final report. "I have good news, there has been no appreciable damage to your horse's legs; she's going to be fine."

"Lord, thank you for Your Grace, it's only through Your grace that we stand and have our breath..."

Mary J. Buch is senior pastor of Breakout Ministries and serves on the Regional Council of the Regional Church of Lancaster County.

The Doors Of My Heart

"Here I am! I stand at the door and knock. If anyone hears my voice and opens the door, I will come in ...." *Revelation 3:20*

Many references in scripture give us reason to believe that the heart matters much to God. In Proverbs, we read that the heart is the wellspring of life. In the passage above, we see the desire of Jesus to have fellowship with us within our hearts. If we have never opened up our lives to Jesus as our Lord, this picture of Jesus knocking on our heart's door is helpful. However, He is also speaking to those whom have lost vitality in their Christian life.

Last year my wife experienced sudden, severe pain in her lower abdomen. I laid my hands on her and prayed for healing but the pain continued to intensify. My wonderful wife was writhing in pain and I was at the end of myself. Before I called 911, I cried out to God in desperation. As I cried out, I remembered a time several weeks earlier that I had disrespected her. I had asked the Lord to forgive me, but I had never made it right with her. As I confessed my wrong to her, the pain immediately broke.

Is it possible that at times we miss God's best for us and don't experience the fullness of His power because of areas in our heart that have not been transformed? Do we only experience partial victory because there are some rooms in our hearts where we do not allow Jesus to enter?

Father, Thank You for sending Your son, Jesus, so that we may have life and have it more abundantly. Lord reveal to me any areas in my heart that are interfering with my experiencing of the fullness of Your love and power today. Cleanse my heart and restore unto me the fullness of the joy of my salvation.

Lloyd Hoover is a bishop of Lancaster Mennonite Conference, executive director for the Potter's House, a leader of reconciliation ministries and a member of the Regional Church of Lancaster County.

Ministering Angels

"Are not all angels ministering spirits sent to serve those who will inherit salvation?" *Hebrews 1:14*

They were forecasting a severe storm starting around four o'clock. All the businesses were closing early. My son called from a friend's house and said he hurt his arm; he thought he needed to go to the doctor. I went and picked him up only to discover that his elbow was pointing in the wrong direction.

I knew it was broken. We rushed to the family doctor, who said that I should take him to the hospital campus immediately and hurry, because the doctor's office will be closing at three o'clock. We made it to the campus, but when we got there I realized I had no idea which building this doctor was in. Everything was very deserted already. We stood there feeling very helpless until a man walking with a cane appeared and asked if he could help us. We told him which doctor we needed to see, and he told us which building to go to.

As we walked outside, I turned for a second to say something to my son and looked back and the man was gone. There was no door he could have slipped into. There were only a few cars left in the parking lot, and he wasn't getting into any of those.

I said to Jason, "That was our angel."

God knew we had no idea where we were to go, and we were running out of time to get to the doctor before he left for the day and before the storm hit. We made it to the doctor's office in time, he set Jason's arm, and we made it home before the storm started. God loves to take care of us.

Thank you Lord for sending Your angels to watch over us.

Brenda Boll serves as an elder, along with her husband, Steve, at Newport DOVE. She is on staff at House to House Publications.

APRIL 17

Road Closed

"If you sinful people know how to give good gifts to your children, how much more will your heavenly Father give the Holy Spirit to those who ask him?" *Luke 11:13*

Ever wonder about opportunities missed and disasters avoided because you heeded "Keep Out" signs and voices? It was late May 1980. Snow was melting in the mountains of New Mexico. I was driving my family at night to surprise friends in Los Alamos with an early arrival.

To save hours, I decided on a shortcut through the mountains. The road was well-paved and everything looked fine–until the "Road Closed" sign. Without much thought and less prayer, I steered around the sign and drove on for another uneventful hour. All of a sudden, our small car stopped in the silent blackness of a chilly moonless night. Hours later at dawn, I witnessed a breathtakingly beautiful scene. I also beheld a sea of mud larger than a football field with foot-deep tire tracks. A desperate situation for me, the foolish father. A delightful opportunity for my faithful Father. With much prayer, family effort, careful maneuvering, and "help from above," I backed the car onto solid ground, drove across the mud field on top of ruts, and proceeded to our destination.

These days I encourage people, especially young people, to embrace a life of adventure, radical faith, and spiritual courage needed to experience joyous beauty and reach a destination that is unreachable within boundaries and norms defined by others. These are extraordinary times. Our Father is even more extraordinary. He gives care, provision, and direction causing a "Wow!" of worship and love to erupt from our hearts and moves us toward great exploits. He is much bigger than even my brash stupidity and youthful arrogance.

Father, in a spirit of humble expectancy and adventure, I ask You to tune my heart to hear Your "Go" when others say "No," to see "Open" where others see "Closed." Give me grace to trust You beyond the signs and warnings of my more reasonable self. Amen

Bruce Boydell leads Lifespan®, serving emerging leaders, businesses, and organizations as coach and consultant.

God Stories 3

Lavish In Revelations

"God intended, out of the goodness of his heart, to be lavish in revelation!" *Isaiah 42:21 (The Message)*

We had been living in this passage of Scripture as we mentored leaders in a church. Time and time again God was "lavish in revelation" as we sought his face in prayer and Scripture!

Three months before "The Call-Nashville," we were invited to join twenty-five people from the church to attend the 07/07/07 event. As we asked the Holy Spirit about attending, he opened a Scripture to us from Isaiah chapter twenty-five. We wanted Scripture that gave us a handle on how God was leading, especially if we were going to travel to "The Call."

We were secure in receiving the middle portion of this chapter: "And here on this mountain, God will banish the pall of doom hanging over all peoples, the shadow of doom darkening all nations. Yes, he'll banish death forever. And God will wipe the tears from every face. He'll remove every sign of disgrace from his people, wherever they are. Yes! God says so! Also at that time, people will say, 'Look at what's happened! This is our God! We waited for him and he showed up and saved us! This God, the one we waited for! Let's celebrate, sing the joys of his salvation. God's hand rests on this mountain!'"

We attended "The Call" and celebrated Jesus, the Father, and the Holy Spirit! We repented, prayed, praised and worshipped God our Father! I saw the "pall of doom" leave as the glory of God descended on Titan Stadium! Thanks be to God for His rich words of truth He had given us in the Scriptures before we attended the event! Such promises we can stand on: a foundation that is immovable, secure, and powerful until Christ returns for His Bride!

To You Jesus do we give thanks for the rich treasure from Your Word! Thy will be done on earth as it is being done in Heaven! Amen

Ray and Louise French intercede for the region from TTWM, Leola.

Meeting Our Needs

"...your Father knows what you need before you ask him."
Matthew 6:8

We were beginning to build in a new community more than twenty miles from our headquarters in Coatesville. We had just hired a site coordinator and were getting him set up with everything he needed to start building our new five-home project. Tom called to tell us that the van that was given to him was not going to make it. I told him to have it looked at by a local repair shop, but it turned out he was right.

I approached our Board of Directors about a used pickup truck I had seen at a local dealer. It was in good condition with reasonable miles and cost only $15,000. After some discussion, they gave their approval and I began the paperwork to get the truck. The next day, a member of our staff asked what I was buying and I told her about our need. She asked me to wait and said that she would make a call to her neighbor who worked for a large auto manufacturer.

A little later her neighbor called, and we discussed the issue and that our board had authorized only $15,000 for the purchase. He told me that he would check the inventory at some local dealerships that he worked with. He called later that day and told me that one of the dealers had gotten in *ten* new vehicles of just the type we were looking for as an extra shipment and that he thought he could make a deal for us. We worked the numbers and soon we had a brand-new pickup truck for the same price as the used one. God knew our needs before we did and shipped a truck to that dealer just for us.

Father, thank you for providing for our needs, known and unknown, even before we ask for them to be fulfilled.

Chip Huston is the executive director of Habitat for Humanity of Chester County in Coatesville and an elder at Paoli Presbyterian Church.

Do Not Touch Me Or My Doll

"The Spirit of the Sovereign Lord is on me, because the Lord has anointed me to preach good news to the poor. He has sent me to bind up the brokenhearted, to proclaim freedom for the captives and release from darkness for the prisoners." *Isaiah 61:1*

One of my goals in my chaplaincy work is to sense what the Holy Spirit would have me do or say as I minister to others. One occasion I especially remember occurred when I was leading a worship service in a psychiatric hospital. I had been invited to lead several hymns and have some special music. I noticed one elderly lady sitting in a wheelchair, holding a doll in her lap. That's not an uncommon sight as at times elderly women find comfort in holding a personal item such as a doll or a stuffed animal.

This particular woman stood out as she was deeply engaged in listening to the service, especially to the music. After the service I made a point to greet this lady. She reached out to shake my hand and thank me for the service. I commented on how she cared for her doll and that brought a big smile to her face. She reached out as if she wanted me to hold her doll. I touched it for I sensed the doll meant a lot to her.

As the attendant was pushing the lady back to her room in a wheelchair, she commented on how I connected in touching the lady and her doll. I didn't realize the impact of the comment until I saw the large sign on the back of the wheelchair. It stated in big letters, "PLEASE DO NOT TOUCH ME OR MY DOLL!" I was glad I hadn't read the sign earlier.

I realized again that as we are sensitive to the Holy Spirit, he helps us connect with people in unique ways even when they may be saying they don't want anyone to connect with them.

Lord, Give me sensitivity to Your Holy Spirit and help me to minister as You direct. Help me to touch people in their areas of need and minister Your love that restores and heals.

Glenn D. Metzler serves as a chaplain in health care at Landis Homes, a retirement community in Lititz.

God's Gift Of Children

"...My God, my God, why hast thou forsaken me?" *Mark 15:34 (King James Version)*

As parents of two children, my wife and I are blessed to have two healthy and extremely active gifts from God. When Esau asked Jacob in Genesis 33:5 to give account for his rather large family, we read that Jacob quickly recognized that children are truly a gift from God by responding that they are "the children which God hath graciously given thy servant." Since the birth of my son four years ago, the impact of God sacrificing His only son on the cross for the redemption of the world has had a more personal effect on me than ever before.

God had to stand by and watch His only son, as he hung on the cross suffering, so that future fathers, mothers, and children could be saved from eternal damnation. As a parent, I get upset when my children have to get a shot at the doctor's office. I cannot imagine the agony God went through watching His will be done. Will God's agony and Christ's suffering be in vain? I only have to look out my backyard at my only son to personally understand the ultimate sacrifice that another parent, God, made for me.

Dear Lord, please remind me every day that my children are a gift from You.

Lee S. Johnson Jr. is president of Lee S. Johnson Associates, Inc., a manufacturer's representative agency selling industrial products to hardware, industrial, and fastener companies in Pennsylvania. The Johnson family attends both Coatesville Bible Fellowship Church and Calvary Fellowship Church.

Be The Best You Can Be

"No one engaged in warfare entangles himself with the affairs of this life, that he may please him who enlisted him as a soldier. And also if anyone competes in athletics, he is not crowned unless he competes according to the rules." *2 Timothy 2:4-5 (New King James Version)*

There have been lots of movies and television shows centered around the military in the last couple of years. There are things that the body of Christ can glean from these productions and from the military itself—discipline, training, being the best you can be, community, comradeship and fighting for each other, just to name a few. In almost every military movie I have watched (I've seen quite a few) the Lord has given me real life applications.

The best forces in the free world are specialized units: Delta Force, Green Beret, Rangers or Navy Seals. Each of these units is only for those who qualify. Only a small percentage of those who try out actually make the cut.

After watching a movie on Special Forces, I felt the Lord ask, "Where are my special forces? Where are those who want to be the very best? Where are those who take on the extreme testing and training to be the best?"

I didn't know how to respond, other than to say, "Lord, I want to be one of your best. But to do that means that I need to submit to the training process. I need to be willing to train myself in the daily disciplines of not only preparing for the army of the Lord but to actually be involved in expanding the Kingdom of our God. To expand the Kingdom will take people of discipline, character, motivation, devotion and commitment to the Lord. My prayer is that you may respond to His call to be the best that you can be to bring the glory and honor to Him.

Father, I pray that You would raise up an army of believers that would stand against the lies of the enemy—those who would fight the powers of darkness that enslave the lives of so many people here in this region. Train, equip, empower and release us to be the deliverers that You have called us to be.

Ron Myer serves as assistant director of DOVE Christian Fellowship International.

Restoration

"Therefore if anyone is in Christ he is a new creation; the old has gone, the new has come." *2 Corinthians 5:17*

My husband, Paul, had grown up in the church but walked away as a teenager. Years later, watching his children come to Jesus one by one and then his wife, caused him to feel like his life was in an ever-tightening vice. Eventually, he made the decision to leave the family.

A number of weeks passed when on a drive to his apartment one evening, he had what we refer to as his "Damascus Road" experience. Stopping at a store, he noticed the clerk wore a button reading "Christians aren't perfect, just forgiven." A billboard on the turnpike read "Know Jesus Know Peace, No Jesus No Peace"; a bumper sticker on a car had a similar message. Putting on the radio to get these images out of his mind, he heard a secular group play "You've Gotta Believe in Something." Paul had struggled for months knowing he needed to either turn back to God or totally reject Him.

Pulling to the side of the road, he tearfully prayed to the Lord to rededicate his life. Back in his apartment, three days of spiritual renewal began. The Lord brought experiences in Paul's life to his mind and reminded him, "I was with you then." Hymns came back. Verses came back. Sobbing would be followed by peace, calm, and deep sleep only to have him awaken and begin all over again. This amazing time led to restoration not only in Paul's relationship with the Lord but also in our marriage and family as well.

I am blessed to be married to a godly man filled with humility, strength, love, and compassion.

Thank you Jesus, that though we may turn our backs on You, Your mercies are new every morning. Great is Your faithfulness.

Kathy Zubik serves as director of client services for Susquehanna Valley Pregnancy Services.

True Wisdom

"I perceived that there is nothing better for [the children of men] than to be joyful and to do good as long as they live; also that everyone should eat and drink and take pleasure in all his toil—that is God's gift to man." *Ecclesiastes 3:12–13 (English Standard Version)*

In 1992, my Grandmother was put in a nursing home. My parents passed on to me her boxes of slides, meticulously labeled. I held each colorful photo up to the sun. One by one, I flipped them into the trash. In one generation, all of Grandma's tours were pure vanity which meant absolutely nothing to me.

The Preacher wants us to feel this kind of vanity about our earthly lives. He felt it after a long life of indulgence. Our neighbors feel it, even if they suppress the truth. Our fellow Christians feel it, even if they ignore the implication. However, our earthly life, if it's in reference to the Creator God, is not meaningless at all, says The Preacher. Rather, it is infused with meaning because God made it for His glory and our good. The vanity we experience is real, but it's not the whole story.

Nor is our earthly reality less sacred than "eternal things." We must reject the apparent spiritual wisdom of despising our bodies, our food, our work and our leisure. These are gifts of God as long as we live. They are not "givens," of course, but loving gifts from our Creator. Today, are you willing to dive into your normal, everyday activities with joyful thanks? If you are, you must be wise. You understand the gift of God.

Father God, I praise You today for all You've created and given for my enjoyment. Forgive me for neglecting to thank You for the simple things. Lead me today. Give me the mind of Your Son Jesus Christ, even as I work, eat and drink.

Rev. Thomas D. Becker lives in Lancaster City with his wife Becky and five children. He now teaches Liberal Arts at Veritas Academy. He is an itinerant preacher and licensed realtor.

.

Follow Me

"My sheep listen to my voice; I know them, and they follow me."
John 10:27

I took a personal retreat to a local camp to get away from the busy-ness of life and focus on God. I was also thinking this would be a great time to write some song lyrics without being distracted.

I spent time in the Word, I prayed, and I was refreshed. Now it was time for me to begin writing a worship song.

I sat in front of my computer, but I had a severe case of writer's block. I was frustrated.

I decided to take a break and go for a hike in the woods.

Not long into my hike a golden retriever puppy came up to me and decided to shower me with affection by jumping on me. I looked down and saw mud all over my jeans —the only jeans I brought with me. I was not happy. I tried to shoo the dog away, but he stayed with me. How was I supposed to hear God speaking to me with this dirty dog at my heels? The dog followed me the entire hike. However, I started enjoying my time with the dog. In the end, I was sad to say goodbye.

Then it hit me. I heard God ask me, "What was that dog doing the whole time?" I answered, "Following me." And that was it. Follow-ing Christ was to be the theme of my song. Just as the dog got things a bit dirty in the beginning, so do we sometimes stumble in our walk with God. Our Father wants to journey with us, not matter how we fail Him. One verse in the song I wrote states, "You are the Shepherd in the night. You are the Savior shining bright."

Father, may we not just believe, but truly follow after You. Even when we mess things up, Your love is unconditionally there, and You never leave us on this journey of life. Thank you.

Gary Buck is worship pastor at Petra Christian Fellowship.

Straightened

"Trust in the Lord with all your heart and lean not on your own understanding; in all your ways acknowledge him and he will make your paths straight." *Proverbs 3:5-6*

At eighteen, I married my dream man. The first year was great but by the second year my husband began to return to some old habits. For the next thirteen years I tried everything I knew to get him to change including a whole lot of praying.

The Amplified Version of Proverbs 3:6 reads, "He will direct ...your paths." There were times when I wanted to leave the marriage, but I continually asked God to direct my path and He continually directed me to stay, so I did.

Finally one night I cried out to God, "He's yours, do whatever You want with him! Lord, I need you to change *me*!" God answered that prayer by revealing to me more of Himself and what I meant to Him.

Not long after that, my husband's life began to change. God was directing his path and turning his focus back to Christ.

God did more in my husband, me, and our marriage than I could have ever asked. Looking back, I don't know if I was put in my husband's life to help change *him* or if he was put in my life to help change *me*.

This year we'll be married thirty years. My husband, now a men's ministry leader, has a passion to help men in their walk with Christ, and I co-lead a support group, encouraging women who are seeking direction in their situation.

God directed my path and made what was crooked straight.

Lord, I praise You that whatever our need is You can give direction and help straighten out our path in life when we acknowledge You. I praise You that You keep Your promises to us. Help me to keep my focus on You and not on what may be happening around me. Keep directing my path today.

Cindy Christman is a women's support group leader at Hopewell Christian Fellowship in Elverson.

The Truth Shall Set You Free

"Jesus said, 'If you hold to my teaching, you are really my disciples. Then you will know the truth and the truth will set you free.'"
John 8:31-32

Many years ago my husband and I went through a severe financial situation. It was the most fearful time of our lives. Fear consumed me with negative thoughts of defeat. I knew I had to be in faith, but my fear level was greater than my faith level. I cried out to God for His mercy and help in times of trouble. (Psalm 121:1) I praised Him for hours with tears rolling down my face. Slowly I began to hear His still small voice. *Cindy, what do you believe? Do you believe I am the same God who raised Jesus from the dead? Yes Lord. Do you believe I am the same God who parted the Red Sea? Yes Lord. Didn't I bring you through before? Why do you not think I will bring you through this time? I don't know Lord. He said, because you do not trust in My Love. My Love will keep you and sustain you through every trial and hardship. Do the Word of God.*

Our life situation was a test and I wanted to pass. A husband and wife prayer team is powerful and we prayed Matthew 17:20 (speaking to every mountain daily); Matthew 18:18 (bind and loose); Matthew 18:19 (prayers of agreement); Mark 11:22-24 (receiving and forgiving your enemies).

God parted our Red Sea and did miracles upon miracles and a few years later we were debt free. Through faith and patience you inherit the promises of God.

Father, thank You for performing John 8:31-32 in our lives and setting us free from adversity. Thank You for the lessons learned; contentment during lack, trust, patience, resting in Your promises and gratefulness.

Cynthia Cotter serves as a Licensed Prayer Minister and Counselor of Redeeming Love Prayer Ministry in Pottstown. Married to Tom for forty-one years, they attend Reading Dove.

I Am The Lord

"Do not fear for I have redeemed you; I have called you by name; you are mine. When you pass through the waters I will be with you...; when you walk through the fire you will not be burned...; for I am the Lord your God." *Isaiah 43:1-3a (New American Standard)*

I received a call from one of my parishioners. I knew immediately from the sound of his voice that something was wrong. "Cindy and Michelle were hit by a drunken driver. They are both dead!" A forty-three year-old mother and an eleven year-old daughter had just been killed by a senseless act. The girl was one of the best friends of my youngest daughter.

As I drove to the home of that grieving family I kept asking God, "Why? How can this happen? What do I say? Am I adequate to meet their needs?"

I flipped on the radio to a station I never listened to, and heard those words from Isaiah 43, "Do not fear for I have redeemed you; I have called you by name; you are mine." When I arrived at the house I mainly listened and cried with that dear father and his one remaining daughter. I then shared the scripture I'd just heard- ancient words that could bring some solace amidst the loss, pain, and questions.

Several days later we gathered as a congregation to mourn and find some Word from God to make sense of the tragedy. Unbeknownst to either the grieving family or me, the worship leader chose the hymn with those same words, "Fear Not, For I Have Redeemed You."

In that moment we were reminded of the providential care of God even while passing through the dark waters and the raging fire. Despite the inward pain, hollow emotions, and glaring questions, there was still hope, for "I am the Lord your God."

Thank you, Lord that You alone are God, and especially in the moments we question You.

Dennis Hollinger, Ph.D. is President and Professor of Christian Ethics at Evangelical Theological Seminary in Myerstown.

Give Thanks

"Give thanks in all circumstances, for this is God's will for you in Christ Jesus." *1 Thessalonians 5:18.*

It was a beautiful day as my wife, my two-year-old son, and I pulled out of the driveway headed for the beach for the weekend. We were on vacation and life was great. We arrived at the beach and prepared for a great day of sun, sand, and surf.

All was going well until my wife decided to get in one last time before we left. As she was coming out of the surf, two waves collided together spraying salt, water, and sand right into my wife's left eye. She couldn't see out of that eye. We flushed it out with three bottles of water and took her to the bathhouse, where she washed it with saline solution. She then took a shower and we left.

We had dinner and then traveled an hour to a hotel in order to visit a pastor friend of mine. We realized at the hotel that she forgot her hair supplies, soap, and bathing suit. I got in the car and went to get some hair gel for her. When I returned to the car, it wouldn't start. I was stuck. Thankfully, someone gave me a ride. We got it started the next day and realized it was only the battery. Then, when coming back to the hotel from breakfast we were locked out. We finally got in, got our stuff, and headed to church. When we arrived, my son tripped over a parking block, and skinned his knee.

When my friend started his sermon, it was about being thankful in all circumstances. We were convicted. We thought back to all the little problems and realized we spent too much time complaining about the problems and not giving thanks for the way God worked everything out.

Lord, I give thanks to You for the good, bad, and hard times.

Ryan Braught, Pastor of Youth Ministries and Nurture at Hempfield Church of the Brethren and a leader of Veritas, an Emerging Missional Community of Faith.

Vision, Passion, Timing

"But if I say I'll never mention the Lord or speak in his name, his word burns in my heart like a fire. It's like a fire in my bones! I am worn out trying to hold it in! I can't do it!"
Jeremiah 20:9 (New Living Translation)

The winds of life have hit my boat many times. Those winds have rocked me back and forth, but I have kept my eyes upon Jesus and He has been my anchor. When I preach and it seems that not even my loved ones come to Christ, I keep my eyes fixed on Him. Through the years, I have discovered three things to keep me walking in God's ways: **vision**, **passion**, and **timing**.

I know that without vision people perish. In rocky moments, when my horizon seems blurry, I bring to mind what the Lord has called me to do. As an evangelist, I do not lose sight of the harvest; I keep focused on Jesus.

The passion is the burning fire—the dynamite power of the Gospel to reach the lost, which propels me beyond my strength, my capacity, and my circumstances.

Finally, when things do not go my way, I remember that the Lord is building His character in me to fit my calling and to prepare me for my position in His Kingdom and in His body—and that process takes time. Then, I can see that in His perfect timing for my life, doors are opened, connections are made, and provision is available. His favor takes me to leaders and drug dealers, to nuns and prostitutes, to rich and poor, to saints and sinners. His will is done and Jesus' name is glorified.

Lord Jesus, thank You for giving us vision that keeps us focused, passion that keeps us moving, and timing that keeps us dying to self—that You may be glorified in us and through us.

Marta Estrada is an author, founder and director of Restoration of the Nations (a ministry under Harvest Field Ministries), and member of Petra Christian Fellowship in New Holland.

May

My Philadelphia Experience

"Oh that You would bless me indeed, and *enlarge my territory*, that Your hand would be with me, and that You would keep me from all evil, that I may not cause pain."
1 Chronicles 4:10 (New King James Version)

Have you ever prayed the "Jabez Prayer"? I had been praying this prayer regularly and even read two books on the Jabez Blessing. In March 2005, I received a form from the Federal Court System. Later a large official envelope arrived. I was summoned to appear April 22 for ceremonies.

The Sunday before, my husband took me on a "dry run." I was so overwhelmed trying to remember how we did it, I sat down and cried and said, "I can't do this." We went through it again.

There were ninety people summoned. The deputy told us twenty-three would be chosen. After break the deputy told us it would be an eighteen-month stint—every Thursday. As the deputy called names, I was beginning to feel some relief.

He continued to "Juror #12" and called my name. My heart sank. Why was the Lord allowing this to happen to me? I sat there trying to look "brave" while wiping tears.

That weekend my emotions went crazy—anger, hurt, fear and disappointment in God, who I felt didn't understand my limitations.

Monday I called the deputy and told him, "I really can't do this and need to be released." He suggested I write a letter to the judge and bring it with me—which I did. During break-time a juror asked a young girl where she was from…. She said Lititz! Neither God nor judge was letting me out of serving, but instead provided a traveling companion.

Even as the Lord stretched me (yes, He did indeed enlarge my territory) He has proven Himself faithful to me. I didn't get out of serving, but the Lord gave me what was best.

Lord, You will never give us more than we can bear. You may enlarge ***my*** *territory anytime You want!*

Nancy Wenger is a Small Group Leader at DOVE Westgate.

God Is Present

"Be still and know that I am God..." *Psalm 46:10*

Friday evening in Kentucky, our church group has just finished a week at the home-repair mission center. Five teams of seven people worked to repair and rebuild houses, foundations, walls, ramps, and to build new relationships with our new friends in Appalachia.

I am sitting on the "porch" outside our center, as I finish writing a letter to a church friend back home. In order to be at my best early tomorrow to lead the drive home, I should be in my sleeping bag.

I am not sure I consciously realize that I am waiting to see if God will show up. The voices of our youth playing cards in the hallway inside grow distant. But the sounds of hammers and saws still echo in my mind. I can still hear us saying good-bye to the family living in the home that we left just a few hours earlier. I wonder if I've done everything as God desired.

But the week is now past. There will be time for consideration, review, and improvement, but not now. Finally even the sounds of my memories fade into the distance and my mind grows still, enjoying the beauty of the stars. It is an uncharacteristically cool Kentucky summer night, but I begin to sense a warmth enveloping me. I realize that God is present. I sense His embrace. Right now, nothing else matters. Nothing at all. I sense God's message for me, "I love you – All is ok - You are in 'the right place' – Bask in my peace."

Jesus, help us all to recognize those times when we need to let the distractions of our physical surroundings and the distractions of our minds fade into the distance. Let us be still and know that You are God. Let us sense Your movement in our lives and hear Your words of affirmation. Above all, let us know what is most important. God is with us. Emmanuel, God is with us. Amen

Allen Keller serves as Youth Pastor at Olivet UMC in Coatesville.

The Secret Place

"He who dwells in the Secret place of the Most High will rest in the shadow of the Almighty." *Psalm 91:1*

Someone said no matter what happens in his life, it only takes him ten minutes to come to a resting place in the Lord. Well, I guess I'm not that mature yet. When the busyness, turmoil, discouragement, or hurt happens, I go to Jesus in prayer, praise, and the Word. It takes a while, but as I pursue Jesus the "rest" comes. What a sweet place—to "rest" in Jesus.

On the busiest of days with oodles of people around, each having many requests, without a moment of quiet, I can dwell in the Secret Place of the Most High. I can transcend the busyness, the turmoil, the discouragement, the hurt, and go to that secret place of my Father and be at "rest" in my heart and my mind.

My Father is so wonderful. He gives us that capability of resting in Him all the time. It's up to us to desire Him, to take that step of asking Him to help us, to have that discipline of turning from the cares of the world, and come to "rest" in Him.

I love that picture of resting in Him. He has His arms around me and gives me all the comfort and serenity I need. We are sitting in a quiet peaceful meadow—just Him and me. We are talking and being together. He is my Father.

Lord, I can't go to the secret place on my own. Help me, Lord, to dwell in that resting place, every day, every hour, and every minute. I love You, Lord.

Yvonne Zeiset is wife, mother, grandmother, and part time secretary-counselor at Columbia Pregnancy Center division of Susquehanna Valley Pregnancy Services.

God's Comfort

"The Father of compassion and the God of all comfort, who comforts us in all our troubles." *2 Corinthians 1:3-4*

In May of 1991, my family and I were planning to return to the U.S. after living four years in Aberdeen, Scotland. With my post-graduate work finished; we were making final preparations to leave.

In the local Scottish neighborhood where we lived was a wonderful Church of Scotland, St. George's Tillydrone. The church was quite small but filled with friendly and sincere Christians. We had made strong friendships. The joy of returning home was countered by the sorrow of leaving these dear saints, many of whom we knew we would never see again.

My gloom was thicker than the cold, dreary weather the North Sea would often toss at us.

The day before our farewell party at the church, I was walking through the blocks of Council Housing on my way to the University. The walkways were lined with pre-World War II waist-high iron fencing to keep the roaming dogs out of the grass. I was in the midst of a long uninterrupted stretch, when I noticed a stooped older woman slowly walking towards me. To my astonishment, as I passed her, she stopped and called me by name. To the best of my knowledge, I had never seen her before.

Startled and uncertain what to say, she warmly thanked me for all the Christian care and love my family and I had given to St. George's, and told me that we will be sorely missed. I asked her if she were coming to the farewell party the next day. She said she would be there. At that, she walked on. Dazed, I continued on. After taking a few steps, I turned to get another look at her to see if I could remember who she was. To my surprise, no one was there.

An angel unawares? Who knows? But God knew my troubled soul and comforted it in a way that only He could do. (Incidentally, she was not at the farewell party.)

I praise You, Father, for Your constant watch and care over me.

Doug Buckwalter, professor of New Testament at Evangelical Theological Seminary in Myerstown.

Perfect Timing

"See, I am doing a new thing! Now it springs up; do you not perceive it?..." *Isaiah 43:19*

Throughout my life, God has demonstrated His faithfulness in unique ways, especially by giving me brand new surprises at unexpected times. One of those surprises was a career change later in my adult life. By the time I reached the age of 50, I had worked in the corporate business world for thirty years and I was manager of a team of software developers. Through those years, my career was both challenging and rewarding. However, by this point in my life, I began to experience a growing dissatisfaction with the ever-increasing stress and demands of the corporate environment. Little did I know that God was preparing me for a significant change in direction.

At the same time, God began to give me a strong desire to focus my time and energy into ministry work. For several years, I had been volunteering as a counselor for Susquehanna Valley Pregnancy Services (SVPS). This work was very fulfilling as I sensed that God had given me a heart for hurting people and had gifted me as a counselor.

Quite unexpectedly during a routine day, I received a telephone call from a dear friend who was a staff member of SVPS. She shared that God had impressed her to inform me of an open position within the ministry. That telephone call set in motion a series of amazing events. Within a few weeks, God opened the door for me to be hired by SVPS and I was able to leave my long-time job with no regrets. What a joy to know that God placed the desires within my heart and then worked out His perfect plan to make them a reality.

Lord, thank You for Your faithfulness and perfect timing in bringing wonderful new things into our lives. You truly are a miracle-working God.

Sharon McCamant, Director of the SVPS Lebanon Pregnancy Clinic, also serves as a ministry leader at the Ephrata Church of the Nazarene Celebrate Recovery ministry.

The Voice

"And you will hear a voice say, "This is the way; turn around and walk here." *Isaiah 30:21 (New Living Translation)*

The equipping ministry where I was employed was closing. As we helped those affected to find alternate means of training, the question remained, "What shall I do?" Numerous friends offered affirmations of what I *could* do. All were appropriate in light of my experience, calling, and gifting. Yet none of them bore witness in my heart; I might have said, "The shoe did not fit."

Then one day I "heard" a phrase rise within me: "Be a resource to pastors." As weeks passed and the ministry was completing its mission, the impression from within strengthened. I realized the Lord was leading me into something without a framework, plan, or salary. Yet the phrase, "Be a resource to pastors," was reshaping me and commissioning me.

My wife, Marian, confirmed the new mission was right for me. Employed in a ministry, also, she proposed, "Give yourself to this for a year, and if it doesn't work out, find a different job."

After a month of much needed rest, I began filling invitations to teach in congregations and meet with pastors in mentoring relationships. That was over twenty years ago. Four months later my schedule was full, and it has been ever since!

Since then the mission has extended from pastors to also enrich directors of ministries and leaders in the marketplace with God's wisdom. Taking the first step to serve pastors locally has taken my feet to serve leaders in neighboring regions and other nations.

We must never discount the impact that God purposes when He gently whispers a simple message to our heart. It may stretch our faith, test our strength, and require our courage. Yet He is trustworthy, and He will enable us to complete what He begins.

Lord, here is my heart; instruct me today.

Keith Yoder, Founder and President of Teaching the Word Ministries, serves on the Executive Team and Regional Council of the Regional Church of Lancaster County.

Religious, But Lost

"For as it is written, 'The name of God is blasphemed among the Gentiles because of you'" *Romans 2:24*

We have lived in Michigan, Arizona, California, Colorado, Texas, and for the past nineteen years in Lancaster. No place on earth compares with Lancaster County, PA! We love it here and thank God for the privilege of living here. Like in no other place we have resided, Lancaster is filled with religious people. Many have a solid, deep relationship with Jesus Christ and trust in His blood and righteousness alone for eternal life. They are contagious Christians! However, through the years we have observed that there are many who are like the folks described by the apostle Paul in Romans 2:17-24. They are religious, church members, and boast of their spiritual advantages. They do a lot of good things, even teaching others.

Their problem is that they have never come face-to-face with their own hypocrisy and guilt before a holy God. Although outwardly religious, they wear a mask to cover their inner attitudes of pride, lust, greed, and anger. They say and even teach one thing, but their souls are ravished. God would say that they are hypocrites and that "the name of God is blasphemed…because of you" (2:24).

Let's examine our hearts today before a holy God and an open Bible to be sure that we are not one of those who are *religious, but lost.*

Loving Father, search my heart today! Show me every bit of hypocrisy that clutters the nooks and crannies of my soul so that I can flee from sin and fall into Your loving and forgiving arms. In Jesus' name, Amen!

David D. Allen is associate pastor of Calvary Church, Lancaster.

Spiritual Alignment

"Those who live according to the sinful nature have their minds set on what that nature desires; but those who live in accordance with the Spirit have their minds set on what the Spirit desires." *Romans 8:5*

D riving home from the office one day, I found my town square blocked off with crime scene police tape. I don't remember ever coming across such a site in my hometown, which basically serves as a bedroom community for some larger surrounding cities. Being inquisitive, I decided to watch the evening local news with my wife. We simply could not believe what we were seeing and hearing.

It seems that a young man, whom we knew personally and who had traveled on a mission team with us years earlier, was involved in a violent crime in the early hours of the morning that day. They had just arrested him hours before the news broadcast. There we sat in tears realizing all this young man and his family would face in the future.

For a season of his life, he realigned himself with those who helped him recover from a rough past and who mentored him into a "new creation" future. He was growing and changing, happy and more fulfilled than ever. As the story goes, he began to drift back to "old" friends and align himself with those who would influence him for the negative. He now bears the consequences for those decisions.

Daily I need to check my alignment with the Father. Daily I need to come into agreement with His will, His purposes and His Word. Have you checked your alignment of late? Spend some time right now and ask Jesus to expose any areas of needed realignment, and I know He will gently nudge you into any needed adjustments.

Father, speak to me now and expose any areas in my life where I am out of alignment and agreement with You and Your Word.

Steve Prokopchak serves on DOVE Christian Fellowship International's Apostolic Council.

Rely On Him

"The prayer of a righteous man is powerful and effective. Elijah was a man just like us. He prayed earnestly [and God heard him]."
James 5:16-18

While the shadows grew long and we turned the boats around to head home to Navy, the Severn River grew increasingly rough. As we got closer, the water became dangerous, especially for three narrow eight-man crew shells with gunnels just inches above the water. It seemed the harder we pulled, the more the waves swelled, and the more they began filling our little boats. Once-synchronized oars began to hit each other.

The last thousand meters past the eight foot high seawall, the rowing became still more difficult as the waves filled our boats. But there was no way out, except to keep rowing. Fear of drowning and hypothermia made concentrating a challenge.

As we neared the boat house, it seemed that the boats would soon be swamped. Suddenly, the wind died, the water went flat, and we rowed up the creek to the boat house. As we put the boats up, I was exhausted and rejoicing just to be alive. Mike, by contrast, was excited for some strange reason. You see, while I had been worrying and pulling with all my might, Mike had been praying with all his. While the rest of us focused on solving our trial with our puny arms and legs, he was focused on another One.

I will never forget seeing the power of God displayed because of the prayers of one man. That day reminds me to look at life's problems as opportunities for the Lord to show Himself faithful. May we remember James' words about Elijah and strive to be as faithful to God. Maybe then our first reaction to tough times will be to rely on not ourselves, but on Him—it's a lot less stressful and a lot more exciting!

Lord, help us to always look to You first.

Gibson C. Armstrong is a vice president at American PowerNet, an energy management company; a member of Calvary Church; and a former member of the PA House of Representatives.

A Word Aptly Spoken

"A word aptly spoken is like apples of gold in settings of silver."
Proverbs 25:11

My dear friend and I were returning home from a weeklong conference. We had about an hour left to visit in the bustling airport before we parted to fly off in different directions. We hoped to have a quiet breakfast and savor the waning moments, not knowing when we could visit again. Lines were long and the tables were crowded. I waited to place our order while she scouted out a table.

The atmosphere was full of tension and tempers were short. The fry cook worked frantically to prepare the orders, the heat from the grill flushing his face. As I waited, a man pushed in front of me to complain that his order was wrong. He began yelling, while his wife demanded the water she had ordered, fussing about the delay. With jaw clenching control, the cook quickly prepared an almost identical dish for the disgruntled customers, and the pair finally stomped away.

I prayed silently for the cook and the recalcitrant elderly couple. I caught the cook's eye as he glanced up to see who was next, and I smiled. His face visibly relaxed as he worked, and I soon had my food tray. "Thank you," I said. "You are doing a great job under pressured conditions. May God bless you."

It was a simple statement, but the reward was the smile and gratitude of a transformed countenance. It struck me how little it takes to encourage and lift the spirits of another person. The man behind me nodded and smiled, too, and for at least a little while, the atmosphere changed.

Lord, help me to be alert to all the opportunities that surround me every day to bless and encourage others, even in the simplest ways in the briefest of encounters. May You be glorified in all things.

Joan Boydell serves as Senior Director of Amnion Crisis Pregnancy Centers, as a consultant with Care Net, and with her husband, Bruce, in Lifespan.

New Every Morning

"...The Lord's lovingkindnesses indeed never cease, for His compassions never fail. They are new every morning..."
Lamentations 3:22-23

I'll never forget that morning. It was a typical day in the life of a mother of five small children. Everyone was dressed and fed, and I was cleaning up the dishes, wiping up spills, answering questions, and reminding the children to share...but there was a problem this particular morning. Mommy was in a *bad* mood.

I could easily justify my awful attitude, but there was this nagging pressure in my heart to stop all of my activity and evaluate my behavior.

At last I surrendered to the obvious leading of the Holy Spirit and plopped myself down on the lowest step of our kitchen stairs. Tears rushed to my eyes and repentance welled up within me. Suddenly, my children were pulled away from what they had been doing and came compassionately to my side. With a circle of sunny faces surrounding me, and little hands patting my back and knees, I poured out my heart saying, "I am so sorry that Mommy has been so irritable this morning, guys. Can you forgive me for being so nasty?"

As if it was the first time I'd ever repented to them, those precious little ones encircled me with their hugs and kisses, showering me with their love. My sin was no longer remembered. Love covered it.

Now, this is the part that's seared into my memory. Hannah, a mere seven-year-old, leaned over and humbly suggested, "Why don't *you* go into the living room and have some quiet time with Jesus, and *I'll* watch the children. Okay?"

The simplest solution to a morning that started out on the wrong foot is to start again . . . the right way!

Thank you, Lord, for Your new mercies every morning. I'm so thankful to be surrounded by love and forgiveness. I am desperate to walk blamelessly before You. Help me, Jesus. Amen

Kathi Wilson and her husband, Mark, co-authors of *Tired of Playing Church* and co-founders of Body Life Ministries, are members of Ephrata Community Church.

God Is A Good God, All The time!

"Every good thing given and every perfect gift is from above, coming down from the Father of lights, with whom there is no variation or shifting shadow." *James 1:17*

We arrived at Victorian manor in Scotland for a two-week pastors' retreat. All eight couples were there at no cost to us. I was struggling with the extravagance of the house and the incredible way that they served us continually, when God reminded me of this verse. In fact, I saw it on a bookmark with my name on it! I began to thank God not only for the blessing that the retreat was to us but also for many other things. Over the weeks following, I saw God's goodness come into focus in a new way in my understanding of God's nature.

I am sure you have heard it said, "God is good, all the time!" That is what this verse says. In God there is no change or shifting of His attributes. His goodness does not flee away like shadows that shift as the sun moves. He is a good God, and there is no time in our lives when He ceases to be good. Even when we are having a difficult time, He has not changed at all. His plans for us, the Bible says, are not for evil but for good. Like David, we should expect to see God's goodness follow us all the days of our lives. David said he would have despaired had he not expected to see the goodness of God in the land of the living. So, give thanks to the Lord for He is good!

Father, when we count our blessings one by one, we are surprised by what You have done! Thank you for Your generous heart toward us Your children.

Barry Wissler is senior pastor of Ephrata Community Church and president of HarvestNET Inc., a network of churches and ministries who partner together for harvest.

God's Timing

"Be completely humble." *Ephesians 4:2*

In the last year of my post-graduate studies in Britain, I had sent out resumes to Christian colleges in the U.S. in hopes of being hired to teach the New Testament. By the time we left in May, 1991, I had two strong prospects.

During this time, my wife and I were asking God to help us discern which of these positions would be best for us.

But pride was quietly taking hold of my heart. And God would have none of it!

The first blow came the week before returning to the U.S. My advisor handed me several pages of final revisions to make in my doctoral thesis.

I thought I was returning home finished. Now I had to tell family and friends that I was still not finished—even after four years!

That summer we lived with our parents in Lancaster, thinking that we would soon be moving to wherever I was hired to teach. God, however, had different plans...my plans were about to fizzle.

The bigger blow came later that summer. Both prospective colleges wanted to hire me. But between a hiring freeze at one and my application getting lost twice at the other, by summer's end neither one had hired me.

By September, there I was, without my thesis done and with no job in sight. My wife returned to nursing full-time, and I was stuck at home being "Mr. Mom."

This was not the road I had planned to travel. But it was the road that God had planned for me.

The only students I would have for the next two years were our two young children. God began to humble me. As my resume sat unnoticed, I was learning the joys of loving and caring for my young, and perhaps my most important, students while waiting on God's timing for the others.

God, I thank you for teaching this student a little more about who You are.

Doug Buckwalter, professor of New Testament at Evangelical Theological Seminary in Myerstown.

MAY 14

Only Heaven Will Tell

"The Lord...not wanting anyone to perish, but everyone to come to repentance." *2 Peter 3:9*

Her name hadn't crossed my mind in more than 35 years! In Canada, where I grew up, she had been a high school classmate...no one close. I sat behind her in a couple of classes. She was tall, thin, Jewish. We'd had some pleasant conversations, nothing deep, as I recall.

When I graduated I never thought of her again, until one night a few years ago. I dreamed about her. I couldn't get her off my mind for weeks after. It was like I ached for her. A name I'd forgotten for decades was consuming my thoughts.

"Lord, I don't know where Malca is. I don't know where the path of her life has led her. But Lord, if she hasn't found You yet, please do whatever it takes to bring her to Yourself." I prayed it over and over, until once again she faded from my focus.

Another couple of years passed. One night while "surfing the net," I discovered a website for my high school's alumni. Her name wasn't there. Then I got the idea (I should have thought of this ages ago, but being over 50, I'm *technologically delayed*) to "Google" some of the names from my past. A few old acquaintances had acquired notoriety. I read about doctors, attorneys, politicians. Then I typed in her name. What came up was a death notice from a Canadian newspaper. I figured it had to be her. She had passed away about 2 years ago.

Even as I write this, there's a voice that says, "Sharon, don't be ridiculous! Pure coincidence! That dream, those prayers didn't mean anything. But there's another softer, gentler voice that says, "I am not willing that any should perish," and, "When you call I *will* answer!"

I won't know until I reach heaven whether Malca made it too. I desperately hope so. And I hope that Jesus might tell me that my prayers for her played an important part.

Lord, is there a Malca I need to pray for today? When a name "pops" into my head, help me not ignore Your nudging. Thank you that as I call, I can rest assured You will answer!

Sharon Charles assists her husband John at Abundant Living Ministries, near Lititz.

God Stories 3

Sometimes God Is Insistent!

"Do not withhold good to whom it is due when it is your power to do it." *Proverbs 3:27 (New King James Version)*

The thought was insistent. It wouldn't leave my mind. "Okay, I thought. It must be the Lord. I had to do it. "Buy LaVerne a bouquet of flowers," it instructed. I bought a cheerful bunch of fresh flowers from the store down the street and headed for LaVerne's home. Now I knew well where she lived but something made me drive right past her place. "Slow down, drive around the block first," the voice seemed to say. I went around the country block that took me through the lovely rolling countryside and in a few minutes was back at her house again. This time I felt I should go in.

I rang the doorbell and LaVerne answered. "Here," I said as I held the bouquet out to her. "I think you're supposed to have this." "Oh, it's flowers from Jesus!" she cried as she took them and showed them to her husband and to the prayer partners who were there to help her in a time of deep distress over someone's giving her a hard time. Her discerning heart immediately knew where they came from. "Jesus sent me flowers!"

Another time when I was baking bread braids, I was again urged to take a big one to their home. The braids are filled with a sweet nut and raisin mix and drizzled with icing and topped with cherries and nuts. I took them to their home but no one was there so I put them on the front seat of their van.

Later they told me they picked up a Russian family at the airport and had nothing to feed them except this bread they found in their van.

Thank you, God for using us in Your work. Thank you for using us to bless others and to bless us through it.

Jackie Bowser attends DOVE Westgate Celebration.

Standing In The Gap

"The prayer of a righteous man is powerful and effective."
James 5:16b

Our excitement increased as the due date of our first child arrived. The supplies were purchased, the nursery was fully stocked, and the childbirth classes were completed. The birth was to take place at home with the doctor, my mother, and, of course, the expectant father at my side. Eleven days later labor started, but after two days of contractions, pain, and complications at home, our first son was delivered in the hospital.

Twenty-two months later I exited my home to be alone on my patio where I irrationally proceeded to tell God that I was not going to deliver our second child, who was now fifteen days past his due date. I had allowed myself to become discouraged and fearful.

As I sat in the beautiful afternoon sun and poured out my fears to God, I suddenly was enveloped by a peace that passed all understanding. Immediately my labor began and I gave birth to our second son, calmly and joyfully.

Due to his 2:00 AM arrival, we were unable to notify anyone. However, before 7:00 AM, my brother in-law and an older friend had contacted me demanding to know why they had felt so strongly to pray for me from 3:00 PM the day before until midnight.

When my faith was at its lowest point, God had impressed others to pray for me.

Am I tuned into God's leading? Would I be faithful to pray and intercede for someone without needing to understand? Is God calling me to stand in the gap for someone today?

Oh Lord, help me to be sensitive to Your prompting and faithful to pray.

Bonnie Greiner is a motivational speaker to women of all ages.

God Will Provide

"Ask and it will be given to you; seek and you will find; knock and the door will be opened to you. For everyone who asks receives; he who seeks finds; and to him who knocks, the door will be opened. Which of you, if his son asks for bread, will give him a stone? Or if he asks for a fish, will give him a snake? If you, then, though you are evil, know how to give good gifts to your children, how much more will your Father in heaven give good gifts to those who ask him!"
Matthew 7:7-11

One day I arrived at work to find a co-worker quite emotional. The landlord was foreclosing unless three months of back rent was paid. Her husband had lost his job, so meeting this demand seemed impossible.

This co-worker came to me for advice. I asked many questions about a budget which I found did not exist and spending habits that were not healthy. I challenged her to attend church that weekend and surrender her situation to God. If she wanted Him to give her guidance, then she needed to make Him a priority.

The following Monday she told me her family had gone to church. She reconnected with God and was willing to accept whatever He brought her way. I congratulated her. We could now watch how God would work. Later that same day she stopped by with tears streaming down her face. A friend offered to cover their back rent! In the days that followed, we rejoiced as God provided a new job for her husband.

Father, we know that asking You for things doesn't guarantee that we'll get them. Sometimes we miss the bigger picture and what is really best for us. You see it all though and promise to give us what we really need—good gifts. Thank you!

Brad Hoopes, an ordained minister, has been in a variety of ministry roles over the past ten years. Most recently he has served as a fundraiser for WJTL radio and as manager of TheCookieSale.com (an effort to feed starving people around the world).

This Is The Way

"Whether you turn to the right or to the left, your ears will hear a voice behind you, saying, 'This is the way; walk in it.'" *Isaiah 30:21*

I had been an at-home mom for several years and my two sons were off to school. I was anticipating that I would remain at home and keep busy with various volunteer opportunities.

One of the places that I felt drawn to was Susquehanna Valley Pregnancy Services. I volunteered in the administrative offices on a monthly basis and enjoyed doing various tasks – data entry, copying, and mailings. In May of 2002, the woman that I was volunteering for asked me if I would consider filling in for her while she was on maternity leave. I wasn't really looking for employment, and my boys would be home for the summer, but I said I would consider it.

As I was thinking and praying about the opportunity at SVPS, I checked with a neighbor to see if she would be available to baby-sit my boys during the summer. She said yes, and I decided that I would be available to fill in for Andrea while she was on maternity leave. But I made it clear that I was not looking to work on a long-term basis.

In the fall when Andrea decided that she did not want to return to her job full time, the job was offered to me. Again, I began to pray for the Lord's direction and to think about how a job might fit into my life. One day at lunch there was some discussion about whether I would stay on with SVPS. I said that I wasn't really looking for a job. One of my coworkers said, "I wasn't really looking for a job when I came here." Another said, "I wasn't either."

That conversation seemed to be the answer I was looking for… the voice behind me saying, "This is the way; walk in it."

Father, thank you for Your still, small voice. Help me to take time to hear You speaking.

Dani Longenecker is an events fundraiser/administrative assistant for Susquehanna Valley Pregnancy Services.

A Seed Of Faith

"...if you have faith as small as a mustard seed, you can say to this mountain, `Move from here to there, and it will move...'"
Matthew 17:20

For years I had prayed for my dad to get saved. Quite honestly, his lifestyle made it hard for me to actually believe he would find Christ. In 1973, he had a very serious heart attack. We were living in Florida, and Dad was in Ohio, but I was advised not to go home because the shock of seeing me could have actually worsened his condition. There was nothing to do but pray. My job was about an hour away from home so my surroundings were somewhat unfamiliar. But on this particular day I was compelled to search for a church over my lunch hour to intervene on Dad's behalf.

I spotted a church and made my way up to the front door, not really expecting it to be unlocked. But to my grateful surprise, it was open! That in itself began to stimulate my faith. As I knelt before the altar, not knowing whether Dad would live or die, I did find the assurance that it was God's will for him to be saved. So, I prayed, "Father, I believe You are speaking to me that You want to save my dad, so I'm asking in faith that You spare his life until he finds You." That was my only point of faith—believing God wanted my dad to be saved. So, I *planted that seed* in faith.

Well, my father recovered from the heart attack. It would be another seventeen years before he accepted Christ, but from that day on, in my mind it was a done deal. At sixty-five years-old, my dad accepted Jesus, and experienced one of the most dramatic conversions I have ever witnessed.

Thank You, Lord, for hearing our prayers, giving us opportunities to plant seeds of faith.

Becky Toews leads the women's ministry at New Covenant Christian Church and is an adjunct professor at Lancaster Bible College.

Entertaining Angels?

"Do not forget to entertain strangers, for by so doing some people have entertained angels without knowing it." Hebrews 13:2

Hundreds of people had gathered for an exciting community day event. There were special singers, speakers, games and food. Many local ministries and area churches were represented, sharing Good News to anyone who would listen. Several prison chaplains and I gave out literature and explained what we do behind the bars of prison.

At the end of the day, as I packed our displays and materials, a middle-aged man walked up to me. I noticed tears in his eyes as he said, "I have a message for you to give to your prison chaplains. Tell them to always keep on doing their work. I'm sure they get discouraged and maybe don't feel like they accomplish much. I am here to say that if only one life is changed by God's power, it is worth it. I am one who was changed."

This man went on to give a few details about his dysfunctional life, how he spent years in prison, and how a chaplain intervened to help him find God. He repeated the request that I give his message to my staff. And then he turned and walked away.

Later when I told this story to our staff, they had many questions. What was his name? What did he look like? Which prison was he in? I didn't find out who he was. Was this gentleman an angel that we entertained unawares? Was he sent to us by God to encourage and bless us? I don't know the answers to those questions. But, I do know we were impacted by his message.

Father, may we watch for opportunities to entertain strangers, to be light and salt to those we meet from day to day. And thank you too for those who come into our lives to bless and encourage us, for Jesus' sake. Amen

Nelson W. Martin is director of Support for Prison Ministries, working with Lancaster County prison chaplains. He also is overseer of a number of Mennonite churches in the Lititz area.

The Next Generation

"Even when I am old and gray, do not forsake me, O God, till I declare your power to the next generation, your might to all who are to come." *Psalm 71:18*

God has purposely placed inside each one of us a measure of His nature and character to be imparted to those around us. Because of His divine nature within us as believers, we all have something of value to offer. Whether we are young or old, God does not want us to give up on our dreams. He has placed them in our hearts for a purpose.

My wife and I were recently invited to a drop-in for dear friends. One of the couples at the party was a retired pastor and his wife who were instrumental in a local revival and church planting. I remember thinking to myself, "Here is a couple who have served Jesus faithfully for well over fifty years."

Even after all those years, they were still passionate about the dreams God had given them decades ago. In fact, in just the last year or two they have begun to see the fulfillment of those dreams. God has given them an open door into a previously closed segment of society. He is using their years of experience to impart wisdom the leaders of a new generation of believers.

Our hearts were encouraged by their example of faith, perseverance and fruitfulness even in old age. Whether they knew it or not, God used them once again to declare His power to the next generation. In fact, it felt like we experienced a little bit of heaven on earth that night.

Dear God, thank You for the saints who have gone before us and paved the way for us to follow. Thank You for their wisdom and example of faith. Please use us to declare Your power to the next generation.

Mark Van Scyoc is a programmer analyst, freelance photographer and Writer, and serves as Mission Director at DOVE Christian Fellowship, Westgate Celebration in Ephrata.

Favor

"For You, Oh Lord, will bless the righteous; with favor You will surround him as with a shield."
Psalm 5:12 (New King James Version)

We had finally arrived in Nairobi, Kenya, late at night, after a *very long* flight. Before landing, a flight attendant's voice instructed each person to be prepared to pay fifty dollars cash for a visa allowing us to enter Kenya. After scrounging in our purses and wallets, we came up short.

The dingy airport terminal appeared deserted, except for a few scattered airport workers and our fellow travelers, who began forming long lines, each waiting their turn to pay their dues, navigate customs and continue on towards their destination. It appeared everyone knew what to do except us! After unsuccessfully attempting to elicit help from several airport employees, we began tackling the paperwork which had been handed to us and cried, "Help, Lord!"

And He heard us! Before long, a professional-looking Kenyan woman approached and asked if we needed help. She proceeded to lead one of our foursome to a remote ATM machine that graciously yielded the coveted dollars. Next, with our passports and cash in her hands, she escorted us to the front of the long lines, spoke briefly to the official who accepted the money, stamped our passports and waved us through. No waiting, no customs, just a nod and a wave of the hand.

We had planned to spend the night in the airport, waiting to catch our flight to Mombassa in the morning. But Nairobi Airport is not a safe place to spend the night! After reserving rooms in a trusted motel, securing a reputable taxi, with plans in place for transportation back to the airport in the morning, this God-sent woman sent us off to catch a few hours of sleep.

Father, You know what we need before we even ask. Thank You for blessing us and surrounding us with Your favor.

Carol Weaver is Director of Post-Abortion Ministry with Susquehanna Valley Pregnancy Services, and serves with her husband, Tim, as a licensed minister at New Holland Family Church.

A Question Of Trust

"The Lord will command the blessing on you in your storehouses and in all to which you set your hand, and He will bless you in the land which the Lord your God is giving you."
Deuteronomy 28:8 (New King James Version)

I was in a very tumultuous time in my life. I was engaged to be married, buying a house, changing churches and generally just trying to figure out who I was. In the midst of this process, God began to speak into my job as well. I heard that same Voice that had led me in so many areas of my life begin to address my dependence on my job for my life. I fought it with everything, but a few weeks later I did the unthinkable. I decided to take the road less traveled and handed in my resignation at my job.

The fear of the unknown began to rise in my heart. Was this really God? Would God say something that others may not agree with? And of course the bottom line question is *"Can He really be trusted?"* It is so easy to trust God when you feel you do everything right. But what if you are unsure?

Miraculously, the house purchase went through anyway, and we became the owners of our new house. Now what? How do we make payments without a job? What about the wedding? Other expenses? Thoughts of us having water and sandwiches at our reception began to cross my mind.

Finally, one night all the frustration came boiling out. I cried out to the Lord how I felt like He got me into this mess and isn't lifting a finger to help us. I showed Him our need and asked for $10,000 to get us through. We were given a gift of $6,000 three days later. The rest came in smaller amounts over time. He truly can be trusted.

Thank You for Your faithfulness in all things. We place our trust and confidence in You.

Shawn Weaver directs The Potter's House, a transitional house in Leola.

Love The Unlovable

"If you love those who love you, what reward will you get? Are not even the tax collectors doing that? ...Be perfect, therefore, as your heavenly Father is perfect." *Matthew 5:46-48*

One night at TNT, I was ministering outside of church to a young lady who was crying and sharing with me how she wanted out of a relationship with a young man who was heavily into drugs and a very angry person. As I shared with her God's grace and love, I looked up to see a very angry young man. I thought he was going to punch me in the face! He shook my hand briefly after I told him I was a minister.

He came back a couple more times - I believe to check on his girlfriend more than to find God. I didn't like this young man; he was arrogant, bitter and cold. I felt conviction to love this young man but I just couldn't. I asked Jesus to give me a love for him.

God started to melt my heart after this young man asked to meet with me. He wanted to get off the drugs and get his life together. We met weekly and I saw God's love and forgiveness break him. God answered my prayer and gave me a real love for him.

Since that time he has become a real brother to me. I love him so much and it delights my heart to see the changes he has made. He has become baptized and continues to grow in faith and love for God.

God calls us to love the unlovable, for they need Jesus just like we do. We must love as Jesus loves.

Jesus, I ask that You give me a love not only for those that love me but for those that hate me. Let me be a messenger of hope, peace, and forgiveness to those that need it. Thank You for Your love for me. May it flow to others.

Mike Wenger, Executive Director of TNT Youth Ministry.

The Great Escape

"The Lord is my strength and my shield; my heart trusts in Him, and I am helped...." *Psalm 28:7*

I was struck to the ground paralyzed with fear. The bull stared at me as he lowered his head to attack again. The full span of his mammoth horns seemed like a bulldozer blade ready to move unwanted debris. He was bellowing, snorting and pawing viciously.

I needed an escape plan. Jumping to my feet, I ran for the edge of the pen. He pursued me with another horn-laden punch that landed me where I did not intend to go. I quickly jumped up to leap along the edge of the pen, into a corner. I couldn't get away from this 1300 pound beast. He was quicker and stronger than I, and I was his sole target. I found myself standing in the corner with his head firmly pressed against my knees. The more I strained to get away, the more furiously he twisted his head and horns to restrain me. I was breathless from my frantic attempts to escape and weak-kneed from fear. I was trapped! So, I surrendered to his painful pressure on my knees as he paused to await my next move. As I stood still, I could only whisper, "Help me Lord!" I felt a slight relaxing in his persistent press. I pondered my next move and managed to squirm loose. I aimed for the top of the fence and jumped over it into safety.

This experience is permanently etched in my memory, along with gratitude to God for His protection. In His miraculous way, He inserted His protective shield at the right place and time.

Lord, I trust You for protection in the everyday activities of life. Watch over me and prepare a shield of protection for this day. Give me strength for all I do. Thank you for Your faithfulness to me. Amen

Nelson Martin serves as an elder of ELANCO DOVE Fellowship, Terre Hill and is on the USA Apostolic Team of DOVE Christian Fellowship. He and his wife, Sue, have three sons.

A Year From Now

"In bitterness of soul Hannah wept much and prayed to the Lord... Hannah was praying in her heart..." *1 Samuel 1:10,13*

Our beloved first-born daughter delighted her father and me with the joyful news that we would be grandparents. Our first grandchild was to be born in July and we could not have been more excited. Weeks passed as we awaited the first ultrasound confirming the "due date." That day was not to be, as suddenly our daughter miscarried.

Grief takes many forms and is certainly a uniquely personal experience. I had faithfully prayed every day for a healthy baby and now felt such a deep sense of loss. I also experienced the added sorrow of seeing the depth of my daughter's grief. The culmination of that grief came when she had to go into the hospital for a surgical procedure.

What could have been the worst day of her life, actually turned out to be a day of remembrance of how God extended His mercy in an incredibly loving way. In the recovery room, my daughter's face can only be described as having the "peace of God." The Lord had removed her sense of hopelessness and emptiness with a *promise.* She knew without any doubt that He placed in her heart these words: *"A year from now when you are in this place, they will be handing you your baby."*

A year later, the gift of a baby girl was given to us from The Lord. My daughter told us that at the moment of her baby's birth, she immediately looked up and although filled with gratitude for her little one, she was even more in "awe" of how God had kept His promise to her. "His promise" is now a happy toddler and we praise Him every day for her.

Compassionate and loving Lord, thank You for blessing us with the desire of our hearts.

Patti Wilcox is Assistant Director, Good Works, Inc., Coatesville, a ministry that repairs homes and restores hope for low-income homeowners.

Can You Hear Me Now?

"Speak, Lord, for your servant is listening."
1 Samuel 3:10

God speaks in different ways to different people at different times. After praying for someone for a long time, one member of our congregation was wondering when God was going to answer her prayers. One day after praying about this person, she looked out the window. The clouds came together and formed the image of a face and shoulders. In the arms of this Person, in intricate detail, was a lamb. God's message, conveyed visually, was that He was caring for this friend and carrying him/her.

God has often spoken to another member, but on two occasions she has heard God speak audibly.

God speaks through His Word, through the counsel of Spirit-filled Christians, sometimes through circumstances, through dreams, once through a donkey. I have had no encounters with talking donkeys, nor have I ever heard God speak audibly. I have never had a vision similar to the cloud picture described above. God does speak to me, but even then it's not always in the same way. There have been times when God has spoken in my spirit, when I have had as clear a sense of the exact words as if I had heard them with my ears. Those instances have been the exception. Usually when God speaks to me He gives a concept, or a knowledge, or a direction, but without specific words. Of course that kind of message is easier to miss than when He is dramatically clear.

I think I probably miss a great deal of what God is trying to say to me. What about you? Often we're going too fast, being too noisy, allowing ourselves to be distracted, or just not expecting God to speak. Like Samuel, let's practice giving God an invitation to speak. Then let's be listening!

Thank You Lord, that You cherish our relationship with You. Help us to hear You, regardless of how You choose to speak. Amen

Joe Sherer is Senior Pastor of Mount Joy Mennonite Church. He and his wife Mary Lou have three daughters: Allison, Melanie, and Carissa.

In A War Zone

"Be self-controlled and alert. Your enemy the devil prowls around…looking for someone to devour." *1 Peter 5:8*

We live in a beautiful area of Lancaster County. As you travel through the countryside in the summer, you will usually see well-tended gardens, flowers, and lush green vegetation. Yet, all is not perfect in this paradise. In my garden, spring began with a plague of rabbits. Under cover of darkness, they feasted on many of the plants and flowers I had painstakingly planted. We tried all kinds of rabbit repellents to no avail, and finally ended up putting wire cages around the plants that survived.

Then in July, multitudes of Japanese beetles invaded. They can be controlled by spraying, but they swarm to any areas that are missed by the spray. So every morning and evening, I'd shake off any remaining beetles and drown them in a bucket of water.

Sometimes we take for granted the peace and security we live under. We forget that spiritually, we live in a war zone. Hopefully, it won't take a severe attack to cause us to be alert and watchful. Granted, the attack on my garden is trivial compared to spiritual warfare. But the principle remains that we must be on the alert and guard our hearts against the enemy of our souls. Our spiritual enemies are insidious, working under cover of darkness, with much more devastating results than the demise of a few plants.

I found some good news in all of this, however. Some of the plants that the rabbits "pruned" survived the attack and turned out to be bigger and bushier than the others. Spiritually, the good news is that when we submit to God, He can turn what the enemy meant for destruction into strength and blessing.

Lord, keep me spiritually alert, and don't let me ever forget that I'm in a war zone. I submit to You and put on Your armor as I go out into the world today.

Jane Nicholas lives in Elizabethtown with her husband, Bill. She works as a proofreader, writer, and editor.

The Gift Of Life

"Thank God for his Son...His gift is too wonderful for words." *2 Corinthians 9:15 (The Living Bible)*

As a recipient of a kidney and pancreas transplant, it is hard to find sufficient words to describe my gratitude to the mother of David, my donor.

Upon query of my surgery, I am always eager to share the transformation that this "Gift of Life" has made on me. My husband Jay, family and friends were so happy that the expected 3 to 5 year wait on the transplant list was only 8 months! Yippee, I no longer was a type1 diabetic; I no longer needed dialysis. We were praising God for an answer to prayer!

Immediately after surgery, I had this overwhelming urgency to write David's mother a letter to thank her for the awesome and selfless gift. I wrote many letters in my head; they gushed of "my" new lease on life, "my" happiness, "my" answer to prayer and on and on about "me." When I put pen to paper, the reality of the cost to David's family was overwhelming. In deep humility, I wrote and rewrote that letter...the words seemed empty and hollow. With a prayer, I placed that letter in the mailbox. Two years have passed and I still long for just the right words to express to David's family so they know without a doubt how deeply grateful I am to them.

While having my quiet time one morning, God spoke to me very clearly. "Nan, when have you ever spent hours pondering just the right words to appropriately express your gratitude to Me? I gave my perfect Son to die on the cross for your sins so you could have the Gift of Eternal Life." Wow, He was right, and once again with meekness I bowed before my God with a grateful heart.

Heavenly Father, thank you for freely giving Your son to die on the cross for my salvation. There are no words adequate, so I offer You my life, even though I am unworthy of Your Eternal Gift. In Jesus' precious name, Amen.

Nan Schock serves as a Stephen Minister at Manor Church, located south of Mountville.

He Can Be Trusted

"O Lord God Almighty, who is like you? You are mighty, O Lord, and your faithfulness surrounds you." *Psalm 89:8*

A psychologist may have labeled it a mid-life crisis. I was in my mid-forties, feeling very unsettled and restless. I had a secure job with good benefits. But, I was ready for adventure, for new challenges—or so I thought!

I often regretted that I had never finished college. So, after much prayer, my wife and I packed some of our belongings, put the rest in storage, and moved to Harrisonburg, Virginia. I became a fulltime college student.

After we were there, I began having second thoughts. What had I done? Why had I left the security of a good job? What was I going to do with this college degree anyway? Academic life seemed so out of touch with the real world. Was I even going to make it?

One day I read in scripture how the Israelites were on the verge of entering the Promised Land but, filled with fear, they rebelled against Moses, begging to go back to Egypt (Numbers 14). How ridiculous! After all the miracles God performed to bring them within sight of the Promised Land, why would they want to go back? Then I realized I was no different. God was providing for our needs. He already worked out so many details to bring us to this point. Surely He would continue to provide. Why would we want to turn back when He had new adventures, new plans for us?

I earned the college degree but, more importantly, I learned again that where God guides, He provides. He can be trusted. After graduation, He led me to a job in Christian retail where I find new challenges every day. He is still faithful!

Lord, we are amazed as we reflect on Your faithfulness. Even when we become anxious, You prove Yourself trustworthy. May we rest confidently in Your care for us, Your children. Amen

Marv Smoker is a manager/buyer for Berean Christian Stores (formerly Provident Bookstores), Lancaster. He and his wife, Rhoda, live in Intercourse and attend Petra Christian Fellowship.

God Stories 3

Seashells

"He gives beauty for ashes, joy for mourning, praise for despair."
Isaiah 61:3

One of my most favorite places to be and things to do is to walk the beach at dawn. The sun just coming up over the horizon takes my breath away with its brilliant pink, purple, and gold. Soon, the beach will be full of colorful umbrellas and people. But for now, it is my special time to be alone with God. Enjoying the solitude, I look for treasures along the shore.

I used to only stop to pick up the perfect seashells until the day God spoke to my heart, "I love the broken ones. They are the most beautiful and interesting to Me." I spot a broken shell and bend to pick it up, and as I turn it round in my hands, I ask God to show me what He means. He speaks softly to my heart, "I see you in that shell." Me? I laugh. He replies, "You've been through some storms in life. The waves have crashed over you time and again; you've been thrown onto the shore and have even been stepped on a time or two. You are broken, but you are still here, special and unique. You have persevered through the storms of life, and you've allowed Me to hold you in the palm of My hand and mold and shape you and even now use your brokenness to help others. And like that shell in your hands, your brokenness is the beauty that I behold."

I fell to my knees on that New Jersey beach, weeping and rejoicing as I saw with new eyes the beauty in my brokenness and in that seashell. Today, whether I am walking along the beach or walking among people, I ask the Holy Spirit to help me see the beauty in the brokenness within and around me.

Thank you Father that You make all things beautiful in Your time.

Sharon Blantz serves as regional pastor of support and care ministries at Worship Center.

June

Joy In The Job

"Consider it pure joy, my brothers, whenever you face trials of many kinds, because you know that the testing of your faith develops perseverance." *James 1:2-3*

I t had been a rough few months. Although much was being accomplished in the work I was doing, I was feeling worn down due to ongoing broken promises.

I felt the Lord had directed me to where I was but I didn't understand why it was not going as I had anticipated.

Several knew of my struggles and had been praying that I would be able to discern His direction.

One Sunday at church, after a particularly frustrating week, a friend suddenly said, "You know what I'm going to do? I'm going to pray for you to have joy in your job."

"Yeah, right," I replied, smiling at the seeming silliness of the thought.

Over the next couple of days, however, things did begin to change and I suddenly started to experience a joy in the job. The circumstances hadn't really changed and I didn't enjoy the situation any better, but there had been a change in mind and heart as to "What, Lord, are you trying to show me in all this?"

The underlying circumstances never improved and I no longer perform that work. I did, however, learn to rely more and more on the peace of the Lord and learn to have patience as He moves me through the maze of life to the place where He wants to bless me today. That became the joy of the job.

Lord, please help me to see You at work in all things today, to know that You can provide a sense of joy even in the midst of despair, and that I need to rely upon You to experience that peace and joy. Amen

Casey Jones, an organization management and grants advisor, resides in Parkesburg. He also focuses on family ministries and those that come alongside the hurting.

Everything And Anything

"Whoever receives one of these little children in My name receives Me and whoever receives Me, receives not Me but Him who sent Me." *Mark 9:37 (New King James Version)*

I committed to go to my daughter's home to assist her recovery following surgery. The body of believers assured me that my elderly roommate and friend would be checked on and kept busy. One friend invited her for lunch. When asked what she would enjoy, I said, "everything and anything." Somehow an idea formed to give her a fresh, new experience. A glorious summer day greeted us and the ride to the home was thoroughly enjoyed. Easy conversation and great food made for a wonderful fellowship time. Following lunch, a son turned to their guest, "Would you like to go for a motorcycle ride?" With little hesitation, the reply came, "Well, I guess so." Quickly the cycle was brought out and helmet carefully placed to protect her. She was told to hang on and off they went. An experienced twenty-something driver and a ninety-plus first-time rider were on their way. Later, she shared with me, "I just hung on tight and it was fine."

Isn't that a picture of a healthy relationship with God? Trusting, dependent, open and hanging on, letting God take us where He wills. The photographs of my Mother on the motorcycle reflect the joy, laughter and ease that a trusting relationship brings. She is a picture of the 'little child' received in God's name…trusting, bold, yet unassuming in this memory.

Father God, I desire to relate with the unconditional childlike trust. I don't want to miss opportunities to explore, expand and enhance the lifetime You have given me. Help me to stay available, ready and willing to do the unexpected and experience all of what You have for me. Teach me, Lord, to be in season and out of season in joy, laughter and play in the moments that You present to me.

Diana Oliphant is a credentialed minister with Teaching The Word Ministries serving with a heart for the region and nations.

Here On Loan

"...Because you have obeyed me and not even withheld your beloved son, I will bless you richly...all because you obeyed me."
Genesis 22:16-18

Our second child, Cameron, was six years old when he was put in the ICU. He developed an illness that was attacking his body in various ways. He seemed to get worse with each passing hour. The final blow was when he developed hepatitis and the doctors couldn't say why.

I felt myself beginning to crumble. What made matters worse was that a boy in Cameron's school died a week earlier, and no one knew what killed him. He was just sick one day and died the next. I couldn't get that out of my mind. I thought, "Is this the same thing? *Is Cameron going to die?*"

At that moment something came over me. I said to God, "God, I want You to heal him. I know You can do it. However, although this is my baby, he was Your baby first. You have just given him to us on loan. I want him to live here with us, but if You want him back, You have every right." I felt a peace come over me, yet my prayer confused me. "Does this make me a bad mother?" I wondered. "Does it seem like I don't care for my child?"

Then God showed me that this is what faith and obedience really is. I was experiencing the ability to trust God no matter what. I was experiencing what it felt like to give up something I loved if it was what God required of me, whether I understood why or not. This must have been how Abraham felt when he went to sacrifice Isaac.

By the next day, Cameron was improving. The doctors said it must have just been a virus. Praise God!

Father, please continue to help me be obedient even when I may not understand all the details.

Melanie Holland is a wife and mother of four, youth pastor, evangelist, and the founder and president of Driven Ministries, Incorporated.

Who Woke You Up?

"Indeed God speaks once, or twice, yet no one notices it. In a dream, a vision of the night, When sound sleep falls on men, while they slumber in their beds, Then He opens the ears of men, and seals their instruction, that He may turn man aside from his conduct, and keep man from pride." *Job 33:14-17 (New American Standard Version)*

I t is such a waste when God speaks and no one notices. I have asked God to open my ears to what He is saying to me, as I believe God is constantly speaking for those who have ears to hear. This passage tells us that God will even speak to us during the night; we see that repeatedly in scripture.

Awaking at night can be caused by various things, but sometimes it is God who wakes us up. Quite honestly I think sometimes God has trouble getting my attention during the day so He will wake me up so I am undistracted. While many dreams have nothing to do with God, I have had a few that have warned me from something that was not His will.

A few years ago, I would wake up repeatedly with the clock reading 3:33. That got my attention but I had no idea why it was happening until one day I noticed Jeremiah 33:3; "Call unto me and I will answer you." God was inviting me to seek Him! Two years ago I woke up repeatedly at 2:22 which gave me a burden to pray for the Route 222 corridor through Ephrata and led to a sermon of a number of texts containing 222. It is important that we test all subjective experiences with scripture, and we must be sure we are not imagining something is God when it is not. But the truth is that God still speaks to us in the night. Sleep well!

Father, we value Your faithfulness in guiding us even if You need to wake us up at night. Thank You for still speaking!

Barry Wissler is senior pastor at Ephrata Community Church and member of Regional Council, RCOLC.

Lord, I Need An Overhaul

"For at just the right time Christ will be revealed from heaven by the blessed and only almighty God, the King of all kings and Lord of all lords." *I Timothy 6:15 (New Living Translation)*

I t was two months since my husband and I had been in a potentially fatal automobile accident, and I was still reeling. I'd seen God move mightily through the accident, but the monumental nature of it upset the rhythm of my daily routines. The one that bugged me most was my waning morning time with Jesus. I was used to an unrushed, lingering time with the Lord, but somehow it had ebbed to a trickle.

I was starving for more of the Lord, but didn't have the strength to shift back into my treasured routine. As I bemoaned and groaned before the Lord, I told Him how I longed to rise early and have plenty of time with Him, and how I couldn't picture this happening without much praying and planning on my part. In the past if my time with Jesus slipped, I could usually count on a fresh start in the New Year, following a season of processing the coming year with Him and receiving His adjustments for me.

But here we were, mid-year, and I needed an overhaul.

I posed this question to the Lord, "How much change could we forge today?"

His reply was, "How much do you want? How much do you need?"

I answered, "I need a ton, as You know."

And He said simply, "I am the King. I am the Lord. Your King. Your Lord."

And suddenly, faith filled my limp sails, I realized God was capable of infusing me with a fresh supply of grace to be with Him, and my morning times with Jesus were reinstated

Father, thank you for being Lord, being King, and being capable of bringing about every change You desire to see in me.

Lisa Hosler serves at Susquehanna Valley Pregnancy Services and with teams uniting for regional transformation.

God's Plans

"For my thoughts are not your thoughts, neither are your ways my ways," declares the Lord." *Isaiah 55:8*

L ast year I was at Creation Festival when the heavy rains caused it to be postponed. I knew it was coming. The night before the announcement, I woke up in the middle of the night to another downpour. I cried to myself, trying not to wake up my friends. *"Praise You in the Storm"* by Casting Crowns was in my head and I knew in my heart that the festival wouldn't happen and that I needed to praise God in the midst of it all.

When the announcement was made, there were tears. We had a worship service and prayed. The volunteers, who had been working on setting up for days, turned around and began to tear down. It was tough to see the disappointed faces.

But God still had plans. We didn't see hundreds of teens flooding the prayer tent as we had in years past…but during our little worship service we learned that someone had made a decision for salvation during set up!

Reports also came in that many youth groups still held events and services that week. One group sent an email sharing about an event complete with camping, music, teaching, hair painting, games, worship and a talent show. They even had communion, a candlelight service, fireworks and a prayer "tent" for those who responded to the ministry times. They said, "We all felt like we had learned more at Creation this year by not being there than we ever had previously!" I'm sure that relationships were formed, seeds planted, and maybe even decisions made for eternity BECAUSE the festival didn't happen.

God's plans were not the ones we had expected …but they were good. His definition is the only true definition of good.

Lord, thank you that Your ways are higher than ours.. Help us to seek You in all that we do and praise You in the midst of what we don't understand.

Stacey Gagne is Office Manager at WJTL Radio.

Handcrafted By God

"For God so loved the world ...." *John 3:16*

D id your favorite team ever come in second? What did you do? Write them off as losers? You always remember who comes in first. You probably know who the first man to walk on the moon was. Who was the second? Who cares? Isn't that our attitude as a society?

What about YOUR imperfection, in sports, school, or work?

As we compete our way through school, we take part in a refining process. We start out crude oil. Only the valedictorian comes out the top of the distilling tower as fine mineral spirits. What if you are spit out at the bottom as tar?

If you did well in high school, maybe you went to college. Every person at college had the same basic qualifications as you. Competition was probably worse. Did you do well, or were you one of the 2/3 who didn't graduate? Either way, most of us find ourselves in the workplace, where we find—more Competition! Competition to get a job. Competition to keep a job. Competition to advance in position.

We never stop competing. It's part of life.

If competition is part of life, then, so is winning, and so is losing. They both come our way.

Most of us can handle winning. What about losing, or placing second? Where do you get your value when no-one besides your mother remembers that you came in second?

GOD.

Don't let the labels the world puts on you stick.

Feel the back of your neck. You may not notice it, but you have a non-removable label.

It reads, "Made in Heaven—Quality Handcrafted by God."

Like a loving parent, God will not forget you no matter how you place according to the world's standards.

Dear Father, thank you for loving us. Whether the world gives us good or bad marks today, may we remember You just as You remember and care for us each moment whether we pay any attention or not. Amen

Allen Keller serves as Youth Pastor at Olivet UMC in Coatesville.

The Picture Of God's Peace

"He made peace with everything in heaven and on earth by means of His blood on the cross." *Colossians 1:20*

The Bible defines peace as the "absence of war," and this "absence of war" has three contexts: the absence of war that occurs between God and me (Romans 5:1); the absence of war between you and me (Galatians 3:28); and the absence of war in my inner world, in my own heart and mind (Philippians 4:7).

Because of what Jesus did on the cross, I don't have to be at war with God. I can have *peace with God*, and I can be reconciled to Him through trusting in His finished work for me.

I can also have *peace with others*. This is a more difficult challenge. However, Romans 12:18 and 2 Corinthians 13 encourages us to be at peace with others.

Because of what Jesus has already done, we can have *peace with ourselves*. Jesus talks in John 14 about that gift of peace. The peace the world offers is made up of empty promises.

Peace is that sense of contentment and confidence in the midst of life's difficulties. Though the storms may be raging in my outer world, my inner world can have peace. That's *God's picture of peace*. The problem is, I have a long list of things that "disturb the peace": traffic, long lines, hostile people, cell phones, stress, noise, information overload, and relational conflict. I'm unsettled about my past and uneasy about my present. In order to conquer my enemies of peace I need to *FIX*:

F - Filter the noise, focusing on Jesus

I - Investigate the truth by reading God's word

X - "X" out the enemies through Jesus and prayer

God grant us Your peace, that we may find solace in life's storms.

Dale H. Engle served as a pastor in the Brethren in Christ Church for thirty years. The above devotional is adapted from his last sermon. He found that perfect picture of peace on June 8th, 2006, when he went to be with the Lord.

Day By Day

"Do not lose heart...inwardly we are being renewed day by day."
2 Corinthians 4:16

I groaned as I headed to physical therapy—again. Following surgery on my foot, I was only two weeks into the process and the exercises were already tedious. Forty times left, forty times right, up and down, around in circles—boring details of all the exercises that I needed to do day after day. Most of them felt insignificant and puny at the time and no outward change was evident. I wanted a strong ankle ASAP. I was not enjoying this day-by-day process.

Until it dawned on me: this was like my relationship with God. I want the result, having a strong connection to my Creator and the change that can produce in my life. But too often, I am so busy looking for that result, I forget about the day-by-day choices that will produce the change I want.

While doing physical therapy, I could not see the muscles and tendons in my ankle gaining strength. Most days, when I finished, it did not feel any stronger than it did an hour earlier. Actually, often it felt tired and weak. I had to go by the knowledge of how the body works and what my therapist told me. These daily exercises would bring the strong ankle I desire.

It is much the same way with my connection to God; most times, I do not see anything happening in myself. While it can be peaceful and calm to read, pray, journal, or be still, I am not holy when I finish. I am still a messy human. Nevertheless, I can choose to believe what God, my pastors, and others I trust say. Day by day, choice by choice, renewal is happening in me.

Spirit of God; help me—day by day—to be intentional in the choices I make to connect with You.

Janet Oberholtzer, wife as well as mother of three teenage boys, serves as associate director for Women of Hope at Hopewell Christian Fellowship.

My Angel

"If I take the wings of the morning, and dwell in the uttermost parts of the sea, even there Your hand shall lead me, and Your right hand shall hold me." *Psalm 139:9–10 (New King James Version)*

I learned to swim at a very early age, both at the pool and the ocean. One sweltering hot summer day, I was bobbing in the waves at Rehoboth Beach and loving every minute. It was late in the afternoon; most of the people and all of the lifeguards had left for the day. My parents were at our spot on the beach; Dad taking a wonderful late-afternoon nap.

Rehoboth is famous for its riptides and sure enough, I got caught in one. Panic set in: I was alone out there and I was frightened. I screamed for help as I was being carried further and further out in the water.

My mother tried to wake my father out of his deep sleep and ran to the ocean. Someone ran past her, dove into the water and swam out to me. I remember thinking that this man was extraordinarily strong; which would have been unusual, as I felt my dad's 6'4", 225 pound strength often. This man got me out of the ocean and laid me carefully on the beach. My mother bent down over me and turned to thank the rescuer: He was nowhere to be seen. My father, who had reached us afterwards, saw no man anytime, anywhere.

The beach was basically deserted at this point, so for him to disappear that quickly was next to impossible. My mother maintains to this day that it was an angel sent to rescue me.

Thank you, Abba, that there is a reason You saw fit to rescue me that day. May I recognize the plans You have for me and fulfill them according to Your Will. Thank you that there is nowhere too far for You to help us.

Wendy Reasner, formerly of Susquehanna Valley Pregnancy Services, is a supervisor at Caron Treatment Centers in Wernersville.

God Will Guide Us

"Your word is a lamp to my feet and a light for my path."
Psalm 119:105

We recently celebrated 20 years of service to our patients and to God at Cornerstone Family Health. Over twenty years ago, Dr. Alice Riden and I had felt called by the Lord to start a family medical practice dedicated to His service. There were some very specific parts of that, including a call to minister to "Jerusalem, Judea and Samaria, and the uttermost bounds of the earth." Our call was to touch our patients right in our immediate area, outreach to the community around us, and finally be involved in some sort of global missions. In the early years, we put in long hours just to feed our families and pay the bills, and it seemed we hardly had time to sleep, let alone see that sort of outreach. We particularly felt led to help send medical professionals to the foreign mission field long term. Our first attempt to do so was unsuccessful. It was discouraging, and it looked like we would never realize the vision we believed the Lord had given us.

Little by little, God was faithful. He provided additional like minded providers and called some to both the foreign and local ministry fields. Now as we look back at 20 years, God has provided opportunities for us to be involved with local ministries like Bethany Christian Services, Water Street Rescue Mission, Susquehanna Valley Pregnancy Services, and others. He has also provided for opportunities for short term trips and long term missions to China, Albania, Honduras, Haiti, India, Indonesia, Bolivia and other countries. If God gives you a vision – stick with it until He tells you to go a different way. It is not always easy (we have an enemy who wants us to give up), but if He gives the path, He will guide us and sustain us on it.

Dear Lord, help us be faithful to the vision that You have called us to, and be sensitive to what other paths You may have for us to go down.

Chip Mershon, MD, is a physician at Cornerstone Family Health in Lititz, and is chairman of the board of elders at the Lancaster Evangelical Free Church.

Replacing The Death Mobile

"A cheerful heart is good medicine, but a crushed spirit dries up the bones." *Proverbs 17:22*

We once owned a vehicle that leaked both oil and gas and had no working horn. This bothered my sister, Cindy, so much that she referred to it as the Death Mobile. Whenever I took her for a drive, she adamantly refused to wear a seat belt because she was convinced we were doomed for destruction anyway.

One day, I totaled the Death Mobile so we were in the market for a new car. We test drove a 1990 Dodge Dynasty and tried the horn. It didn't work. I thought this was hysterical, and I laughed and laughed as we repeatedly tried to beep that horn to no avail during the entire test drive. Finally, as we pulled into the car lot, it beeped. Instantly we knew the car was ours.

In all the years we owned that car, the horn never stopped working. The Lord used His sense of humor to show us the car He had picked out just for us.

Lord, I thank you for laughter and for the spirit of joy You have given to us.

Stephanie Eshleman serves with her husband, Kevin, at Ephrata Community Church.

Not Overtaken

"He who dwells in the shelter of the Most High will rest in the shadow of the Almighty. I will say of the Lord, he is my refuge and my fortress, my God, in whom I trust. Surely he will save you from the fowler's snare and from the deadly pestilence. He will cover you with his feathers, and under his wings you will find refuge."
Psalm 91:1-4

As a child, I memorized many scriptures from both the Old and the New Testaments. I found that memorizing verses helped to get God's truth into my heart and my mind. Those truths would then come to mind at opportune times.

One special time that scriptures came to mind occurred during a season of life when I was struggling with deep depression. I was working hard at issues and trying to fight off the darkness, but it still felt overwhelming at times. I remember clearly one morning when I got awake and said that I didn't have the strength to fight anymore and that if the darkness comes, it comes.

I still got up and went down to the kitchen to make breakfast for the family. As I walked into the kitchen, I had an impression that Jesus was turning on a record player inside my head and playing a record there (before the days of cassette tapes and CD's!).

All day long, with no effort of my own, the words of Psalm 91 played themselves over and over in my mind and heart. I was aware that Jesus was my refuge and my fortress and that He would deliver me. I could trust Him to answer me and be with me in trouble.

As these words played within me throughout the day, I was strengthened. I still had work to do on my journey of healing, but the darkness did not overtake me. I had the assurance that God would deliver me and bring me through.

Lord God, thank you for being the one who delivers in times of trouble, for being the one in whom I can trust.

Betty Metzler serves as a counselor at Petra Christian Fellowship, New Holland.

JUNE 14

God Is Orchestrating My Day

"...but you know both God and who he works. Steep your life in
God-reality, God-initiative, God-provisions."
Matthew 6:33 (The Message)

We slid the last box in the mini van as the first rain drops
plopped on the tail gate. I was moving from Mt. Gretna to
Leola using the installment plan: a van-, car-, or truckload
at a time whenever a friend volunteered to help. My windshield wipers
tapped a hurried rhythm as the rain became a torrent.

I called ahead to Leola—was it raining?

Not yet.

Willing hands and strong backs were waiting to help unload. And
as the last box was pulled from the van, the rain arrived. Such perfect
timing could not be accidental.

That invisible orchestration happened over and over during my
change in location: all my friends arriving, from different directions,
ten minutes early one day and both twenty minutes late the next so that
no time was lost.

Even my moving date proved God's hand was at work. My friends
weren't available to help the weekend I had hoped for which was very
good: I discovered a development-wide garage sale had been planned
for that weekend. Imagine the confusion and stress of loading vans and
trucks among swarms of bargain hunters.

To see God at work in the ordinary events of our days bring a
reassurance unlike any other. The Creator of the universe is interested
and involved with every area of my life. My security and peace thrive
when I see God "orchestrating" my day. I imagine Him, conductor's
baton in hand, summoning people, signaling weather, and selecting
events so that all flows in harmonious rhythms.

*Father, open my eyes to see Your hand at work in the ordinary events
of my day.*

Ruth Morris is a small group leader at The Worship Center and special projects
writer for Loving & Caring, Inc.

God Stories 3

"Please Father Me"

"…My son, do not regard lightly the discipline of the Lord, nor faint when you are reproved by Him; For those whom the Lord loves He disciplines, and He scourges every son whom He receives." …All discipline for the moment seems not to be joyful, but sorrowful; yet to those who have been trained by it, afterwards it yields the peaceful fruit of righteousness." *Hebrews 12:5-6,11 (New American Standard)*

In this generation, many young people feel fatherless. My wife, Valerie and I live and work on one of Youth With A Mission's campuses where we disciple young people. Many of them ask us to "father" them. We discovered that there is a connection between fatherlessness and lawlessness, and between fathering and discipline.

Recently, one of our staff ladies who had been abandoned by her own father, asked me to "father" her. So I gave her a task that was too big for her but a job that I knew she was capable of. (Fathers provide opportunities for their children to grow, often giving them a task too big so they can accomplish it with God's help and with coaching.) After a few days of work, this young lady was upset and completely overwhelmed with the task. She was angry and refused to talk to me, but I felt impressed of the Lord to gently but firmly challenge her, telling her to keep trying, and to change her attitude.

Often times when you don't have a father, you don't learn the necessary discipline and self-control in your life. You learn that no one will pay attention to you unless you exhibit bad behavior, so you end up developing bad habits to get attention for all the wrong reasons. This can lead to lawlessness where there are no boundaries. To be fathered is to be disciplined for your good. It means some pain and discomfort now but wonderful fruitfulness in the future. Thankfully this young lady connected the idea that my firmness in confronting her attitude and work was because I wanted to see her expand in her abilities. After a few days, she came back and thanked me for being firm with her; she then finished the task and grew stronger in her capacity.

Heavenly Father, help me to receive Your discipline and instruction for I trust and love You. I know that You have my best interest at heart.

Bill Landis from Lancaster County, serves with Youth With A Mission as the Caribbean Regional Director.

Divine Encounter

"The wolf also shall dwell with the lamb…and a little child shall lead them." *Isaiah 11:6 (New King James Version)*

To me, the beginning of motherhood meant putting my missions career on hold. God had other plans in store to use my baby to open doors of international ministry. When friends from Germany were visiting, we promised them authentic Pennsylvania Dutch food. As we arrived at the farm of our Amish hosts, we were surprised to find a limo instead of a buggy. Inside, seated around the table were ten Iraqi guests.

As the meal began, I excused myself to feed my son. Our Amish hostess escorted me as I shared how excited I was to see the international guests.

"This is a divine encounter!" I exclaimed.

"So you are a Christian, just like me?" she asked.

I said yes, I grew up Mennonite and am a follower of Jesus. She embraced me saying, "Oh, good! I was praying that God would bring the right people to minister His love to these Iraqi guests." "I'll be praying for an opportunity!" I answered.

As always, my smiling son stole the show. The only Iraqi woman asked to hold him and she began pulling out pictures of her grown "babies". We shared stories of our children and soon I was in tears telling her how much my heart breaks for her people.

"My prayers are with you. Jesus loves you." I said through my tears. Our conversation drew the attention of the room. This freed our Amish hosts to also share about Jesus' love and their prayers for peace in Iraq. In no time, we were all singing "Amazing Grace" together, followed by a German worship song and an Iraqi dance. We gathered together for an Amish supper but the Lord allowed us to partake in a communion feast like none we could ever imagine.

Lord, You are able to do immeasurably more than all we can ask or imagine!

Deb Muenstermann, apart from serving as a mother, leads a mom's ministry at ACTS church in Lancaster and helps oversee their small group ministry.

The Groom

"…as the bridegroom rejoices over the bride, so shall your God rejoice over you." *Isaiah 62:5*

Weddings—the best place on earth to glimpse the embodiment of *purity*. Every eye is on the bride walking down the aisle; except my husband, Bob, and me...

We like to look at the *groom*'s face as he awaits his bride. We enjoy the transformation from nervousness, to anxious expectancy, to that boyish grin that lights up his whole face, reflecting his inner joy!

On June 23, 2007, Bob and I attended our only son, Joshua's, wedding. We fervently watched the very typical and still marvelous transformations. However, Joshua's countenance filled with joyous emotion as he struggled to fight back obvious tears. (That was our cue to look quickly at Kari, Joshua's bride, lest we too lose our composure.)

Jesus refers to Himself as the bridegroom. And He calls us, His church, His bride. Does Jesus, like many earthly grooms, anxiously wait, expecting soon to see His beautiful bride? And when Jesus does cast eyes upon us, will He, too, break out into a huge boyish grin because He knows His wait is now over? Will His excitement be as great, knowing that we are now forever in His presence? Will He be overcome with deep emotion, like He showed with the death of Lazarus because He loves us so much?

Just as Kari prepared herself for her groom, we the Church must also prepare for our own wedding day. Our wedding garments must be washed and white as snow. Is Jesus Christ your Lord and Savior? Are you earthly husbands ready to present your wives as having no spot or wrinkle before God? Are we, as wives, honoring our husbands as lord? Do our earthly marriages reflect the servant-leader and respectful-helper relationships of the God-head? Are we truly ready?

To our Bridegroom, Your Bride looks forward to our wedding day. How we long to see You face to face!

Tamalyn Jo Heim has been married 30 years to her best friend Bob.

Choices

"He has put eternity in their hearts...." *Ecclesiastes 3:11*

E arly one morning on a summer day on one of the worst blocks of Reading, Pennsylvania, two young men were having a conversation. They were discussing how serious life was and how they were fearful of getting involved in the gangs and drugs that infested their neighborhood. They talked about how they needed to find the answer to life's problems, but they were unsure of where to turn.

That night they were invited to a party. I'm sure girls would be waiting for them, alcohol, probably drugs, and more of life's problems. But that morning they weren't sure why they made the decision, but they committed not go to the party that night.

It was that very night that we had a major outreach right on their block. Over 30 churches in our city were partnering with the Nicky Cruz Outreach and TRUCE team to minister the life-changing message of Jesus Christ in over 15 different high need areas of our city.

As they listened to the music and they heard the message, they began to ask questions and realized that this was the answer for which they were looking. That night they joined with over 50 other people in making Jesus Christ their Savior and Lord! They could have been at a party ruining their lives, but instead the angels hosted a party in heaven on their behalf because they found new life in Christ.

Lord, let eternity call out today in the hearts of the multitude of people in the valley of decision and lead me in their path to share the good news!

Craig Nanna lives in Reading with his amazing wife and three kids, and together they serve as Sr. pastors of Reading DOVE Christian Ministry Center. Craig also serves as the director of the Reading Regional Transformation Network.

Exactly Enough

"And my God will meet all your needs according to his glorious riches in Christ Jesus." *Philippians 4:19*

When I began serving at Water Street Rescue Mission, I frequently heard others on staff relate how God had met various needs. It was exciting to realize that I was now serving somewhere close to the "front lines" and able to see God's provision first-hand.

One day I realized that I had run out of spare computers and parts. I calculated we needed about twenty computers to make the necessary replacements. But we didn't have the funds to go buy twenty computers. I hadn't "formally" prayed about it, but it was certainly on my mind as I conversed with God in trying to figure out what to do. Then the phone rang. A local business had recently upgraded their users and had twenty computer monitors that they'd like to donate. I enlisted a couple of helpers and we took a truck over to pick them up.

The next day my phone rang again. This time it was another enterprise that also had recently upgraded their users and had some computers they'd like to donate—but they didn't have any monitors. Could we still use them? Then God dropped the other shoe. "How many computers are we talking about?" I asked. "Twenty" was the reply. Hallelujah! Neither of these companies knew what the other was doing, or that we had any need. But even in the mundane area of technology, God was supplying our every need. And now I had a story I could share with the rest of the staff....

Father, thank You for providing what we needed before I asked for it or let anyone else know about it. You have shown me that in every area, the ordinary as well as the deeply spiritual, You know our need and delight in providing it in ways we can't imagine

Larry Newby is formerly the Information Technology Manager for Water Street Rescue Mission. He is now semi-retired.

A Widow's Mite

"They gave out of their wealth; but she, out of her poverty, put in everything—all she had to live on." *Mark 12:44*

While leading a short term construction team to Ecuador, God allowed me the privilege of meeting Juan, a man with a "widow's heart."

Juan, a Quechua Indian, worked alongside the team every day as we endeavored to build a church. We were given the job of tying re-bar together in sections with small pieces of wire. These were later to be covered with concrete laid between the foundation forms. The tool we were given to twist the wire was a bent, rusty nail. However, Juan had made a tool that was key shaped with a pointed, curved hook at the end that worked much better than our bent rusty nail. No matter how hard we tried, Juan could out tie us by a long shot with his homemade tool.

At the end of our short term, as we were saying goodbye I saw Juan coming toward me, dressed in his usual attire, nearly soleless shoes, holey shorts, and a tattered t-shirt, the same clothes we saw him in everyday. He was wearing a smile from ear to ear, as only a Quechua Indian can wear, and had one hand held behind his back. He brought out his hand and placed in my hand his key-shaped tool! I was overwhelmed with emotion. To my "Why?" Juan simply answered, "This is for you so that when you get to your home you can build yourself a house."

Here was a man, living under a lean-to, made of scraps collected from the city dump, with one set of clothes on his back, giving me his only tool! I saw a widow's heart that day and that key shaped tool hangs in my garage where I see it everyday to remind me of this man that gave all he had.

Joe Nolt serves as a volunteer two days a week at the DOVE Mission International office and is a member of DOVE Christian Fellowship Elizabethtown.

Everyone Deserves A Second Chance

"Solomon aptly said, 'Many waters cannot quench love; rivers cannot wash it away....'" *Song of Songs 8:7*

Like most of our serious clients, Russell could barely stumble through the doors of the Water Street Rescue Mission. He had sold his life off for a steady handful of pills; a price that could no longer purchase relief. Dark shadows haunted Russell, reminding him of his life's most painful memories; memories of a wife who now belonged to another and of a daughter and granddaughter who had grown up, without him; memories of countless broken promises.

On Russell's first day with us, he met Chuck (men's counselor) who simply began loving him to our precious Jesus. Imagine my joy, when Chuck called to share the news that Russell had accepted Jesus, flushed the pills, and was going to join our Christian Life Recovery Program (to change his life). For nearly 1½ years now, Russell has been following Jesus, "by faith". He has surely relished the tender moments, when God would touch him in a deeply personal way, but mostly Russell has trusted Jesus, as he takes "one more" painful step of recovery.

Yesterday, I was blessed to attend a wedding with Russell. His daughter had invited her changing dad (and me) to share in her day. Imagine the immense joy on Russell's face, as a long line of relatives and friends from his past (relationships he thought were utterly destroyed) came up to shake his hand and to hug him, welcoming him back into their lives. And imagine a beaming Russell, as his daughter came with a welcoming hug saying, "Daddy, I have always wondered if you would be at my wedding but you came and you're doing so well. I'm so proud of you." Now imagine a happy man being hugged by a lovely little granddaughter (who he only held as a baby).

It was interesting to note that the scripture Russell's daughter chose for her table gifts was the very first scripture Russell memorized, "Love is patient; love is kind...." How apt are the words of his former in-laws, "Everyone deserves a second chance, Russell."

Norm Lowry serves as Learning Center Coordinator at Water Street Rescue Mission.

Road Trip

"Not that I have already obtained all this, or have already been made perfect, but I press on to take hold of that for which Christ Jesus took hold of me...toward the goal to win the prize for which God has called me heavenward in Christ Jesus." *Philippians 3:12,14*

There's nothing I enjoy more in the fall than a road trip! Last year we headed toward Columbus, Ohio, where my husband, Brad, had lived for several years. We took a tour of the area and visited friends, enjoying the colors of autumn. It was my first time seeing where many memories were made for Brad.

We stopped at an apartment building Brad had stayed for a few months as a college student. He was amazed how much the condition of building had improved. When he had lived there, the section of town had a bad reputation. The pizza shop would not even deliver there because it was considered too dangerous of an area! It was hard for me to imagine with the current crisp white paint and shiny doorknobs on the brick structure.

We stopped by another house where he had lived. The outside looked fairly nice, but inside doors were missing from cabinets and rugs were torn up from the floors. Brad was rather dismayed at the current state. It looked like for many years things had been left to deteriorate.

It's hard not to see a parallel for my own life. The road trip our lives go on. What's really happening? Is my walk with God left with little or no care taken? Am I seeking to make improvements in my character? Does my attitude need a fresh coat of paint or a complete renovation? It is good to pull over and check out my true condition from time to time!

Father, thank You for Your Word that gives us many signposts to successfully navigate through life! Help us be careful to maintain our walk with You and with those around us.

Sarah Sauder works as a graphic designer and serves on the youth leadership team with DOVE Christian Fellowship International.

His Strength Or Mine

"But He said to me, "My strength is sufficient for you, for My power is made perfect in your weakness." Therefore I will boast all the more gladly about my weaknesses so that Christ's power may rest on me." *2 Corinthians 12:9*

"A wicked man puts up a bold front, but an upright man gives thought to his ways." *Proverbs 21:25*

Years ago, approximately 1955, when I was thirteen years old, I was riding my bicycle down a country road feeling like I was a really hot kid on top of the world! A convertible passed me with two guys in it and they made some insulting yells to me. Well "tough me", was not going to take that, so I yelled back at the top of my voice, "Shut up!" They slammed on the brakes and started backing up toward me. My legs got so weak from fear that I literally fell in a ditch. They saw, "mission accomplished" and took off!

This lesson not only taught me something that day, but I've been reminded many times that the only real strength I have is the inner stability provided by the Holy Spirit.

Dear Lord, help each person reading this to realize that You are Commander of heaven's armies and that we find strength by leaning our weaknesses on You. Amen

LaMarr Sensenig is an elder at Lancaster Evangelical Church in Lititz.

She Sees Me When I Can't See Myself

"When he was still a long way off, his father saw him." *Luke 15:20*

While at the rescue mission in Jacksonville, my boss met with city officials before the Super Bowl came to town. They had a keen interest in knowing what was going to "happen to the homeless" when the Super Bowlers visited Jax. They were concerned that the "unhidden" homeless in our midst might disturb the partygoers from out of town. They, like many, believed it best that the homeless and troubled were out of view—and out of public awareness.

I am encouraged to know that God sees us and loves us when we are "out of sight." Way before any of us came to know Jesus, God already knew us and was urging us to consider Him. Amazing isn't it?

Everyday I see fellow staff members "noticing" residents. On any day of the year, at any time of the day there is someone being fed, spoken with, and ministered to. The staff and volunteers bring dignity and respect to each of these who have long been "in the shadows of life." And in so doing, the staff dramatically models the reality that God sees us when "we are afar off."

One of our older, African-American residents was speaking passionately to me about her relationship with Cheryl, one of our young counselors. Of Cheryl, she said this, *"Cheryl sees me when I can't see myself!"* I was humbled when I heard this and reminded of the sacred privilege of loving those broken and hurting. Cheryl's compassionate eyes, her thoughtful words, her loving silence, her embracing acceptance, and her authentic and vulnerable relationship with this once hidden older woman reveals that Jesus sees her and has not "passed her by." May you be encouraged today, Cheryl, to persist in loving those around you in such an open and defenseless way! Jesus loves *you*, girlfriend, in word and deed!

Lord, help me see others as You see them.

Steve Brubaker is the Director of Residential Programs at Water Street Rescue Mission.

God Help Us!

"He shall call upon Me and I will answer him: I will be with him in trouble, I will deliver him and honor him." *Psalm 91:15*

I couldn't believe my eyes—fire in our woods! I cried out "God, help us. You said if we call upon you, you will answer." My husband had come home from dinner that March evening, and before he took off his coat, had taken the trash out to burn in the burn-pit of our wooded home. Forty-five minutes later we discovered over a ¼ acre of our "yard" was ablaze.

We continued to call upon the Lord as we fought the fire awaiting the fire trucks. My husband was feverishly raking wet leaves over the burning ones. When the first fire truck arrived, I went into our home to continue praying. About 7 minutes later I returned outdoors only to learn that John had collapsed to the ground after he stopped raking. His heart had stopped beating and he ceased breathing.

About the time he went down the second fire truck pulled up. Four caring and skillful firemen quickly resuscitated him while the others put out the fire.

In the emergency room that night, John seemed to have quickly recovered. But tests the next day revealed that 2 previously inserted stints in the center of his heart had closed—100% and 70%. He under went by-pass surgery and beautifully recovered under God's obvious grace and blessing.

What we soon realized was that the fire did absolutely no damage and was easily cared for. It did, however, provide a safe place to expose the condition of John's heart stints. God's timing was so evident. The first fire truck carried no resuscitation equipment but just as John was falling, the second fire truck pulled up fully equipped to meet the pressing need of the moment.

God is good!

Father God, You are everything You say You are and You do everything You say You'll do. Fully good. Fully God. I worship You with my whole heart.

Ann Gibbel is involved with prayer in our region.

Love Them

"And the King shall answer and say unto them, 'Verily I say unto you, inasmuch as ye have done *it* unto one of the least of these my brethren, ye have done *it* unto me.'" *Matthew 25:40*

D id you ever walk by a street person and look the other way, hoping they wouldn't notice or speak to you? Society teaches us that this is an acceptable reaction to poverty and homelessness. In fact, we've become so comfortable with poverty and homelessness that we hardly notice their end results.

I interact with our clients daily and I can tell you that each one of them has a life history similar to yours and mine. Often the only difference is one bad decision made along the way.

I recently had the privilege of having my teenage step-son (Daniel) spend a day with me at Water Street Rescue Mission. He spent several hours working with one of our clients (Don) and they developed a real connection. Driving home that day, Daniel said "I really like Don, he's a great guy!" The thought that came into my head was: how would we have reacted if we'd met Don on the street instead of at the Mission?

We can't all work at a rescue mission, nor should we, but there is more you can do. I invite you to take a moment to consider your reaction to poverty and homelessness, based only on one idea: there's a real person of God's creation under the rags and dirt. You don't have to give money, cars, or time to our clients or those on the streets, but I invite you to consider giving them love, respect, and most of all, your prayers. Look them in the eye and say hello, you might be surprised at the good it does for both of you.

Dear Lord, help us to see the value You have created in others, just as You have created the value in us.

Scooter Haase is the Director of Operations at Water Street Rescue Mission.

Opened Doors

"[One may hear God's voice] in a dream, in a vision of the night, when deep sleep falls on men while slumbering upon the bed." *Job 33:15 (Amplified Bible)*

The Lord seems to use dreams in my life quite a bit. I was having warning dreams of my inheritance being stolen, with literal mountains of sand in my way and people stealing stuff from my house, but I didn't understand how to deal with it exactly.

The word of the Lord came to me saying, "Read Zechariah 4:1," which referred to being awakened in the Spirit (understanding the dreams) and verses 6 and 7, which refers to speaking "grace, grace to the mountain" and it will become a mole hill. The Lord also took me to Mark 11:23, which refers to speaking to the mountain to be plucked up and cast into the sea. This was the word of wisdom the Lord used to help me. Proverbs 18:21 says that death and life are in the power of the tongue, and they who indulge in it shall eat the fruit of it (for death, or for life). So, I literally spoke to the mountain (of human obstacles) and things standing between me and my destiny in God, and literally within minutes, I had two separate phone calls that opened doors to make room for my gifts.

I'm thankful that God's grace is sufficient, even when the enemy tries to steal, kill and destroy our inheritance in Him. He has come to give abundant life. Let's be those that walk in their full inheritance, as we cooperate with God's will for us. He will never leave us or forsake us. Let's chose to trust Him even when things don't seem to be going right, knowing that He is the author and finisher of our faith.

Father, thank you for communicating to us Your will for our lives and even protecting the destiny You have given to us by dreams and visions. You said You help us both to will and do of Your good pleasure. We want to fulfill the reason we were born into this world. We declare: If God be for us, who can be against us? In Jesus' name, Amen.

Dorinda Kaylor is a regional intercessor, minister at the Healing rooms and at the Lancaster prison.

Rhythms Of Grace

"Are you tired? Worn out? Burned out on religion? Come to me. Get away with me and you'll recover your life. I'll show you how to take a real rest. Walk with me and work with me—watch how I do it. Learn the unforced rhythms of grace. I won't lay anything heavy or ill-fitting on you. Keep company with me and you'll learn to live freely and lightly." *Matthew 11:28-30 (The Message)*

Have you ever had an ongoing relationship that could be compared to screeching chalk on a blackboard? You almost dread the necessary encounter. What about supervisors or co-workers who criticize, complain or do their work without integrity? It tarnishes the quality of your day. Even in the church, there are times when our own ideas of what should be done runs contrary to leadership and something within rises up on the inside.

How many mini-crises have hit you that required adjusting your wants to facilitate the needs of another? Irritation and frustration rush in to flood you. Then there are the times that we react and do not respond as the Lord teaches. The results are not His, but poor fruit produced out of our soul, our carnal self.

Reflect on the promise above. Listen to the words of the Lord. Drink them in. Allow the Holy Spirit to write them upon the table of your heart. Take them into your lifestyle. The unforced rhythms of grace are available to each of us, and we can learn to walk in that.

Father, Your word says that we are to walk with an easy yoke and a light burden. Teach me how to live in the unforced rhythms of Your grace. Your grace, Lord is sufficient for me. Let my life be grace-filled during the calm, the winds and the storms of life. Abounding in grace and abiding in You, I shall be an expression of Your image.

Diana Oliphant is a credentialed minister with Teaching The Word Ministries serving with a heart for the region and nations.

In Jesus' Name

"...In My Name they will drive out demons...." *Mark 16:7*

Tonight our destination was Kensington, a poor neighborhood of Philadelphia. Years ago it was a nice place to live, but now its streets are comprised of boarded-up factories, with the working poor living in row homes and their children playing among discarded needles and trash. Those trapped in addiction and prostitution live in the many abandoned houses in the area.

It's nighttime, and local stores are barred shut. Crack is so very cheap. We see ones strung out on heroin, and young women, once beautiful, driven to prostitution to support their addictions.

At a busy drug corner, we get out of the van, open the back, and set up to serve a hot dinner to these precious ones. It is here that I meet a man who is bent over and stumbling. He becomes very quiet as we pray for him. I knew something was wrong. His breathing got more and more shallow. I call 911.

Rubbing his head, I tell him, "Come on Guy, hold on, help is coming." I tell the operator, "Hurry, he's coding!" A crowd gathers... "Does anybody know this man; does anyone know how many bags he has used?" No one answers. Some men try to rouse him, his eyes open briefly and then roll back and he stops breathing. I yell to the team, "He's gone, don't stop praying." Boldly, a team member rebukes the spirit of death, in the name of Jesus. He immediately draws a breath. The crowd breaks into applause. He continues taking shallow breathes. The ambulance arrives, and transports him to the hospital conscious and talking.

Tonight, this one was ripped from Satan's hand. Life reigned. The Light prevailed over the darkness.

Lord, help us today to boldly walk in the authority, You, have given us in Your Name!

Joetta Keefer from DOVE ELANCO serves with Hands of Hope, a ministry to the homeless in Philadelphia, meeting physical, emotional, and spiritual needs of hurting people in a practical way.

Wedding Clothes

"And why do you worry about clothes? See how the lilies of the field grow. They do not labor or spin...If that is how God clothes the grass of the field...will he not much more clothe you, O you of little faith?"
Matthew 6:28-30

Three out of four weddings in our family created 'God Stories' in the clothing department. When our eldest got married, we were halfway across the country in Bible School with limited resources. My dress came about through lovely fabric given by his future in-laws and God's faithful help to this rusty seamstress to create the dress.

When our eldest daughter married, I shopped and shopped with no satisfactory results for the mother-of-the-bride dress. Then, while she shopped for bridesmaid dresses at a name-brand outlet, I found it as I casually looked through rejected dresses in the dressing room. My size, it was gorgeous with lovely accents! And only $25! How God was that?

When our youngest married, she was on the other side of the country (Washington) and planned to be married in Montana near the YWAM base where she'd met her husband-to-be. Two months prior to the wedding, we headed west for a week to meet the young man and his family. We carried with us her sister's bridal gown that she had dreamed of wearing some day. We soon realized that it wasn't going to work. After earnest prayer (and some initial mother-of-the-bride panic), we discovered a bridal shop about a block away...going out of business with all gowns half off. The halter neck line of the gown was a long-time favored style of the bride. God faithfully enabled this rusty seamstress to make the alterations in our limited time on a sewing machine borrowed from our future son-in-law's mother, even supplying a special attachment needed for the task.

Father, You faithfully clothe us with garments that pass away. Help me to fully trust You for the white robe of Your righteousness for that final wedding feast.

Ruth Ann Stauffer from Leola, is the wife of Al, mother and grandmother, and prayer leader associated with Teaching the Word Ministries.

Photo by Amy Barley

July

God's Protection

"For He is the Living God and He endures forever; He rescues and He saves; He performs signs and wonders in the Heavens and on the earth." *Daniel 6:26-27*

One day while driving home with my family, I saw a storm approaching and felt a darkness, not only a physical darkness of clouds, but a spiritual darkness as well. We prayed for protection.

When pulling into our driveway, I asked my husband to move the car. I believed a tree was going to fall down. He moved it and proceeded to the house.

I remained at the car gathering packages, feeling an immediate urgency to go to the house. As I began walking, I suddenly heard a loud "crack" and saw my husband standing on the porch. Our eyes locked as I screamed, "The tree cracked!" Then, looking up I saw the tree coming down on top of me.

The tree was enormous. There was nowhere to run. I just stood still. I closed my eyes and said, "Lord, I know you can deliver me!" Then I thought, "Lord, I'm coming home!" I thought of my husband and son and how much I loved them, but I knew I was going home to Jesus, and I knew one day they would also.

I stood there with my eyes shut waiting for the tree to hit me, but it never did. I felt a "swoosh" of air over me and then utter silence. I asked the Lord, "Lord, did it fall? It hasn't hit my head yet." I opened my eyes and found myself standing in the middle of this enormous tree. I remember being gently lifted and walking out of a mass of limbs and branches.

I don't know how or why my Lord chose to deliver me that day. I only know it was His grace alone that held me in the palm of His hand.

Lord, thank you for Your mighty hand that protects us each day.

Leah Davis, Servant of Christ, and one who delights to sit in the shade of He who calls Himself the Bright and Morning Star, Member of Life Center Ministries International, Harrisburg.

Is There Joy In Your Journey?

"Work hard and cheerfully at whatever you do, as though you were working for the Lord rather than for people. Remember the Lord will give you an inheritance as your reward, and the Master you are serving is Christ." *Colossians 3:23 (New Living Bible)*

'm sure we all get discouraged at times. We all get tired on the journey. I remember one day driving home from a stressful meeting. I was mulling over some unfinished work which had me feeling drained emotionally and physically. Before I realized it, I started a "pity party" for myself.

Suddenly I became aware of the words of a song that was on the cassette I had just inserted. It was an older tape that I hadn't listened to for a long time. But it spoke of joy in the journey, even amidst struggles and tears. As we help each other, we climb to higher ground and make progress on the journey.

Suddenly, I was feeling better. We are not working for people, but for God and His Kingdom. But persons can and do encourage us. They help us on, through tears and joys, toward our future with God. Remember, whatever you are facing today, a reward (inheritance) is coming if we are faithfully serving our Lord Jesus Christ.

Father God, help us to work for You this day, knowing You are Lord and King of our lives. Thank you for Your presence in our journeys of life, giving us peace and joy as we walk with You. Keep us in Your care. Amen

Nelson W. Martin is an overseer in the Lancaster Mennonite Conference. He also is director of Support for Prison Ministries. He and his wife, Anna Mae, live near Lititz.

God Will Make A Way

"'For My thoughts are not your thoughts, neither are your ways My ways,' declares the Lord." *Isaiah 55:8*

In July 2003, my employer needed some volunteers to go and work in England for a month. When my manager asked me whether I wanted to go, I said I would not be able to since I was a single mom with two teenage children.

After my manager left my desk, I kept thinking about this offer. I really wanted to go. Then the thought went through my head, "If God wants me to go, He would work it out." So I went and added my name to the list. Needless to say, God wanted me to go. I did not even have a passport. God worked everything out. I found out on Tuesday that I was leaving the following Sunday. Everything was in order in time.

But when I found out who was in my group to go to England, I was not a happy camper. One particular woman really worked on my nerves. Four weeks in England meant being around her seven days a week. However, God knew what He was doing. Being with her for that much time, I got to know her better. I also better understood why she reacted the way she did. After we got back from England, we actually became friends and began doing things outside of work together.

This trip was a lot of firsts for me. Flying in a plane, riding a train and subway, and being out of the country were all first-time experiences. The last Sunday we were in England, we took the Eurostar and went to Paris for the day. I even got a ten-year passport for free. God sure blessed me while I was doing my employer a favor.

Lord, I'm so glad that Your ways and thoughts are not my ways and thoughts. You see the big picture and respond accordingly. Thank you for not always doing as I ask.

Julie Gehman serves on the Prayer and Ministry teams at Ephrata Community Church.

Where Did That Come From?

"But seek ye first the Kingdom of God and His righteousness, and all these things shall be added unto you." *Matthew 6:33*

On the way to my second meeting of the morning, I remembered that my bank account was resting on empty. I didn't have enough cash available to treat my friend, a dear elderly pastor to breakfast!

Arriving at the place of meeting about a half hour early, I thought I would just order coffee and then ask my friend to pick up the check this time and explain my "forgetting" to bring cash. Suddenly, the thought occurred to me that because I had gotten up early for my first meeting, I had neglected to have my quiet time with God. I determined that I would invest the entire waiting time in His Word.

While reading and praying in Psalms, and turning the pages of my Bible from one Psalm to another, I discovered a twenty dollar bill tucked neatly in the fold between two pages. Unbelievable, I thought! God has provided again! Passages like: "Oh, ye of little faith…" and "ye have not, because ye ask not…" went through my mind as I lamented my doubting of God's provision and His concern for me. I wiped tears away from my eyes as I rejoiced and reflected on His faithfulness. My time with my dear friend and brother was a time of added joyous blessing as I shared with him how God had used our meeting to teach me that morning, to always seek Him first and to trust Him for everything in my life. To this day, I have no idea how that money got into my Bible; however I do know from where it came!

Father God, thank you for Your faithfulness. You are faithful even when I am fearful, doubting, and showing my lack of faith in You. You are Jehovah Jireh....My Provider! Thank you!

Richard Taylor is a missionary with The Navigators in the Church Discipleship Ministry and is on the board of Life Transforming Ministries in Coatesville.

Yard Sale

"Be still, and know that I am God; I will be exalted among the nations, I will be exalted in the earth!" *Psalm 46:10*

I enjoy going to other people's garage sales, but I dreaded having my own. This time, though, my oldest daughter, Bobbi, and my daughter-in-law, Kari, helped me price items and arrange them on sheets of plywood that my husband had set across sawhorses in our garage.

My objective was not to make money, but to inexpensively provide needed items to others, leaving me with fewer things to get rid of somewhere else.

Much to our surprise, our 5-10-25-cent table emptied very quickly. Bobbi remarked that people were more likely to spend their coins on "junky" dirt-cheap items than spend an equal amount of money for one higher-quality item.

This philosophy culminated with a woman buying a set of twin sheets I had priced for $1.00 (I knew that the pillow case had tears in it that I had mended). I started to say, "If you need a twin size, I have another set of sheets for only $3.00 that's of higher quality over..."

"I like *this* color," she interrupted, and off she walked.

I smelled a spiritual lesson: How often does my arrogance get in the way of listening to the Owner when He tries to tell me something that is clearly in my best interest? How often do I settle for second best or even the bottom of the junk pile when instead, if I was patient and obeyed the Master, I would not have to settle for shallow, fleeting outward appearance but for the deeper inner quality of a gift from the Master's hand?

Dear Lord, help me to "be still" and remain dependent on You. Please forgive my arrogance and independence when I think I know better than You. Help me to realize that You love me and know what is best for me.

Tamalyn Jo Heim and her husband, Bob, have three daughters, one son, one son-in-law, and one daughter-in-law—all of whom like a bargain.

Let God Handle It

"Behold, I am the Lord, the God of all flesh. Is there anything too hard for me?" *Jeremiah 32:27*

I started a new job in March of 2006. In June of 2006 I began having back problems and by the end of August, I found myself in the hospital. I had to go out on disability from the end of August to the beginning of November. I went back to work on November 7, and the pain increased to the point that I had trouble walking, sitting, and standing.

I went back out on disability on December 7. My disability was 70 percent of my salary, but this time God had a "ram in the bush" to provide for the difference. I was diagnosed with degenerative disc disease. Surgery could be performed to replace the disc, but there was only a fifty-fifty chance that it would work. I began pain management. In the meantime, my disability leave was coming to an end, and I knew that I would not be able to return to work. I let my employer know that I would not be returning, and I sent in my letter of resignation. I was trusting God to work it out.

I received a call and learned that they had talked it over with the president of the company who asked what I would be doing. They told him that I would probably have to find something that I could do from home. His reply was, "Then let's give her something to do from home!" They helped set up my home office, and I started working as an independent contractor from home on April 4, 2007.

If He can do it for me, He can certainly do it for you! Whatever you are facing in your life right now, let God handle it!

Thank you God for orchestrating every detail! I praise You for Your provision and Your favor! I know that there is nothing too hard for You!

Ava Williams serves as Music Ministry Director at New Life In Christ Fellowship in Coatesville.

God Our Healer

"Praise the Lord, O my soul, and forget not all his benefits—who forgives all your sins and heals all your diseases." *Psalm 103:2-3*

In my congregation there is a young woman named Michelle, who has been married for over ten years and has been severely diabetic since she was a teenager. Due to her diabetes, she could not see well enough to get her driver's license. She asked my wife and several others in the church to pray for her eyes to be healed, since she was going to go for her learner's permit again. She had failed the eye test the first time she applied. The big day came and Michelle passed her eye test and got her learner's permit. We, as a church body, rejoiced with her.

But Michelle had another desire that was even greater for her than driving. She and her husband of ten years wanted a baby. Michelle thought that if God can heal my eyes so that I can drive, He can also give me a baby. Michelle long ago had given up the idea of having a baby, since her doctors said that due to her diabetes, it would be impossible. Again, Michelle asked several people to pray, and pray they did. We serve a God of the impossible, and the God who delights in doing what man says can never happen, came through again and Michelle became pregnant. And after nine more months of prayer, she delivered a beautiful healthy baby girl. God is indeed our healer.

Jesus our healer, thank you for forgiving all our sins and healing all our diseases.

Patrick W. Wilson serves as pastor of Living Truth Fellowship Church in Christiana.

Androgynous Or Andrizesthe?

"Be on your guard; stand firm in the faith; **be men of courage**; be strong." *1 Corinthians 16:13*

The words "be men of courage" are the words "quit you like men" (King James Version). Both phrases are English attempts at conveying the meaning of the Greek word *andrizesqe*, found only in this place in the New Testament Scriptures.

On the other hand, "androgynous" is a word that has come to be increasingly used to describe our modern society. Based upon the compound Greek word *androghnos,* this word speaks of humans that have "the characteristics or nature of both the male and the female…neither specifically feminine nor masculine" (Webster's Dictionary). The pop singer, Michael Jackson, would be considered by many to be the premier androgynous man.

In his book, *The Church Impotent: The Feminization of Christianity*, Leon Podles describes the way in which the church has increasingly become a place of feminine domain. This is reflected in the fact that, in general, more women than men attend church. It is also evidenced in the way that many churchgoing men have become feminized. The point is that men, including men in the church, have increasingly become androgynous. All the while, the apostle Paul has challenged men to be "andrizesthe"—men of courage, men of strength…MANLY MEN.

We need godly, masculine men. In a day and age when increasingly boys are being raised by their mothers and crumbs (men who come and go out of these boys' lives), the need for godly masculine models of manhood are desperately needed in the church. Boys without dads can easily grow up to be men without masculinity. And that was apparently a concern to the apostle Paul.

Lord, please help us to buck the trends of our world by presenting a Christianity that has in view the conversion of the world, including the conversion of men to godly manhood. I pray in Christ's name, Amen.

Doug Winne is the senior pastor of Lancaster Evangelical Free Church, Lititz, where he has served for well over twenty years. He and his wife, Ruth, have five children, ages 8-23.

Mind The Gap

"At his gate was laid a beggar named Lazarus, covered with sores and longing to eat what fell from the rich man's table. Even the dogs came and licked his sores." *Luke 16:20-21*

"Mind the gap," the electronic voice said over the intercom. Mind the gap. I was standing in the Underground in London waiting to get on one of the train cars when I heard this voice. The voice called for us to be aware of the space that existed between the platform and the step up into the train car. Since that day in May, I have thought of that voice and that statement, "Mind the gap." I began to think about this in regard to the parable that Jesus tells in Luke 16, the parable of the Rich Man and Lazarus.

This parable is the only parable that Jesus ever told where he named one of his characters. Interestingly enough, it was a poor beggar who was given a name. This I believe is an amazing example of God's love for the poor and the oppressed. Did you know that there are over two thousand Scriptures that talk about poverty and God's heart for those in the midst of poverty? God has a heart for those who are hurting. Martin Luther King Jr. said it best when he said, "Injustice anywhere is a threat to justice everywhere." God has a heart for the single mother struggling to make ends meet and for people who are facing injustice every day.

God calls His people to stand up and to mind the gap between rich and poor, between those who have and those who have not, and between those who oppress and those who are oppressed. God calls us, the church, to serve and bless our world. How will you mind the gap in your own life, in your church, and in your community?

God help us to mind the gap and work for justice everywhere.

Ryan Braught is Pastor of Youth Ministries and Nurture at Hempfield COB as well as leader of Veritas, an emerging missional community of faith.

Why Settle for Good When God's Plans are Best?

"We can make our plans, but the Lord gives the right answer. Commit your actions to the Lord, and your plans will succeed." *Proverbs 16:1,3 (New Living Translation)*

In July 2007, to my complete surprise, one of my three business partners wanted to leave and go out on his own. I immediately began to think of all the details that needed to be worked out and the impact this would have. In a small company every person has a vital role in its ongoing success, so to lose a key person would require major adjustments and decisions. The decisions we needed to make would not only affect the personal lives of the owners but also the lives of seven other employees who were counting on us to do what was best for them.

The two other partners and I began to plan how we could work out all the details. After a few weeks and numerous discussions, we came up with a plan.

On August 15, one of my partners had a meeting with the person to present our plan. When he left the meeting, he called me with a completely different plan—a much better one.

The next morning I read Proverbs 16 for my devotions, and I was overwhelmed to once again experience how much our loving God cares about every detail of our lives. The fact that He would send me a confirmation so clear and so timely was just awesome. Verse 9 states "We can make our plans, but the Lord determines our steps."

We serve a God who truly cares about every detail of our lives. Seek God first—His plan is always best.

Lord, thank you for Your faithfulness even at times when we try to figure things out on our own. Give us the desire to always seek Your will first for our lives. Thank you, Lord, that You are able to do immeasurably more than all we ask or imagine.

Larry Hess and his wife, Lois, attend DOVE Westgate Celebration.

Getting Along

"May the Master of Peace himself give you the gift of getting along with each other at all times, in all ways. May the Master be truly among you!" *2 Thessalonians 3:16 (The Message)*

The other day I stopped for lunch around two o'clock in the afternoon. I had eaten a bite earlier, but since I was rushing off to an appointment, I didn't eat enough. I thought it'd be nice to catch some quiet time, reading and refueling. It was not to be.

The hostess seated me next to two mothers with their kids. I think the kids needed a nap, because they where whiny and defiant. Every once in a while one of them would scream—one of the children, not one of the mothers. That, of course, frustrated and embarrassed the mother, who then tried to use me as a tool. "That man is probably trying to have a quiet lunch and get some work done and *you are disturbing him*!" (She got that right.) Actually, the mother was being firm and reasonable, but the child remained disagreeable. He had no interest in getting along with anyone. Mercifully (for me), the mothers gathered their chicks and headed out for the next relational challenge.

Relationships, even with those you love, are sometimes a challenge. Being in right relationship requires work, and it often requires help. I love the way *The Message* translates Paul's words: "May the Master of Peace himself give you the gift of getting along..."

I am reminded that I cannot have a right relationship with God without God's help, and I reasonably assume that I cannot have a right relationship with my loved ones without God's help. "Getting along" is a gift that God gives to those who belong to Him—the gift of His unconditional love. It is often said that the family that "prays together" (or the secular variation, "plays together") stays together. I would amend that. It's the family whose members stay close to God that stays together. Without knowing the Master of Peace, you cannot know peace.

Lord, plant Your peace in my heart!

Dr. Stephen Dunn is the lead pastor for the Church of God of Landisville, which is celebrating 175 years of ministry in Lancaster County.

Look Out For The Interests Of Others

"Let nothing be done through selfish ambition or conceit, but in lowliness of mind let each esteem others better than himself. Let each of you look out not only for his own interests, but also for the interests of others." *Philippians 2:3–4 (New King James Version)*

I was a young pastor at the time. My overseer and two individuals had scheduled a meeting with me to share their concerns of things they saw in my life that were less than best. I was convinced that if they could see the whole picture they would understand that I was not a bad guy. I was really trying to do my best. If only they could see my heart, I was convinced that they would agree with me and drop their accusations. The whole meeting was very painful for me. We ended with somewhat of an agreement but I was not convinced that they understood where I was coming from.

They had no sooner left the room than my overseer placed a loving hand upon my shoulder and said these words that I will never forget. "Ron, I think you will go much farther if you are more concerned with trying to understand than by trying to be understood." Those words had a major impact upon my life to this day. How often we cut in when people are talking because of the important things that we have to share, sometimes not even listening to what they are saying because we think what we have to say is more important. When we try to understand what the other person is dealing with, it will go a long way in the relationship-building process. I have found that most people are not willing to listen to me until they know that I have heard them. I think that is part of what Paul means when he says that we are to esteem others better than ourselves. I learned a lesson that day that has proved to be very beneficial as I relate to many people from many different cultures.

Lord Jesus, help me today to focus on understanding others rather than trying to be understood myself. Help me to see the importance of valuing others and preferring others before myself.

Ron Myer serves as assistant director of DOVE Christian Fellowship International.

Jesus Is Holding Us

"...I will fear no evil, for you are with me...." *Psalm 23:4*

It had been a challenging couple of months for my husband and me. We were expecting our second child, but the prognosis that we had received for his survival was grim. We would often listen to worship music together as a family. The TV was turned off, the lights were dimmed, and words of praise would saturate our souls. Our two-year old son, Cole, was absorbing every bit of it, too. He was especially drawn to a song by Matt Redman called "You Never Let Go." Before we knew it, he was belting out the lyrics. He would dance around our living room singing welcomed words of hope.

I carried our baby to full-term, but he only lived for four hours after he was born. Cole decided that it was a good time to sing, "You Never Let Go" to his little brother, Luke, and the rest of the family that had gathered to meet him. The words spoke about walking through the valley and God's perfect love casting out all fear as He never let us go. The song soothed our hearts and minds.

It was so precious to be reminded that Jesus is always holding us, even through our darkest valleys. It was even more precious that God used our beautiful two-year son to tell us!

Jesus, You are all we need. Thank you for never letting go of us.

Brie Stoltzfus, wife, mother, pharmacist and elder in The Lancaster Micro Church Network.

He Will Never Leave Us

"Blessed be the God and Father of our Lord Jesus Christ, the Father of mercies and God of all comfort, who comforts us in all our tribulation, that we may be able to comfort those who are in any trouble, with the comfort with which we ourselves are comforted by God." *2 Corinthians 1:3–4*

After finding out with great excitement that we were going to have our second child, my wife made an appointment to go for an ultrasound at 20 weeks into the pregnancy. After the ultrasound, we were told that our child had a rare condition that would limit his ability to develop healthy lungs, and that he would only live a short time after birth. We were given no hope of his survival. This news was obviously devastating for us. It is difficult to express in words the many thoughts, questions, fears, that went through our minds.

But over the next weeks and months our hope increased! We truly experienced God's care through His body, the church, in ways that brought encouragement and peace. We knew that God's power was well able to heal our child.

That fateful day to meet our boy came nearly five months from when we had first been told that our child wouldn't survive after birth. Luke Michael was born on September 25, 2007. He was then too quickly gone after the four precious hours that we were able to share with him.

This journey was unlike anything that I have ever experienced before. It's been a mixture of the most overwhelming pain and struggle that I have ever felt, while feeling an intimate connection with our loving and compassionate Father in heaven. We truly have felt comfort from God, and through the church, just as 2 Corinthians 1:3-4 describes. Although our journey is not over, and we may never understand God's ways, we know that He will never leave or forsake us.

Thank you, Lord, for Your peace and Your presence.

Mike Stoltzfus gives leadership to a group of house churches called the Network.

Divisions

"Without wood a fire goes out; without gossip a quarrel dies down."
Proverbs 26:20

A congregation once known for its unity had become divided. Half wanted the senior pastor to leave, and the other half said the associate pastor had to go. Things got ugly. Like the church at Corinth (2 Corinthians 12:20), there was "quarreling, jealousy, outbursts of anger, factions, slander, gossip, arrogance and disorder."

Bill (not his real name), now in his late seventies, was asked to come back on the church board to help with the problem. He took the elders and pastors to lunch individually. As they met, he told each a bit of gossip "he had heard" about the matter, but asked that it be kept confidential. Bill completed his meetings with each man then waited. Soon he had his answer. He called them all together and made a shocking announcement: "Gentlemen, I know the source of vicious rumors that have spread throughout the church." Bill had told the same "confidential" story–one he had totally fabricated—to each man, but each time he told it he changed one key detail. When someone in the congregation whispered the rumor in Bill's ear one Sunday, he knew immediately which man had leaked it!

Sadly, the mere exposure of the gossiper was not enough to restore unity. Efforts at reconciliation failed. Two pastors were forced to resign; many who sided with them left the church. The "little leaven that leavened the whole lump" had to be painfully excised. Today Bill's church, though significantly smaller, is united again and poised to move forward by the grace of God.

It is so easy to pass on hurtful gossip. These "morsels" taste so delicious to us, but they are so deadly to the Body of Christ. Instead, let us gossip "good gossip" about one another for the sake of Christ!

Lord, keep our tongues pure.

Dr. Bruce Mawhinney is senior pastor of Wheatland Presbyterian Church (PCA) of Lancaster, Pennsylvania. He received his M.Div. from Pittsburgh Theological Seminary, D.Min. from Westminster Theological Seminary (California). He is the author of *Preaching with Freshness*.

Putting Him Above All

"What good is it for a man to gain the whole world, and yet lose or forfeit his very self? If anyone is ashamed of me and my words, the Son of Man will be ashamed of him when he comes in his glory and in the glory of the Father and of the holy angels." *Luke 9:25-26*

Many years have passed since that Physical Anthropology class. Although I loved animals, in no way was this instructor going to convince me I had evolved from an ape! To make matters worse, "No A's given in my class."

All semester he delighted in referring to creation and Christianity as a lot of hocus-pocus, branding believers as weak, in need of a crutch. I told Mom that I wanted out. Simple response, "It's always good to know what the opposition has to say." Taking the challenge, the next day I sat in the front row. A large magnificent pewter cross dangled from my neck, silently challenging this professor.

I was dumbfounded to hear that our final project would count for one-half of our grade. Not wanting to lose my A average, I immediately decided to do my project on chimpanzee locomotion, the professor's "first love." He even let me use his personal library.

Two nights before my presentation, I was overwhelmed by an incredible urge to rip up all my research and, instead, present an artistic display of the biblical days of creation. "Even if I had time to switch gears, Lord, You know I cannot even draw a laudable stick figure!"

I unveiled my monstrous poster of Genesis in front of the class to a deafening silence. I stood there mute and momentarily paralyzed. Then suddenly, my heart started beating again and I heard myself exclaiming the miracle of how God had created Adam and Eve. The rest melted into a blur.

When my grades arrived, I jumped with joy as I beheld what God had done. The simple "A" was displayed with a brief note: "Due to the beauty and thoroughness of your project, I have given you an A. Congratulations."

Dear Lord, may I never be afraid to proclaim Your glory. Amen

Janet Medrow is Assistant to the Director at National Christian Conference Center, Valley Forge, Pennsylvania, and deacon at Great Valley Presbyterian Church, Wayne.

The Missions Benefit Auction

"We are assured *and* know that [God being a partner in their labor] all things work together *and* are [fitting into a plan] for good to *and* for those who love God and are called according to [His] design *and* purpose." *Romans 8:28 (Amplified Bible)*

The day arrived for the Youth Missions Benefit Auction. All the money raised would be used specifically for mission projects. It was with extremely mixed emotions that I contemplated what the day would hold for me.

My family and I had already decided that it was time for me to give up driving; hence, there would be an auto for sale. I heartily agreed to donate it to the auction fund.

Some other donated items were handmade quilts; handcrafted furniture; attractive little birdhouses; time to do such things as yard work, painting, babysitting; and much more.

I needed help from heaven to keep my composure as the auctioneer read a description of the car and called for bids. So many precious memories flashed through my mind. I recalled the hundreds of miles and time spent with my late husband in that car–some happy, some serious, and other relaxing fun times.

It was not long before the sound of the gavel sounded. Just a short time later, I felt a tap on the shoulder and someone said, "I bought the car for my sister and brother-in-law who will be home on furlough from their missions work soon. It will be theirs to use while they travel to various mission-related activities. When they return to their mission field, the car will be made available, as needed, for other missionaries."

I never cease to be amazed at how God works out plans for His glory if we submit to His will.

Lord, help me heed Your every word, commands that I have read and heard, as You reveal Your will each day, help me to follow and obey. Your lovingkindness never ends and neither do the prayers for friends.

Grace Newswanger is a member of Manor Brethren in Christ Church, mother of four, and grandmother of six.

Choose This Day

"...choose for yourselves this day whom you will serve...."
Joshua 24:15

The year 2004 was a transitional year for me. Of course, as is the case in most transitions, it began the year before with a small prompting from God that my time was finishing up in my position at my church. God was asking me to take a step of faith and join my husband in his business. For most of that year I kept quiet about the prompting, but eventually I shared it with my husband.

Once it came out, we began praying together about the timing of the move. One thing you should realize is I was the one that brought home the "secure" paycheck. I carried the benefits. This was a big step for us. We began praying about the timing in January of 2004. Then we prayed in February, in March, in April–you get the picture. All along God was saying, "Step out in faith." We wanted the burning bush!

We finally reached a point that summer when we knew we were nearing the area of disobedience. Fortunately, we chose to obey. We stopped delaying the decision that needed to be made. But in the process I came to appreciate the long-suffering of God and how He will not force us to obey Him, serve Him, worship Him, or love Him. He gives us the power of choice. *We* choose whom we will serve! That became so real to me that summer. God wasn't going to make me obey. He loves us so much; He gives us the choice. And may we choose *this* day to serve Him, to love Him, to worship Him, and to honor Him.

Father, thank you for Your desire to be in relationship with us—a relationship built on choices. Help us, with the gentle promptings of Your Spirit, to make choices that please You.

Kathy Nolt works alongside her husband in business. She is also an administrative assistant for the Regional Church of Lancaster County.

Grandpa Fred And Grandma Millie

"…we are compassed about with so great a cloud of witnesses… let us run with patience the race that is set before us."
Hebrews 12:1 (King James Version)

We loved having Grandpa Fred and Grandma Millie, retired missionaries, at our house during weekend meetings at our church. Grandma Millie had special children's stories and Grandpa preached to the congregation. He was not only a missionary but also a doctor, with many stories to tell. We were so glad they got to stay with us!

Because they had parented seven children and now were also grandparents, we gravitated toward them like magnets. They graciously adjusted to our noisy, busy household while we served them and tried to make them as comfortable as possible. They warmly shared themselves with us in their own unique way. Our children loved them like grandparents.

They were preparing to leave us and the children were preparing to go to school. Our daughter began to complain of a sore throat. Grandpa Fred kindly reached into his pocket and pulled out two pills and gave them to her while hugs and goodbyes were given. She later said she was fine and walked to school with her brothers just a few hundred feet down the road.

I had to wonder if those pills were candy and if his heart knew all she needed was a bit of a grandpa love touch. The key was, she was satisfied, and we had come to trust both of them, so all was well.

They have long since passed on to Glory, but we will see them again in heaven. Now they are joined with that great cloud of witnesses with Jesus and are cheering us on as we fulfill our service to the Lord.

Thank You, Lord for their love, instruction and insight for us as young parents needing encouragement. Now help us to reach out with that same grace to other parents where You would give us opportunity, Amen

Naomi Sensenig and her husband, LaMarr, attend and serve at Lancaster Evangelical Free Church in Lititz.

Planting Faith

"The Kingdom of heaven is like a mustard seed, which a man took and sowed in his field; and this is smaller than all other seeds, but when it is full grown, it is larger than the garden plants and becomes a tree, so that the birds of the air come and rest in its branches."
Matthew 13:31–32

I was going through a very frustrating time in my life and walk with Christ. My walk with the Lord felt distant and distracted. I was still reading my Bible, praying, and worshipping, but I felt very distant. It was as if He had left me. I felt lonely. This continued for weeks; my frustration grew. How could I be so far from the Lord? I'm a pastor. I still had to do my job, even though I felt this distance. Something had to give. Then it did.

Through God's Word, I learned that it was time to increase my devotion to Him. What I had done in the past was no longer enough. It was time for my walk to gain some conviction. I needed to plant new seeds of faith in order to mature. Even if my faith was as small as a mustard seed, though by this point in my life I believed it to be greater, I still had to plant the seed for my faith to grow. It was time to stop relying on the past and its glory and move toward what God had for me *now*! I was stuck in a rut, but I dug the hole and rested there. God is more concerned with where we're going than where we've been. He needs to be Lord of our future.

Dear Lord, help us to plant our faith in You and walk it out with conviction and Your purpose. Help us to focus on Your Kingdom and not our lives. Release us from our own created business. May Your Kingdom come and Your will be done in our families as it is in heaven. Amen

Aaron J. Durso is the pastor of LOVE Christian Fellowship and the vice-president of the Birdsboro Borough Council.

Fresh Bread

"...I am the bread of life. He who comes to me will never go hungry, and he who believes in me will never be thirsty." *John 6:35*

A few years ago my family and I spent a month living in Central Asia. It was a great opportunity to be immersed in the culture and experience everyday life. One of our favorite memories was going out to buy fresh bread every morning. It was a flat-bread, baked in a clay oven and served piping hot. It smelled so good that it rarely made it back to our apartment without someone nibbling on it.

We soon came to realize how important bread was in that society. At the beginning of every meal the host would take bread from the center of the table, break it, and set out pieces for everyone to share. Right there in the midst of their culture was a picture of Jesus, the bread of life, whose body was broken for all to partake.

It reminded me how God is drawing all men, women, and children to Himself; people from every tongue, tribe, and nation. He has already placed eternity in their hearts and is waiting for us to partner with Him to share His love with them.

We all have a role to play in fulfilling the Great Commission whether it is sharing God's love with our neighbors, supporting a missionary, praying for their ministry, or serving overseas ourselves.

Dear God, thank you for calling us to share Your love with men, women, and children of every tribe, tongue, and nation. Give me Your heart for others around me and around the world. Use me to touch someone's life in a special way today.

Mark Van Scyoc is a Programmer Analyst, Freelance Photographer and Writer, and serves as Mission Director at DOVE Christian Fellowship, Westgate Celebration in Ephrata, PA.

His Directed Path

"Trust in the Lord with all thine heart; and lean not unto thine own understanding. In all thy ways acknowledge Him, and He shall direct thy paths." *Proverbs 3:6-7 (King James Version)*

During the last five years, my wife, Nadine, and I heard many testimonies of miracles and prayer requests. These were given to us not in the four walls of a church, but off the beaten path in eastern United States as I attempt to prayer walk across our nation on the American Discovery Trail. Sometimes the Holy Spirit leads us to those who need prayer.

One day, we made a detour off the trail. Shawnee, Ohio became a boomtown in the 1870's because of nearby coalfields but prosperity only lasted into 1920's. Since that time, the town has seen a gradual economic and population decline. With two opera houses and many other businesses, the town was the showplace of Perry County, Ohio. Now with a population of over six hundred people, there are no gas stations, markets, clothing stores or doctor's offices that I noticed.

After prayer walking along Main Street, we decided to eat at the only restaurant in town. Since we were not locals, the waitress, Theresa, asked why we were in the area. Nadine told her that we were prayer walking across America. After she went back into the kitchen, I heard her tell someone, "They're prayer walking across America." That someone was Shelia, cook/waitress/ manager/dishwasher/owner of Shawnee Village Restaurant. Shelia came out of the kitchen sat with us and asked, "Before you leave, can you pray for me?"

Since she works seven days a week and cannot attend church on Sunday morning, Shelia had been praying that the Lord would send someone to pray for her. For two hours, we fellowshipped and prayed for her. The Lord honored her prayer.

Father, in the name of Jesus, guide us to those who need prayer and give us the words to comfort them.

Jim Shaner, member of Praise Fellowship Church in Downingtown, is founder of One Nation Under God - Walk Across America.

Airborne Canoe

"For He will command His angels concerning you, to guard you in all your ways." *Psalm 91:11*

For many years, we have made it a practice to begin any road trip or adventure with a prayer asking for God's protection, for His angels to surround us.

Once again with prayer, we set off for a family camping vacation, heading north on the interstate. Although we drove in heavy rain, our spirits were "sunny." We had great expectations for this family time of campfires, s'mores, and canoeing.

Driving in the left lane, surrounded by traffic, I glanced out the rearview mirror. Astonished, I saw our canoe, always safely attached to the roof rack, airborne behind us. Fearfully, I realized this could be a deadly situation, and somehow managed to slow quickly, pulling into the center median.

Tom took over driving, as we turned around to head back. In a short distance, he pulled off again. There was the canoe, still attached to the rack. Rather than flying straight back into oncoming traffic, we are convinced God's protective angels pushed the canoe sideways, landing it safely in the grassy median.

While waiting for the service to "tow" the canoe, we received a call from Cousin Kevin, a cross country trucker on the road in Texas. While I had been driving, Tom had been talking with Kevin. After losing the signal, he was trying to reconnect when the canoe went airborne. Amazingly, the signal connected to Kevin's voice mail, and soon he heard the whole event. Ready to call 911, he listened further, and realized we really were safe.

Not only had God protected us and our fellow travelers, our canoe was undamaged by its flight and landing! Even God's "back-up" plan was in place with Kevin ready to help all the way from Texas.

This was truly a miraculous event!

We praise You, Lord, that as we call on Your Name, You are always ready to rescue and protect us.

Tom and Linda Page are members of Lancaster Evangelical Free Church where they are involved in Men's and Women's ministries.

One Sleepless Night

"Oh the depth of the riches of the wisdom and knowledge of God!
How unsearchable His judgments and His paths tracing out."
Romans 11:33-34

One of the many lessons God is teaching me is to trust Him when His ways defy explanation. When sleep escapes me, I have tried to trace His path and I cannot. I have tried to fathom His unfathomable ways, and I cannot. I have encountered situations that seem to be contradictory, and I could not understand.

As I was searching and asking God "why and how", He showed me in His Word, Proverbs 16:1 (LBT), "We can gather our thoughts, but the Lord gives the right answer." Verse 9, "We can make our plans, but the Lord determines our steps", and verse 33, "We may throw the dice, but the Lord determines how they fall." Because God cares about the anguish of my soul (Psalms 31:7), I am grateful and encouraged when David said in Psalms 31:14, "But, I am trusting you, Oh Lord, saying you are my God, my future is in your hands." And verse 24, "So be strong and take courage all of you who put your hope in the Lord!"

It was a wonderful moment for me when I finally realized that I do not have to explain the will of God. My part is to simply obey it. Then, I could sleep!

Oh God, forgive me for worrying and doubting Your knowledge and involvement in every detail of my life now and in the future. Thank You for Your Word that instructs me to cast my cares on Jesus because He cares for me.

Dick Shellenberger, Lancaster County Commissioner (2004-2007).

39-Gallons-Per-Minute

"Speak to the rock before their eyes, and it will yield its water."
Numbers 20:8

I n October of 1999, I was building my first house. I was walking with the builder on the property one day and I asked him, "How do you know where to drill for the well?"

He replied, "The well-driller will come out and perform "water dowsing" around the property to determine the best location for the well, then drill where his water dowsing shows him."

I questioned, "Water dowsing? Don't you mean water witching? I don't want that done on my property. Can I choose where I want him to drill instead?" My builder replied, "Yes, you can. However, if there is no water where we drill, you will have to pay for all the fees associated with the re-drilling." I said, "God found water for Elisha in the Bible, He will find water for me, too."

I walked around the property asking God to show me where to drill. After a few minutes, my eye was attracted to a spot at the top of my driveway. As I walked near it I pointed and declared, "I claim 39-gallons-per-minute right here in Jesus name!"

The builder smiled and chuckled a bit then marked my location. I went on my way to work.

Later, I received a call from the builder. He said, "We've drilled 200 feet and found nothing. What do you want us to do?" I replied, "Keep drilling. There's water there."

I received another phone call from him an hour later. He said, "We went 280 feet deep and have a 40-gallons-per-minute well here." I asked, "How accurate is your measurement? Could it be 39-gallons-per-minute instead of 40?" He said, "Yes. I suppose it could." I finished, "Then it is!"

God is looking for a mouth to stand and declare His word. Is yours available?

You are the God who hears and speaks. May our mouths give Yours a voice.

Jimmy Nimon is the Executive Director of Gateway House of Prayer in Ephrata.

Nothing Is Impossible With God

"I am the resurrection and the life. He who believes in me, though he die, yet will he live. *John 11:25 (American Standard Version)*

M ost people I have spoken to can relate to at some point worrying about death. "How does it happen? When do we realize we are dead? Is it really like a long tunnel? Do we feel things differently?"

Well, I had been brewing on this question for a long time. I had gotten in the pattern of asking "How sure can I be that I will live on after death?" Knowing that a body decays in a coffin, it was hard for me to understand how God can resurrect it all. How do I reconcile what I believe with what I can observe? It had become quite a faith obstacle for me. I had been to seminary and I know all the Biblical answers, but I still had a hard time really grasping it all.

I have experienced something like God's voice at several times in my life - out of nowhere, like lightning, a train of thought hits me and I recognize God is speaking to me. I was wondering how God can give us life again. Then a completely contrary thought hit me. "John, I did it before, I can do it again." This made no sense to me. And then, like a warm aftershock the meaning became apparent.

I had no problem with the faith step of God creating this world - obviously we all didn't come out of nothing. If God is responsible for creating all of this out of nothing, why couldn't He do this again with a set of rotting bones?

How foolish it was for my faith in God to be shaken by something I couldn't comprehend. It is exactly things that I cannot comprehend that should bolster my faith in God.

Thank You for the reminder that nothing is too hard or impossible for You.

John Wilkinson is the Senior High Pastor at LCBC (Lives Changed By Christ, Lancaster). He and his wife, Nikki, and 3 children Tyler, Aedan and Kylie live in Mt. Joy.

Sacrifice

"Then God said, 'Take your son, your only son, Isaac, whom you love, and go to the region of Moriah. Sacrifice him there as a burnt offering on one of the mountains I will tell you about." *Genesis 22:2*

There have been many times in my life when God has called me to lay down my desires at the altar of sacrifice. This has been true in major life events such as: finding a husband, the conception and birth of our first child, and purchasing our first home, as well as in the little things, such as my plans for the day. While it is not a guaranteed formula, my experience has been that once I finally get to that place where I'm willing to lay it down, God comes, picks it up and says "Here you go, now I know you are ready - your heart is right."

We serve a God that longs to give us the desires of our hearts, however He cares much more about our hearts than our desires; if our desire is no good for us, or our motives are wrong, or the timing is off, God loves us enough to say "no" or "wait." Times like these can be frustrating and cause us to doubt; Satan will whisper "Did God really say...?" We will be tempted to pick up our desire and try to do it our way. Abraham could have easily rationalized disobeying God, but he would have missed out on seeing God's provision and a tremendous increase of faith. What is the "Isaac" in your life that God is calling you to lay down?

Father God, I lay down my desires at Your altar, believing that You want what is best for me, and will bring it to pass in Your time. Holy Spirit, I pray that You would match the desires of my heart with the Father's; comfort me as I wait on Him. In the mighty name of Jesus, Amen.

Emily Yoder is a wife, mother, and teacher serving in Lancaster City with In the Light Ministries.

Ask And You Shall Receive

"Until now you have not asked for anything in my name. Ask and you will receive, and your joy will be complete." *John 16:24*

Almost everyone who knows my husband, Al, realizes his hobby of watching weather and keeping weather statistics. Some time ago, he received a message from the Lord that he was to pray expectantly in the area of weather. This encouraging word affirmed that his weather interest was a gift from God, not just a personal choice.

During the summer things started to dry up. Lawns turned from green to tan to brown. Corn leaves became pointed and narrow as the stalks reacted to the lack of rain. In early July, Al prayed for 2 inches of rain in our area. Several days later, rain came. He recorded exactly 2.83 inches and quietly praised and thanked God for this confirming answer.

By the end of the end of July, things began to wither again. He was reminded of the previous prayer and answer, so he prayed once more for 2 inches of rain in our area. Again, on the third and fourth day following a simple prayer recorded in his journal, he measured and recorded 2.13 inches in his weather records.

Al is quiet, gentle, and unassuming. His prayers were neither intense nor prolonged, just a sentence or two in his journal and recognition of a faithful Father.

To what area of life do you seem to be highly attuned? Consider that God may have specifically given you that sensitivity in order to allow you to release His will and purposes in that area through your prayers cooperating with Him.

Father, let me see my natural interests as expressions of Your interests. Use me to release Your will and purposes through cooperation with You as Your will was done through our Lord Jesus Christ.

Ruth Ann Stauffer from Leola, is the wife of Al, mother and grandmother, and prayer leader associated with Teaching the Word Ministries.

Our God

"...the Lord is the great God, The great King above all gods. In His hand are the depths of the earth, and the mountain peaks belong to Him. The sea is His, for He made it, and His hands formed the dry land. Come, let us bow down in worship...." *Psalm 95:3-6*

As I prepare for each class that I teach, I try to be mindful that I am a servant of the Lord, positioned by Him in this place at this time with these particular people. Because this generation desires personal relationships, I structure my classes so that students have opportunity to talk with one another and with me about what they are learning and experiencing.

The day following a reading assignment where students read a fictional piece by Langston Hughes, a renowned African-American writer, I began the discussion by saying, "Tell me something that stood out to you in this story." Immediately a young man raised his hand and said, "This story made me want to know Christ more than anything I have ever read."

I knew this student was not a believer in Christ and I certainly wasn't expecting this response about a "secular" story in a secular setting. When I asked him what there was about the story that prompted that response in him, he answered, "Because at one point in the story, Christ came down from the cross and walked with a homeless man."

After class, I said to God, "How did you do that? There was no way I could have planned for or made that happen." I have seen God work in ways like this over and over again. He keeps reminding me just to partner with him on a daily basis—whether in my classroom or in the hallways or even in rush hour traffic—and He will do wonderful things!

God, show me how to join forces with You to convey Your love and compassion all day every day.

Marian Yoder, an assistant professor at Harrisburg Area Community College, leads a breakfast discussion group for women in the marketplace.

Declaration Of Faith

"Your mercy, O Lord, is in the heavens; Your faithfulness reaches to the clouds." *Psalm 36:5*

When our 17-year-old son left home and moved to Tennessee, my heart felt as if it would break for the pain of it all. As I cried to the Lord, He gave me Psalms 27 as my scripture. My Bible's subtitle for that scripture is "An Exuberant Declaration of Faith".

The Lord is my light and my salvation; whom shall I fear? The Lord is the strength of my life; of whom shall I be afraid?

When you said, "Seek My face," my heart said to You, "Your face, Lord, I will seek."

I would have lost heart unless I had believed that I would see the goodness of the Lord in the land of the living.

"Wait on the Lord; be of good courage and He will strengthen your heart; wait, I say, on the Lord."

What did I have to fear? The Lord is my light, my strength, and my salvation. He wants me to draw near to Him, to seek His face. He wants me to believe that He is working in the heart of our son. He asks me to wait, to be of good courage, and He will strengthen my heart.

Now over two years later our son has come home. God is so faithful. The prayers of God's people have been answered. I have sought the Lord's face and drawn closer to Him. I have been strengthened. He has worked in our son's life.

Dear Lord, You are so faithful. Your mercy, O Lord, is indeed in the heavens; Your faithfulness reaches to the clouds. Praise Your Holy Name.

Yvonne Zeiset is wife, mother, grandmother and part -time secretary counselor at the Columbia Pregnancy Center division of Susquehanna Valley Pregnancy Services.

His Voice Rules

"The voice of the Lord is over the waters; the God of glory thunders, the Lord thunders over the mighty waters." *Psalm 29:3*

If it wasn't the stench of sewer water drenched carpet or gnats buzzing around in constant procession, the ninety-degree heat and humidity in July might have put me over the edge. The weeklong blame game over a sewer backup into our office had me on my last nerve! The landlord had finally called informing me they were sending someone out. As the conversation ended, the crackling of distant thunder could be heard.

Within minutes, the blue skies of summer gave way to an imposing darkness. A torrential downpour amidst booming thunder commenced. "Brownwater" began to emanate from multiple points. Racing to save belongings, my mind was full of frustration over delays in reopening the Transformation Center plus the displacement of programs, worship services and staff.

Suddenly a bolt of lightning like no other I had witnessed caught my eye. It seemed to last seconds and its glow created a surreal image of blinding light. Though indoors, my instincts dominated and I darted behind our coffee bar. I will never forget the image. My mind refreshed and a portion of Christ's words (Luke 10) replaced my thoughts: *"I saw Satan fall like lightning from heaven. I have given you authority to trample on snakes and scorpions and to overcome all the power of the enemy; nothing will harm you."*

As the water poured inside and hail pounded outside, I was peaceful and assured. I'm reminded that even when trying to navigate the deceptive tactics of snakes and painful, evenly deadly, stings of the scorpions, even when Satan himself is too close for comfort, our faith in the power and authority of Jesus Christ, His redeeming blood and our eternal destiny with the Father in Heaven, is our joy!

Today and in each day, Thy Kingdom come, Thy will be done, on earth as it is in heaven.

Bill Shaw is the Executive Director of Life Transforming Ministries in the city of Coatesville.

Photo by Irene Briner

Relentless Pursuit

"You have given me the shield of your salvation, and your right hand supported me, and your gentleness made me great."
Psalm 18:35 (English Standard Version)

Have you thought you had finally mastered something or overcome a besetting sin? You have probably soon discovered that God was not through working. "Gentle" is not the first word that those in the know would use to describe me— not that I haven't had some gentle moments or done gentle things. I'm a guy who plans and pursues results. You've met the type. For some years God has been softening my heart and reshaping my approach to people and projects. My wife and two adult children, all truly gentle people, are often His instruments. The changes have been recognized.

Now for the rest of the story. Two days ago, I arrived at my church to meet with two pastors. On arriving, I was told by a young woman serving in the office the she had called about an hour earlier and left a message rescheduling the meeting. What next emerged from my heart and mouth bore no evidence of the paragon of kindness and gentleness that I had become. I publicly corrected, instructed and vented my self-righteous irritation. Later that day it began to dawn on me, partly through the gentle questioning of my wife, that God had set me up for some instruction of His own.

The path of humbling, confessing, asking forgiveness lay before me—a path I took the next morning. What freedom to know I don't have to excuse or rationalize my boorish behavior. What joy and peace to know that my God is relentlessly pursuing His plans to make me like His Son. He's not through with me yet, but He will have His way, and that's more than okay.

Father, thank you for strengthening me by Your gentle, yet firm and loving hand. Thank you that You will fulfill Your purposes and plans in my life, for Your glory.

Bruce Boydell serves emerging leaders, businesses, and ministry organizations through Lifespan® Consulting and Coaching Services.

Agreeable Disagreements

"…and if in anything you have a different attitude, God will reveal that also to you; however let us keep living by the same standard to which we have attained." *Philippians 3:15-16*

I once knew a Board member of a local college — a gracious man, a champion of God, family, and business; in that order. It was my privilege, as a college administrator, to observe a passionate exchange among Board members involving this man. Both individuals articulated their positions, argued voraciously with legitimate documentation and logic, then followed with a vote.

I honestly don't recall what the issue was, and how the vote ended, but remember quite vividly the sight of this man's imposing frame rising up from the table, walking across the room and warmly greeting the opposing Board member with a handshake and a smile. He exhibited care and value for a person that disagreed with him. He knew the secret of how to agree to disagree. He kept living by the same standard to which we have attained.

It's a lesson I have sought to emulate in my own life, though admittedly, I am still on the learning curve. What a wonderful statement to the world it would be, and many times is, if/when the world knew Jesus' followers as the people who deeply and consistently loved one another.

Father, help us to be honest in our opinions, to communicate effectively and graciously, and to remember the superseding family relationship which allows us to greet one another in love. Help us/ me to sacrifice self-righteousness and to consider others more important than ourselves. Thank you for the promise that You will be the One to clear up our flawed understandings.

John Zeswitz currently serves as Executive Director of Ministries for LCBC's Lancaster campus. Prior to that, he served 15 years at Lancaster Bible College and Graduate School in a variety of senior leadership capacities. He and his family reside in Lititz.

Choosing To Give Thanks

"...give thanks in all circumstances, for this is God's will for you in Christ Jesus." *1 Thessalonians 5:18*

On the morning of our fourth wedding anniversary, we heard the doorbell ring. It was our neighbor telling us that during the night someone had decided to throw paint remover on many cars on our block, including one of ours. Great! On top of that, our 1 ½ year old son had the croup, so we were tired from caring for him. My husband was soon out the door, off to his work at our local hospital. And, me? I was left to be home with a sick son. What a great anniversary!

Since my husband was working a 12-hour shift that day, I took our son on a walk after dinner. As I was pushing that stroller (and pitying myself), I was reminded of something my parents told me growing up. "Give thanks in all things." Not *for* all things, but *in* all things. I was trying my best to give thanks, but I'm not sure I passed that test as I walked down the sidewalk talking to God. "Thank you Lord that I have a loving husband...(yet under my breath continued on)...who has to work so late on our anniversary! Thank you that we have a wonderful little son...who's sick right now! Thank you that we have a nice home as well as two cars...that just got vandalized!"

I kind of smiled to myself as I knew God read through my fake gratitude. I asked Him for strength to truly give thanks. The truth is, He was working in my heart through those circumstances and I pray next time I pass the test more faithfully.

Lord Jesus, I ask for grace to give thanks, no matter what comes my way today. I know You will honor a heart that is full of gratitude and I choose to praise You no matter what.

Cindy Zeyak is a homemaker as well as a worship leader at The Door Christian Fellowship. She lives with her husband, Ken, and son, Brennan, in Lancaster City.

Fear Not; FEAR NOT!

"Call on Me in the day of trouble…." *Psalm 50:15 (New King James Version)*

All I could do was cry, "Jesus! Jesus!" I kept it up, not knowing what was going to happen but knowing deep down if I were going to make it through this, it would be only because Jesus helped me. But the most amazing thing happened...I actually felt the prayers of my anxious family. I can't explain it but I knew what it was.

The emergency room doctor and his nurse tried to get the needle into a vein in my upper chest to insert a lead into my heart to get my pulse up from twenty beats a minute before it stopped altogether, but they were having problems. Finally they used the plates to shock my heart. I awakened to find myself being loaded into an ambulance for a trip to another hospital where the cardiac facilities were better. Since it was Friday evening of Mother's Day weekend, the operating room staff was mostly gone so they opted to let me wait until a full staff would be there Monday. I had all sorts of things go wrong. Machinery failed; instruments failed; even the call button in my room failed.

When I finally did get into the OR, the doctors told me there was a chance they would have to remove my collarbone to remove a plug that was inserted into an artery instead of a vein. I prayed earnestly that I could keep my collarbone and they could do their job. I watched the clock tick by the minutes until they successfully got everything fixed and a pacemaker implanted. I was awake through it all but between God's grace and the medication, I was relaxed.

I don't know why my heart had a complete block...my "electrical system" failed to get the stimulus from the group of cells above the heart down through the heart muscle to initiate the beats but God allowed it and made an alternate manmade system. I have a full life and can encourage many who must have this procedure.

Are you fearful today? Call on Him!

Praise You, God, for all You do for us in all our daily lives and trials. Surely, we may "fear not!"

Jackie Bowser attends DOVE Westgate Celebration.

Transformed

"And we, who with unveiled faces all reflect the Lord's glory, are being transformed into his likeness with ever-increasing glory, which comes from the Lord, who is the Spirit." *2 Corinthians3:18*

We were recently involved in a remodeling project that lasted for two and a half months. In some ways it was an exciting time for our family knowing that our new addition would be enjoyed for years to come. Yet there were days also when the inconvenience of living in our basement, along with the noise and all the dust, slowly wore us down.

Eventually we got used to being in the basement and settled in for the long haul. In some ways, I think I got a little too settled and almost lost sight of the finished product. About two months into the project, the kitchen and floors were installed, and I was reminded of the original vision. It was exciting to see things finally start to come together as the transformation neared completion. It turned out that the temporary inconvenience was worth it in the end.

It makes me think about the times when God is at work in our lives transforming us into his image. It can seem inconvenient and downright uncomfortable at times. If we get too focused on our shortcomings, we may even lose sight of God's purpose for our lives. But we must not lose heart, for before too long we will begin to see glimpses of His glory being reflected in our lives.

Dear God, help me not to lose sight of Your work of grace in my life as You transform me into Your likeness with ever-increasing glory. Fulfill Your plans and purposes in my life today.

Mark Van Scyoc is a Programmer Analyst, Freelance Photographer and Writer, and serves as Mission Director at DOVE Christian Fellowship, Westgate Celebration in Ephrata.

Voice Of God

"Therefore, since we are receiving a Kingdom which cannot be shaken, let us have grace; by which we may serve God acceptably with reverence and godly fear. For our God is a consuming fire."
Hebrews 12:28-29 (New King James Version)

It was a typical Sunday morning. I walked into church, ready for worship and the Word. As I was walking toward the sanctuary, I heard a teenager tell someone that he had a terrible headache and wanted some Tylenol. People hear conversations like this every day, and I thought nothing more about it. As I sat down, this same boy sat right in front of me. As we worshipped, I heard a still, small voice telling me to pray for the boy. I was a young Christian, still learning to hear and obey the voice of my Father. I thought it was my own voice and promptly ignored it, reasoning that he just had a headache and he'd be fine without my silly prayer.

I will never forget where I was when I received the news a few days later that the boy had a brain aneurism that same Sunday and died the next day. I was in a restaurant, eating with my family, ran to a secluded area, and sobbed until no more tears would come. I was filled with guilt and shame. I had heard the voice of my Father, but did not recognize or obey it. How could I live with this?

Then, the same still voice said to me, "Wendy, I know all things. I knew I was bringing him home with Me. It's okay. Use this lesson to know My voice and not hesitate to obey in the future." Needless to say, I do not ignore that still small voice anymore.

Thank you, Abba, for teaching me to hear and listen to Your voice. May we always listen and obey when we hear You. We praise You for Your everlasting grace.

Wendy Reasner, formerly from Susquehanna Valley Pregnancy Services, is a supervisor at Caron Treatment Centers in Wernersville.

Chasing After God

"Come, let us bow down in worship, let us kneel before the Lord our Maker." *Psalm 95:6*

My baby has just begun crawling. Forward, with purpose, and not backward as before. She once took joy, lying on her back, as I got on my hands and knees crawling to her, in a giggly anticipation of the final "pounce" at the end. She has now matured and is delighted that she can crawl in exploration. (Enter cabinet latches and stairway gates.) One of the few commands she seems to understand and obey is "Come to Mommy." She will stop whatever she is doing to crawl to the beloved attention-giver.

I wish I could be that obedient and come to the Lord when He calls! You see, I could easily walk over and pick her up, but where is the fun in that anymore? She not only appreciates the opportunity to use her maturing skills, but she also builds her strength as she crawls. And it may sound cliché, but there is joy in the journey. She has to spend that time focused on me to get to me.

If Noel, the cat, happens to walk between us, you can be sure my daughter will notice and possibly even change her course to follow. But trust me, there is no reward in that! As fascinating as the cat may be, she scratches and just cannot hold a baby like I do. So take joy in chasing after God today as He calls you. Although He called us first and came to pick us up from where we were sitting, at some point, we have all squirmed out of His lap. Now that we know where He is, He will strengthen us *through our coming to Him.* So set your sights on Him, and motor on over. There's a big hug at the end.

Father, I run to You! Take me up in Your arms and comfort me with Your strength. Amen

Tracy Slonaker is a wife, mother of three, and Director of Christian Education at Harvest Fellowship of Colebrookdale in Boyertown.

The "Return" Of The Lord

"He has showed you, O man, what is good. And what does the Lord require of you? To act justly and to love mercy and to walk humbly with your God." *Micah 6:6-8*

I was on a missionary trip to New York City. I was down to my last fifty cents. During the church service, I felt compelled to put my last fifty cents into the offering bucket. The next day, I received a card from a friend. When I opened the card, inside it was a fifty-dollar bill. The Lord used what was in my heart when I put that fifty cents in the bucket and He blessed me.

Basically what I am saying is, examine your heart when you come to the Lord. The Lord already knows, but when you give an offering, know what is motivating your heart.

Lord God, I ask that You help us to examine our hearts and help us to give You our first offerings.

Amy Rhoads serves on a support team for the Taproot micro church, Lititz.

Sit Right Here

"Let us go to His dwelling place; let us worship at His footstool—arise, O Lord, and come to Your resting place, You and the ark of Your might." *Psalm 132:7-8*

"**D**addy, sit right here!" implored my two and a half year-old daughter, pointing to the end of the sofa right next to where she was playing on the floor. She was not asking me to do anything for her; she just wanted my presence close by. To her, it was not enough that I was in the same room. Even my presence at the far end of the sofa was too distant. She wanted to content herself *right by my feet.*

As I heard the appeal of my little girl, something stirred within my spirit: Is *"Abba (Daddy), sit right here!"* the cry of my heart? Is my heart so set on being in the Father's presence (right next to Him—without even the length of the sofa between us) that I refuse to be content unless I am right by His feet?

The Psalmist (in the verses recorded above) echoed that sentiment and plea. Throughout Scripture, the Ark of the Covenant was a symbol of God's presence and power. In essence, the Psalmist was crying out, *"Abba, sit right here! Come close in this very place with a mighty demonstration of Your Presence."*

Will I—will you—refuse to be content with even a "sofa-length" distance from the Father? Will we take the posture of a child, imploring with humble boldness, *"Abba (Daddy), sit right here,"* crying out for Him to come close with a mighty demonstration of His Presence?

Abba, sit right here! Burn within my heart an insatiable hunger for Your presence and a desire to be at Your feet. Come close with a mighty demonstration of Your Presence—in my home, my church, my workplace, and my community—for Your glory!

Dwane Reitz, prayer coordinator at Global Disciples in Lancaster, is an elder and missions director at Petra Christian Fellowship, New Holland.

Yes, Lord!

"God told Abram: 'Leave your country, your family and your father's home for a land that I will show you.'" *Genesis 12:1 (The Message)*

L ike Abram, there have been many times when God has instructed me to get up and go to a place that is often unfamiliar to me. I can choose to be obedient and go forth or stay behind in the land of familiar and miss the many blessings that accompany obedience.

There's a story of a group of monks that traveled through darkened hallways. The only light available to them was from candles placed on their shoes. The monks could only see exactly where they were standing.

I was reminded of the true meaning of obedience and the journey the Lord has me on at Chester County Women's Services Medical. Many times He's only given me enough direction to follow with true obedience trusting Him to tell me when to get up and go, when to pick up my foot and where to put it down. I've often prayed, "Lord, please tell me where You are taking me in this journey." Sometimes He tells me specifically what His plans are. Other times, I can hear Him say, "Trust Me my dear child. If I were to tell you, it would be too much for you to bear at this time."

True trust leads to true obedience. Do we trust the Lord with all our heart? Do we believe He loves us and wants to bless us as it says in Jeremiah 29:11? Abram had this faith! It is my desire to follow God in true obedience as Abram did. When God says, "Get up and go," I want to say, "Yes Lord!"

Father, thank You for Your promise of a hope and a future. Thank You that You love us so much You have plans to prosper us and not to harm us. Please help us to live this life in true obedience to You. Amen

Karen Pennell, Chief Executive Officer of Chester County Women's Services Medical in Coatesville and West Chester.

Who Will They Say YOU Are?

"By this shall all men know that ye are my disciples, if ye have love one to another." *John 13:35 (King James Version)*

As a member of the Christian Motorcyclist Association (CMA), it has been my privilege over the years to ride many miles as an ambassador for Christ, sharing the love of Jesus and, as CMA's slogan says, "changing the world one heart at a time."

In addition to serving at secular biking events and other outreach efforts, one of the most effective ways of "shining our light'" when traveling is by displaying what is known in the biking world as "colors." These "colors" are patches sown onto jackets, vests, and other outerwear—worn both in the Christian and secular arena—helping to distinguish one group from the next.

When a bunch of noisy cycles and hungry bikers roll into a restaurant, it usually gets the attention of personnel and patrons alike! Having noticed the unique patch, people often approach the group with questions, eager to hear what CMA is all about. As a result, there are many opportunities to pray with individuals and let them know that Jesus loves and cares about them, personally.

No matter where our activities and interests take us, we can display His 'colors' as we journey through life. The Bible says that people will know we are His disciples by the love we have for one another. Our attitudes, words, and deeds help to identify us as followers of Christ. We can all ponder, "who will they say **we** are?" after having been in our company.

Lord, I desire to leave the imprint of Your love wherever I go. Please help me to be mindful of my words and actions so that You will be glorified in my life and so that others will be drawn to Your love and salvation through me.

Richard Place has served in various leadership positions within the local CMA Chapter for many years. He and his wife, Ann, attend Dove Christian Fellowship, Elizabethtown.

Seeds We Sow

"So shall my word ... not return unto me void, but it shall accomplish that which I please...." *Isaiah 55:11 (King James Version)*

I love my job as a nurse in a doctors' office. I have opportunity to welcome the patients, communicate with them briefly, and set them at ease as they wait.

Several weeks ago, I escorted an elderly woman and her adult daughter to an exam room. As children, this daughter and I had spent hours playing together at the local park. It was fun after many years to renew our acquaintance. Minutes after I had left the room and continued to escort other patients to their exam rooms, Sherry, the daughter, flagged me down.

"When we were kids and we would play at the playground, you were the first person who ever told me what it meant to be saved." Sherry said.

"I did?" was my stunned reply. I could not remember sharing my faith with her as a child, but was delighted that she could remember the details.

"Oh, yes," she replied. "My church never talked about being saved, so it was new information for me. But some time after you shared with me, a summer evangelist held a Good News Club for the neighborhood children. One day I was the only child who attended. That teacher led me to Jesus. I understood what I was committing to because you had already shared the gospel plan with me. I thought you would like to know that."

How sweet that God would use me as a young child to plant seeds of His Word in a playmate's heart and that later He would bring them to fruition in her life.

Needless to say, I moved through the remainder of my workday with a grateful heart.

Thank You, Father, that Your word continues to be powerful and life-giving today. It will not return void, but accomplishes what You please. May we be faithful to share Your word with a needy world around us. In Jesus' Name, Amen.

Mary Prokopchak is a R.N. at Susquehanna Family Health Center and is a cell leader at DOVE Elizabethtown.

Minister His Love

"Practice what you have learned …and model your way of living on it, and the God of peace will be with you."
Philippians 4:9 (Amplified Bible)

Two of our sons are in elementary school. I'm fortunate to be able to help in their classrooms. This gives me a chance to get to know the children whom my boys share about. I encourage them to love even those not easy to love and to be friendly to their classmates. I explain "they may not have a home life-like you have."

Last year, the younger son, Sean, had a challenging boy in his class. Sean did become friends with him. After several times helping in his classroom, we started praying for this boy. Then this year, when classroom assignments were posted, this boy's name appeared with Sean's name in his class. I admit, I was frustrated! What little faith I had in our prayers.

Before school began, testing was scheduled. At this time, we met this boy with his dad. I overheard his dad updating his information because Dad now had custody. He appeared to be more engaged with his son than the mother had been, and his son has improved.

Now our older son, Jared, has a boy in his class who isn't behaving well. Helping in his class, I experienced much disruption. Why didn't I think to begin praying immediately?! We started praying for him and for wisdom for the teacher. Already Jared's new friend is doing better. We regularly pray for both sons' teachers and classmates in our family devotion time.

Our children, in their youth, can be a little Christ in their world. They can minister His love to their classmates and teachers.

Dear Lord we pray for our children, their friends, classmates, and teachers. Thank you, Holy Spirit, for Your guidance in praying for them. Give our children strength and courage to minister Your life to those around them.

Millie Stauffer walks alongside her husband, Clair, in the Refreshing Leaders Ministry, encouraging and building up leaders around the world.

A Clear Sense Of Identity

"...I know where I came from and where I am going." *John 8:14*

Finish this sentence, "I derive a clear sense of personal identity from _____." When I was growing up, I would have really struggled with that question. I had no clue as to where an identity would come from for me. "Why am I here?" "What can I do?" "Where am I going?" No logical response would surface and it left me open and vulnerable to whatever came along.

Jesus was constantly taunted by the Pharisees and one day He found Himself confronted with a particularly nasty line of questioning. It seems this time they were trying to provoke a negative response concerning His personal sense of identity. They were questioning the validity of Jesus' testimony. Could He speak on His own behalf without the normal set of witnesses? Jesus, undaunted, let them know that His testimony was valid because He knew where He came from and He knew where He was going (John 8:14). And then He said, "I am one who testifies for myself; my other witness is the Father, who sent me" (John 8:18).

Back to me. At the ripe old age of seventeen, I found this One who knew who He was, and the process of finding out who I was and why I was here was set into motion. A clear sense of identity causes us to be able to walk in God's vision for us undaunted by the evil one's temptation to lose our identity in something or someone else. It is not your accomplishments He's after, your degrees, or your possessions; it's your heart. When He has your heart, we will not need to perform for or try to please men for a personal sense of worth because we will know that we are His son or daughter (Galatians 1:10).

Thank you, Father, that I am loved and approved of unconditionally by You. I have Your approval and I know where I have come from and why I am here.

Steve Prokopchak serves on DOVE Christian Fellowship International's Apostolic Council.

God's Messenger

"Are not all angels ministering spirits...." *Hebrews 1:14*

During the spring of 1992, I found myself deeply immersed with my work. I was involved with many commitments, extended travel, and desperately seeking God. My heart's desire was to serve God through my employment, but I was unable to discern God's wisdom in managing my responsibilities as husband, father, employee, Sunday school teacher, and church leader. I managed to put on a smile, but inside I was discouraged and tired.

At the end of a week of meetings in Florida, I arrived at the airport for my return flight home, feeling more discouraged and worn out than ever. As I sat down and closed my eyes, the man next to me tapped my arm to get my attention. He was of Indian descent and immaculately dressed. The very first words that he spoke thundered in my ears and it was as if God Himself had entered my presence.

He said, "I see the Holy Spirit on you. God has heard your prayers and I am to encourage you that God sees your heart and is making a way where you see no way." I looked at him and could see the love of God exuding from his being and pouring over my parched spirit.

As we spoke, this gentleman related that he was to be on an earlier flight, but while he was waiting at the gate, God spoke to him to take a later, less direct flight, and that he was to touch the life of whoever sat beside him. He boldly obeyed.

God had used this servant to connect me with Him once again. My days ahead took on fresh, God-given perspective, and the assurance that God was intimately involved in every detail of my life. Since then I've pondered—was this really a human encounter or could this have been an angelic being sent by God to minister to one hurting child?

Thank you, Lord, that You always cause us to triumph!

Peter Ragaller serves as Manager-Strategic Relations with Teaching The Word Ministries.

God's Protection

"...Now choose life, so that you and your children may live and that you may love the Lord your God, listen to his voice, and hold fast to him. For the Lord is your life, and he will give you many years in the land...." *Deuteronomy 30:19–20*

Several years ago, a friend and I traveled to her sister's home to pick up a kitten. My friend held it as we drove. In the past, I would speed up in order to get to work on time. As I grew older, I realized how reckless I had been and changed this habit.

That day I drove down the road at a leisurely pace, at least ten miles below the limit. There wasn't much traffic and so my friend and I chatted and enjoyed the crisp October day. About a mile or two before we reached the traffic light where we would cross Route 30, a clear urgent thought told me to "speed up." It wasn't an audible voice, and it seemed like a strange request, not something I would tell myself. But I obeyed, speeding up ten miles per hour faster.

When we got to the traffic light, it was green and we crossed. As soon as we were safely on the other side, a speeding SUV hit something and turned onto its roof, sliding and coming to a stop exactly where our car would have been if we had stopped at the red light.

Immediately, I recognized God's protection. He had spared Jean and me and a tiny black kitten (now our nine-year-old cat). I am always amazed at how God is "in the details." He has proven Himself over and over.

Heavenly Father, thank you for Your protection, Your faithfulness, and the love You show in so many ways. May we always be open to hearing and obeying Your guiding voice. In Jesus' name, Amen.

Sharon Neal is involved in children's, Women's Bible Fellowship, and the shepherding team ministries at Lancaster Evangelical Free Church, Lititz.

Cleared Path

"In his heart a man plans his course, but the Lord determines his steps." *Proverbs 16:9*

Fifteen minutes away from home, I began to experience pain. We were on our way home from the Philadelphia airport after working with orphans in Ghana, West Africa. My husband, Glenn, and I felt confident that we had accomplished our mission to encourage and love our missionary friends and present a VBS at the orphanage. It had been a learning and growing experience to witness life in Africa. Although I had been a little apprehensive before going, God had assured me twice that He was with me.

As I prepared Psalm 23 using Phillip Keller's book "A Shepherd Looks at the 23rd Psalm, I was comforted at how much the good shepherd does for his sheep. He carefully chooses the paths, clearing the way, preparing the pastures, all because he loves the sheep. We shared that with those precious children who had experienced things beyond our comprehension. We trusted the Holy Spirit to make a path to their hearts.

We finished our assignment and began our long path home. Africa is far away from Pennsylvania. Seven hours from Ghana to London, a five hour layover, then another seven hours to Philadelphia. So I was so grateful that we were close to home when I began to experience pain. Two hours after arriving home I was in the emergency room. A tumor on my liver, that was unknown to us, burst.

Our Shepherd had led us and kept me safe all those miles and hours. He spared my life and allowed me to get back to the United States and to Lancaster County, where I could receive the physical, emotional, and spiritual care best for me. How good and faithful my Shepherd is.

Lord Jesus, my Good Shepherd, You love and care for each of Your sheep. Help us remember that we might plan our way but You choose our steps. Thank you for Your tenderness, gentleness, and plan.

Christina Ricker is a wife, mother, grandmother and one of the sheep of Petra Christian Fellowship.

Intercession

"The Lord is not slow about his promise, as some count slowness, but is patient toward you, not wishing for any to perish but for all to come to repentance." *2 Peter 3:9*

While on vacation a few years ago, I had a chance to sit contemplatively, with my heart open wide to the Lord, by a lake that was surrounded by extremely exclusive houses. I was having time with the Lord, and I was simply enjoying the sights. As I innocently pondered the neighborhood, a viciously narrow-minded thought erupted within me, "Families that can afford to live in a place like this have so much abundance–such freedom of choice–how blinding such wealth can be. They *can't* be in touch with how needy they really are."

"Do you really think so?" I heard whispered deep within my heart.

"It's gotta be close to impossible for them to come to terms with their need for a Savior," I muttered silently to myself.

Then, as suddenly as I had clumped these strangers into a category of people who'd never be drawn to Jesus, I was struck with a thought that was *not* my own: *"Will you pray for revival to break out in this place?"*

Talk about a crushing question! Dissolved in tears, devastated to rediscover the deceitfulness of my heart, I began to weep for the many families who called that place their home. As I interceded, I became increasingly aware of God's incredible heart of compassion for *all* people. So poignant was my experience, I expect a great move of God to stir that precious neighborhood one day.

How relieved I am to know that God's love far exceeds my own.

Forgive me, Lord, that I dare to pass judgment upon those You want me to pray for instead. Cultivate Your perfect love in me so that I'll intercede with compassionate confidence, knowing You don't wish for any to perish. Amen

Kathi Wilson and her husband, Mark, co-authors of *Tired of Playing Church* and co-founders of Body Life Ministries, are members of Ephrata Community Church.

Show Us Your Goodness, God

"Then Moses said, 'I pray You, show me Your glory!' And God said,
'I Myself will make all My goodness pass before you...'"
Exodus 33:18–19

While reading Exodus 33, one of my favorite chapters, I noticed something I had overlooked for years. As you may remember, God just told Moses that His presence could not go with them. Moses prevailed upon God to send His presence saying that it was His presence that distinguished His people from all other peoples. God agreed to go with Israel, and Moses then asked to see God's glory. God's response is very interesting and this is what I had overlooked for years: God said, "I will make My goodness pass before you."

We often pray that the Glory of God will be manifested in our lives and region. But here is a clue to how God answers that prayer: He reveals His goodness. Of all the various attributes and aspects of God's nature, it is His goodness that He chose to parade before our eyes.

We often use the word *goodness* to mean ethical righteousness, as when we tell our children to be good! But that is not the meaning of this Hebrew word. While God is certainly righteous, this word has more to do with God's generosity and His good will toward us. The word is translated joy at times and speaks more of His personality and heart toward us. Later in Exodus 34, the Scripture says that God is "abounding in goodness." God is good, all the time!

Father, we are so glad that You are a good God. We admit that years of sin have made us reluctant to really believe that at times. Please forgive us for doubting Your nature. We ask that You would let Your goodness pass before our eyes also. Amen!

Barry Wissler is senior pastor of Ephrata Community Church and president of HarvestNET Inc., a network of churches and ministries who partner together for harvest.

Every Tongue And Every Tribe

"Who shall not fear You, O Lord, and glorify Your name? For You alone are holy. For all nations shall come and worship before You, For Your judgments have been manifested." *Revelation 15:4*

"Hello, is this Mrs. Heeeems?"

I wanted to shout, how can people get such an easy, short last name like "Heim", all discombobulated?

Living in northern Louisiana at the time, my husband, Bob, suggested that since we were the only "Heim" listed in the phone book (and probably the only *German* name in the book at that), the local French-background people wouldn't know that you pronounce the *second* vowel in a German name. Bob jokingly reminded me that I had butchered Beauvais, and Thibodeaux when we first moved there. Well, duh! In my alphabet, we pronounce the letters "s" and "x."

Having grown up as Pennsylvania Dutch in Schuylkill County and now living in Lancaster County for 8 years, my family will always enjoy our familiar German ancestry of *gut* Lebanon bologna, red beet eggs, *nitsy* or *rutchey* children, red barns with silos, and *red up* houses.

For 23 years as a military family, we had been "foreigners," scattered to the four corners of the United States: we came to appreciate and enjoy Texas hospitality and barbeque; Maine humor, lighthouses and lobster; upper Michigan's tight-knit (survival) community amid harsh winters; Nebraska's spirited passion for red [Cornhuskers]; Kansas' spiritual oasis with the pioneer-trails setting as the backdrop; California's star-shaped piñata (it held our children's stocking gifts one Christmas), and Louisiana's "fixin' on fixin' red beans and rice with crawfish etouffee." These variations are within the United States!

I look forward to heaven when we can see, hear and experience all the cultures, ethnic groups, and tribes from throughout the world. If there is just one tribe absent, the rest of us will be missing out.

Dear Father, many times differences can be frustrating and form barriers between people groups. Help me to see beyond the surface hindrances and focus on the distinctness and uniqueness of others, because You created us and love us all.

Tamalyn Jo (Heinbaugh) Heim plans to barter her shoo-fly pie and Dutch Blitz skills for … a flight in a Waodani-piloted airplane in heaven.

Open Our Eyes

"Do you not say, 'Four months more and then the harvest'? I tell you, open your eyes and look at the fields! They are ripe for harvest."
John 4:35

I admit that at times when I look at our society I perceive it as resistant, disinterested, and often cold to the gospel. Yet when we look at people through the eyes of Jesus, we are able to see beyond the surface to a deep hunger for God.

I recently had my eyes opened in a fresh way to the ripe harvest and open hearts around us, when several people decided to set up a prayer station on the streets of Lancaster City. A small table with a banner that read "Prayer Station" became the place where Jesus began to meet people in a special way. Amazingly, many that walked by began to respond to the invitation to pray for their needs. Within a short period of time, a number gave their lives to Christ and others began to share some very deep needs and hurts. For those few hours, the street became God's altar of ministry and a holy place.

How often we pass people on the street or in the grocery store and assume they are not interested in hearing about our God. If we could only see their hearts as Jesus does, we would see all kinds of hurts and longings. Underneath the exterior are people searching for something that will meet the inner cry of their hearts.

People may react to what they perceive as dead religion, but they are ripe toward genuine love and concern for their needs.

Lord Jesus, I ask You to open my eyes to see what You see and to soften my heart to love like You do. Show me the opportunities throughout my day to pray for people as they express their needs.

Lester Zimmerman is pastor of Petra Christian Fellowship, Apostolic Leader of the Hopewell Network of Churches, and council member of the Regional Church of Lancaster County.

Trusting The Lord In Dark Times

"I am still confident of this: I will see the goodness of the Lord in the land of the living." *Psalm 27:13*

I enjoyed seeing the movie, "Amazing Grace" although I'm glad the director didn't graphically portray all that the African captives had to bear on the trip over. It was a bit easier on my conscience not to have to linger on the great suffering those on the ship endured.

Yesterday, I was able to speak to a young female resident in a way that I would speak to my daughters. I was amazed at how she was riveted to my words as I spoke. I don't think what I said was terribly profound. Yet it was a great opportunity to fill the void left by a father who wasn't there with hope that she might better know the Father who is always there.

I felt sad hearing the news of the latest shootings in our community: I was sad for a little girl, who is thankfully headed toward full recovery, sad for a young man who is dead, sad for turf wars and the presence of drugs in our community, sad for young people out late groping for an elusive adulthood, sad for the role models of the day that champion bluster and self-interest.

I remember G. K. Chesterton's quote, "Certain new theologians dispute original sin, which is the only part of Christian theology which can really be proved." This statement is sad, real and profound, when we see the suffering around us. The goodness of the Lord is the antidote to fear in our troubled world. We must trust the Lord, and He will strengthen us. Trust Him today!

Lord, help me seek You when things seem bleak.

Steve Brubaker is the Director of Residential Programs at Water Street Rescue Mission.

Just Call Me Dennis

"But God forbid that I should boast except in the cross of our Lord Jesus Christ..." *Galatians 6:14*

I was recently introduced to a new minister from a neighboring church during our church's Sunday service. I wanted to be sure that I was referring to him by the proper and appropriate title, so I asked him if I should call him reverend, doctor, or pastor? He gave me a warm hand shake and very humbly replied, "Just call me Dennis." I was impressed and pleasantly surprised at this man's humility. It was refreshing to talk with him, because he was not caught up in titles or what name he had made for himself. He was simply happy to be a servant of the Lord.

This conversation was a good reminder to me that all that I am that is good comes from God. It is Him that deserves the glory. I am simply one of the vessels He uses to display His glory, and I can do that so much more effectively when I have a humble attitude and am focused on pleasing Him.

Oh Lord, help us to know that we can best reflect Your glory by keeping a humble attitude. Please work this humility in us today. Amen

Sarah Erk serves the Lord with her husband, David, at New Covenant Christian Church in Washington Boro.

Handicapped Or "Handi Capable"

"I can do everything through Christ who gives me strength."
Philippians 4:13

The continual sound of the bell ringing overpowered my phone conversation with one of our patients trying to set up a dental appointment. Glancing up from my computer screen and scanning the waiting room area I saw who was holding the door open. Grace flashed me a smile as she struggled to get through the door. Using her backpack to hold the door open she placed her walking stick on the hardwood floor to steady her partially paralyzed body as she stumbled through the doorway. Several patients offered assistance, but she refused. As she seated herself, I chuckled as I read, **HANDI CAPABLE** in bold letters across the front of her purple t-shirt. Holding up her right leg she drew my attention to the swimming fish pattern on her matching colored leg brace and gave me a "thumbs up."

When Grace was in her early 50's, a stroke left her partially paralyzed, changing her life dramatically. Being a very determined individual, after months of rehab, she began swimming again and currently swims at least 20 laps 3 times each week. Her goals to drive, cook and to be as independent as possible have all been accomplished. Grace is a delightful patient and brightens any day with her engaging smile, outgoing personality and "can do" attitude.

I was impressed with the fact that mankind is all handicapped in some way—spiritually, physically or emotionally, but as a follower of Christ I am to live my life "handi capable" in the Spirit. He gives me everything I need to live independent from sin and to be free in Christ as I daily yield the handicapped areas of my life to Him. Like Grace, I do need desire, discipline and determination to accomplish all He has for me on this earth.

As Grace stood and turned around, I read the back of her shirt, "If I need help, I'll ask." Let's admit we need help today and ask our perfectly capable God.

Father, help, I need You! I don't want to live my life handicapped, but in Your strength and power.

Coleen Gehman is a wife and mother and serves as deaconess at Lancaster Evangelical Free Church.

Show Me The Way

"The Lord said to him, 'Who gave man his mouth? Who makes him deaf or mute? Who gives him sight or makes him blind? Is it not I, the Lord? Now go; I will help you to speak and will teach you what to say.'" *Exodus 4:11-12*

For years my husband and I have been praying for direction for our lives. Direction for jobs, financial decisions, which mission field He would have us serve in, which school to send our children to…the list goes on. I have been praying individually for direction for my career and how to use the creativity that God has given me.

God led me to the book of Exodus through a Bible study at church. In reading about God's calling on Moses to lead the Israelites out of Egypt, I recognized very real similarities to my own life and doubts that I carry.

Like Moses was led early in life to be a rescuer, I was led early in life to be a writer. And like Moses at the burning bush, I came up with excuse after excuse as to why I couldn't write. "I'm not that good at it." "It's too scary; I can't handle the inevitable rejection." "What do *I* have to say?" "Who would want to read my writing anyway?"

As the Lord was with Moses, so too was He patient with me and slow to anger through all of my doubts and questions. God gave Moses his brother, Aaron, to help him speak; in the same way, God has given me siblings in Christ who stand beside me and encourage me as I move through my journey as a writer.

Lord, help me to be obedient when You reveal Your will for my life. Thank you for those You have placed in my life to lift me up along the way.

Jennifer Hamilton is a word missionary. She is married to Jason and mother of three beautiful children. She attends Lancaster Evangelical Free Church in Lititz.

God Will Never Forsake Me

"Do not fear, for I am with you; Do not anxiously look about you, for I am your God. I will strengthen you, surely I will help you, Surely I will uphold you with My righteous right hand."
Isaiah 41:10 (New American Standard Bible)

The Lord recently brought this verse to my attention, no doubt to encourage my overwhelmed heart and mind. I recall the first time I heard these reassuring words. I was twenty-three years old and had recently received Christ as my personal Lord and Savior. Struggling with the desire to end my life, I had great difficulty believing that God could love and forgive me. Those early months as a new Christian were traumatic. I was hospitalized due to the fragile condition of my emotions and mind. Yet my heavenly Father remained faithful and began to heal me as His Word started to take root in my heart. However, there was the underlying fear that He might abandon me.

I was abandoned at the age of eight at a Boston hospital where I faced surgery alone. What a terrifying experience! Coupled with regular threats of abandonment by family members, I became an anxious, insecure person. Then the unthinkable happened. My father abandoned me when he divorced my mother. My world was shattered! Do you see why it was difficult for me to feel secure in my heavenly Father, trusting Him for my well-being? Yet repeatedly in the Bible God promises His eternal, faithful love to His children (Jeremiah 31:3). Would I believe Him?

A few years ago, I was struggling with a significant issue as I was praying in the chapel of a medical center. The inaudible command came, "Sing!" With reluctance, I reached for a hymnal and randomly (providentially) turned to "O Love That Wilt Not Let Me Go." I realized the bottom line: my need to believe my heavenly Father when He says, "'I will never desert you, nor will I ever forsake you'" (Hebrews 13:5). Yes, God is a faithful Father!

Heavenly Father, thank you for Your unfailing love and faithfulness. May those who have experienced abandonment find their security in You through the Lord Jesus.

Susan Marie Davis is a student at Lancaster Bible College and a member at Calvary Church in Lancaster, where she serves with her husband Karl on the Cambodia Initiative Team.

Who Am I?

"...Have I been with you all this time...and yet you still don't know who I am...?" John 14:9 (New Living Translation)

"**M**om, there's cheese in that. You know I can't have dairy!" My son was hovering over the stove, watching me prepare dinner for the others, becoming more and more frantic. Of course I knew. He had been on a dairy-free diet for years. I also knew that, unseen to him, I had already prepared his favorite, a meatball dinner, ready to be brought out at the right time.

I put the stirring spoon down. "Look at me," I said. "Who am I?"

"Mom, of course," he replied, exasperated. This was not the answer he wanted.

"Yes, I am. As Mom, have I ever let you go without dinner?" I continued. "No." Was it getting through? "Can you trust that I'll take care of you—can you just relax and trust *me*?" I said.

"I guess so," he responded, shrugging his shoulders.

How often these interactions teach me about my relationship with my heavenly Father. I feel so frantic at times when I see His answer for others but not for myself. What does my response reveal—do I really think He's unaware? Uncaring? Incapable? The waiting time between my awareness of my need and my awareness of His provision is a time to stand on the truth and embrace faith in *who He is*. He has given forethought. He has promised to care for me. *"Who am I, Cindy? I have your answer tucked safely away in my pocket. Can you trust that it is a good plan—a plan to prosper you and bring you a future and a hope? (Jeremiah 29:11) Will you trust Me?"*

Lord, You are the I AM. Thank you for Your patience in teaching me Your ways and leading me to a deeper level of trust in You.

Cindy Riker, mother of four, is involved with her husband at Teaching the Word Ministries and is also a Bible study facilitator at Change of Pace.

A Wave Of Blessing

"This is the day the Lord has made; let us rejoice and be glad in it."
Psalm 118:24

B eing new to the area, I didn't think much about it when I gave my customary wave to folks who were driving by during my regular walks around the community. After all, I had been doing it for years.

However, except for a few out-of-staters and truck drivers along the main highways, there wasn't much response other than blank stares. Some expressions indicated a precursor to an unhappy day at the office.

Over time, however, reactions seemed to change. Now, a couple years later, I not only receive return waves and smiles from a great majority of the people I see, but many now initiate the greeting. Since many of these folks seem to be ones I have not seen before, their cheerful responses, hopefully, have resulted from one person passing a friendly wave on to another.

I also have learned a couple lessons in my travels. When my waves and smiles are enthusiastic because I am having a great day, the return waves and smiles seem to have more expression. And, when I force myself to reach out on a down day, my frame of mind soon becomes brighter and I find myself being blessed.

Lord, help me to display Your joy to others today that they might see Your blessings in their lives. Amen

Casey Jones, an organization management and grants advisor, resides in Parkesburg. He also focuses on family ministries and those that come alongside the hurting.

A Long And Satisfying Life

"He who dwells in the shelter of the Most High will rest in the shadow of the Almighty." *Psalm 91:1*

Cancer! I received this sudden and piercing diagnosis the week of my 37th birthday. I immediately began to search the scriptures; "Father, what are You doing in this?" I'd learned to meditate in the scriptures and wait for the voice of God, but as I reviewed the many scriptural promises of healing, His voice seemed silent.

Healing was not unknown in our fellowship. Once after we prayed for a little girl with a tumor wrapped around her spine, the tumor simply popped out when the surgeon made his first incision!

Now as we waited on God I declared, "Lord You are my refuge and my fortress." I continued reading Psalm 91, searching for a word from my Heavenly Father: "Surely He will save you from the deadly pestilence." But God's voice was not there, so I read on: "no harm will befall you, no disaster will come near your tent." Still heaven was silent. "Where is Your promise for me, Lord?" I continued reading this marvelous Psalm, but through every verse, like Elijah on the mountain, God's presence was not there.

Then it happened; "Because he loves me," says the Lord, "I will rescue him: I will protect him, for he acknowledges my name." A still small voice whispered to my heart: "You love me, Lee, this promise is for you." I continued reading, "He will call upon me, and I will answer him; I will be with him in trouble, I will deliver him and honor him. With long life will I satisfy him and show him my salvation."

God spoke again, "My will is to take you through this, and my promise is a long and satisfying life." Today, I rejoice in fourteen years of cancer free fellowship with my Heavenly Father.

Father, I trust in You and embrace Your good plans for my life! I anticipate with joy the daily unveiling of Your satisfying purpose for me.

Lee Ritz is pastor of Hampden Mennonite Church in Reading and serves on the leadership team of Reading House of Prayer.

Seen And Unseen

"Now faith is being sure of what we hope for and certain of what we do not see." *Hebrews 11:1*

It was a difficult year. I never would have predicted the events that took place in my life. Fortunately, none of it caught God by surprise and thankfully, He can see what we cannot.

In February, I was told my position at a local ministry was being eliminated and I was no longer needed. I couldn't believe the words I was hearing. The shock and hurt piercing my heart was intense. Didn't the Lord remember how much I had sacrificed to join this ministry five and a half years earlier? But I had felt God leading, so I had followed.

It took over a year of unemployment, before God brought me to my next assignment. During that year, my morning times with the Lord became sweeter and longer. As I crossed paths with new people, new areas of ministry opened up for me. My faith increased and a peace and grace, despite my circumstances, surrounded me. God doesn't waste anything, does He?

He sees the whole picture of our lives from beginning to end, while we only see and experience one moment at a time. I've come to realize that is how it should be. If it wasn't that way, I know there are deep waters I wouldn't choose to walk through. If I knew about them, there would be blessings I would want early, before I would truly be ready to handle them. With God's help, we can truly be sure of what we hope for and certain of what we do not see.

Father, help me to trust in the sovereignty of Your ways, even when I don't understand. Give me the grace I need to trust in Your perfect, loving care for me in every circumstance You allow in my life. May Your will be done and not mine.

Deb Roggenbaum is a team member at Elexio, a business dedicated to advancing the gospel by developing websites for churches, ministries, and mission agencies (www.elexio.com).

Tomato Thief

"Love your enemies, do good to those who hate you." *Luke 6:27*

As a young teenager, this teaching of Jesus took on practical meaning. For many years I helped tend a produce market stand. One of our regular customers was a middle-aged woman who bought a few tomatoes every week. She became my "enemy" as each week I listened to her complain while she aggressively sorted through the pile of home-grown tomatoes, squeezing each one firmly enough to bruise.

One Saturday, my "tomato enemy" once again began sorting through the beautiful quantity of tomatoes. I waited on her grudgingly, fuming as I watched her deliberately squeeze each one. My attitude wasn't helped as I witnessed her steal two tomatoes, dropping them into her basket. Needless to say, I was angry, but I finally had the opportunity for vengeance!

I quickly informed the owner. I wasn't prepared for his reply. He instructed me to get a large paper sack, fill it with the nicest tomatoes, and give them to her freely. Furthermore, tell her she doesn't need to steal any of them. If she can't pay, we will gladly supply her, free of charge, all the tomatoes she needs.

I did what I was told, even though I wanted to retaliate and serve justice. But that act of kindness did something for us both; it changed our hearts. In the ensuing weeks I developed a strange friendship with my new "friend" as I learned to know her name and that she was a single mom struggling to raise a handicapped son.

Could it be that our witness for Jesus would win the world if we all just showed a little more kindness to those difficult people in our lives? If we desire to win souls for Christ, it will only happen by melting their hearts with kindness not hammering them with revenge.

Lord Jesus, in Your loving kindness You have taken me off the judgment seat and put me on the mercy seat. Help me today to love my enemies. Amen

Wesley D. Siegrist pastors Erb Mennonite Church, Lititz.

Photo by Mark Van Scyoc

GAP
TOWN CLOCK

September

An Open Heart

"May the favor of the Lord our God rest upon us; establish the work of our hands for us—yes, establish the work of our hands."
Psalm 90:17

The date was May 18, 2005, and I had hit a low point. I was tired of pouring into people in our neighborhood and seeing little fruit for my labor…tired of my own feeble efforts to advance God's Kingdom…and frustrated at my own ability to "love my neighbor sincerely."

I remember crying out to God in my journal, wanting to quit…wanting to move my family out of the neighborhood where we lived, in southwest Lancaster City. The vision had been clear in the year 2000 when we moved in…but now I needed a fresh word, another affirmation that we were where God wanted us.

As I was reading Psalm 90, the whisper of the Lord came, "*Jennie, keep the door of your heart open.*" I weep even now as I write this, because it was the word that my spirit needed to hear at that moment. To me, it meant to keep the door of my heart open, to trust that the "end of the story" had not been written; and with the Lord establishing the work of our hands, there were still more chapters of hope that He wanted to write. The part that I needed to embrace was "faith" to keep my heart open and to keep walking forward.

That was two years ago, and although there have been some times of discouragement, I feel like there is a freshness to live and minister in the neighborhood where God has placed us. We fixed up a more permanent home on our street, and it doesn't seem like God will move us anytime soon!

How thankful I am Father that You give us what we need and that You establish the work of our hands.

Jennie Groff lives with her husband and four children in Lancaster City where they help to give leadership to an emerging network of house churches whose focus is reaching those that don't yet know Jesus.

Look Up

"The heavens declare the glory of God; the skies proclaim the work of His hands." *Psalm 19:1*

Relax. Having completed the creation of earth, water, and mankind in seven days, God is still in control. Individuals are prone to ask the centuries old question, "Where in the world is God?" Especially in light of constant disappointments. People, observing the steady rhythm of earthly suffering, refuse to believe that a Royal King, an all-loving Creator is still interacting with His creation. This is an understandable sentiment. Children are left unprotected; wars ravage brothers, sisters, mothers, and fathers; the desire for more money controls our minds and distorts our realities; and people die daily. Disconnection catches us all like a transparent spider web trapping its prey day in and day out. Did the stairway to heaven collapse?

Act. Move towards the clear message of Jesus Christ's eternal and complete work of salvation for you. Know God by daily breaking through the traps of distraction and discontentment. Find the path lit by His Word; spend time every day nourishing your empty soul with the fruit of absolute truth. You will never be the same. Purify your heart, and you will see the traces of His presence everywhere. Know God. See God. Feel God. He is everywhere; He is in the falling snowflake, the sudden smile from a baby, the soft touch of a gentle hand, eye contact with someone who really knows you.

Look. Move closer to simplicity, stillness, and connection with God and others. The Creator's life force will connect with yours. Slow down to breathe in the mighty power of God. It will come as a still small voice calling your name and revealing His nature, love, and glory to you. Imagine being the treasured work of the Creator of the universe, the work of His holy hands.

All is well; rejoice in the eternal hope that is God. Amen

Joanne Stauffer is an English Professor at Lancaster Bible College, Lancaster. She watches the skies proclaim the glory of God from her Willow Bend Farm neighborhood with her husband, Gary, and her daughters, Angela and Evelyn.

Good Gifts

"Every good gift and every perfect gift is from above, and comes down from the Father of Lights, with whom there is no variation or shadow of turning." *James 1:17*

Sometimes it's easier to see and focus on the big events or extraordinary incidents and I forget the "God Story" that is mine every day. God is so amazing that even though He is the creator of all that I see, He is my Father. He knows and cares about everything in my life. He is the one who gives all good gifts and who showers me with blessing upon blessing. He is the one who is constantly making Himself known in great big, obvious ways but also in small day-to-day ways that I often overlook and take for granted.

I've been considering the "God Story" of my everyday life…

I have the gift of life just to wake up in the morning.

I have the gift of sight to see the color and beauty around me

I have the gift of hearing to listen to the sounds of nature.

I have the gift of health and strength to breathe and move and experience God's creation.

I have the gift of the Holy Spirit. He is always with me giving wisdom and discernment and direction.

I have the gift of the Word. It is always true, always certain, always sure.

I have the gift of family and friends. When times are difficult, I have support; there is someone to listen and pray. When things are going well, I have someone to stand with me, someone to rejoice with me.

If I will look and listen, I will see and hear and experience a "God Story" every day.

Father, thank you for Your good and perfect gifts. Thank you for Your heart toward me. Thank you for demonstrating Your presence and Your love every day in my life.

Lauren Charles is a writer and business owner serving in prison ministry in Lancaster.

Seeking God First

"Yet at the same time many even among the leaders believed in him. But… they would not confess their faith for fear they would be put out of the synagogue; for they loved praise from men more than praise from God." *John 12: 42–43*

Normally a very outgoing and social person, I was given a "spiritual wake-up call" a number of years ago when I found myself pulling away from people and ministry opportunities. After years of outreach to our neighbors, God was on the move. So why was I ready to relocate to a cabin in the mountains never to be seen again? The answer came when a friend said, "Teresa, you need to get away with God and ask Him why it's so hard for you to say no." I knew what she meant. People would call for counsel, stop in, or ask for help and without much thought or prayer my answer was usually yes. I was on the verge of burnout. As I got away, the Lord led me to the above verses and it was like an arrow to my heart. I couldn't say no because the fear of man was guiding my life not the fear of God. I wanted "people approval" rather than "God approval".

So began my journey to a life of more healthy boundaries and seeking God first *before* saying yes. Am I still busy? Yes, but now there is a God-directed order to all I do and abundant joy as I walk with people. What freedom it has brought to me and my family! Sure, there have been bumps along the way. But what a life of peace is available to us as God-followers when we seek God first in all we do and look to Him alone for our affirmation.

Lord, You know how easy it is for me to look to others for approval. Help me, God. Help me desire Your praise, to know You are pleased with me, above any other praise this world or others have to offer.

Teresa Groff serves in various ways at The Door Christian Fellowship where her husband, Dave, is pastor.

God's Grace

"For the grace of God that brings salvation has appeared to all men."
Titus 2:11

I was ministering with several people in the front of the church after the Sunday morning service. A mother approached me and said her son would like to speak to me. It was very typical to find friends in the center aisle sharing what God was doing in their lives. Her son, being handicapped and in a wheel chair, was at the back of the sanctuary. As I worked my way toward the son, he saw me coming and nearly leaped from his wheelchair. Being overjoyed, he couldn't speak and his mother told me he had received Jesus during the past week and desired to be baptized. Our church doesn't have a baptistery so I made arrangements at a nearby retirement village pool two weeks later for his baptism.

Baptism is a time of celebration and this Sunday afternoon many from the church were present. The manager from the retirement village met me and said the policy did not allow handicapped persons in the pool. I explained that the father would go in the pool with his son and that the boy enjoys water. She gave permission to proceed. As we baptized the boy, there was a peace and joy in the room like I have never experienced before. I remember as the boy came out of the water how his whole face and body glowed with a joy that seemed heavenly.

It was only a few days later he developed a fever. A doctor visit confirmed an infection and we as a church turned to prayer calling on God for healing. God had prepared another saint to meet his Maker in glory.

As a pastor, I thank the Lord for opening my eyes in time to see how His hand works and to see the saving grace only He can give.

God, may You continue to open my eyes to Your hand that is preparing the Church as a bride to meet her Maker.

Pastor Glenn Hoover, along with his wife, Ginny, gives leadership to Carpenter Community Church, Talmage.

Tea Party

"But thanks be to God who always leads us in His triumph in Christ, and manifests through us the sweet aroma of the knowledge of Him in every place." *2 Corinthians 2:14*

"Now we have received, not the spirit of the world, but the Spirit who is from God, that we might know the things freely given to us by God, which things we also speak, not in words taught by human wisdom, but in those taught by the Spirit, combining spiritual thoughts with spiritual words." *1 Corinthians 2:12–13*

The sweet fragrance of tea filled the room as we sat at the table waiting to begin our tea party. In walked Marty (not her real name), with her Bible, insisting that we have devotions. She opened it to page one hundred and two and wanted me to read. I heard myself saying, "Sure, we can have devotions with our tea. That's a good idea!" On the inside I was crying out, "Come, Holy Spirit! Show me what You have here in Leviticus that will minister life to these dear friends."

I don't remember the lesson He had for my friends, but I do remember that He gave a beautiful life application that was perfect for what we were experiencing that day. The lesson for me that day was loud and clear: "Call to Me, and I will answer you, and I will tell you great and mighty things, which you do not know (Jeremiah 33:3)."

Holy Spirit, thank you for Your faithfulness! Father, Your plans and Your ways are so good. Help me to lay aside my agenda today. I want to take time for tea with You, to listen for Your voice and follow Your direction as I go through this day. May I be a vessel filled with Your aroma for all You bring my way today. Amen

Liz Ingold works for Friendship Community and is involved with prayer ministry at Petra Christian Fellowship.

Spiritual Stall Cleaning

"Where there are no oxen, the manger is empty, but from the strength of an ox comes an abundant harvest." *Proverbs 14:4*

I grew up on a farm and spent plenty of hours doing less than pleasant tasks like cleaning out the cattle stalls. Isn't it great how at times the Bible is so blunt about practical aspects of life and at the same time so clear about the spiritual truth?

Have you ever thought of yourself as an "ox"? If we're living in God's barn and working for Him, we have to allow Him to clean out our garbage. Our lives have stuff in them that we need to allow Him to remove in order for us to be healthy and useful oxen. Things get pretty messy before a harvest can be brought in. We must be willing to let go of the personal agendas, ungodly beliefs, false comforts and idols that end up causing a spiritual separation from God.

The following scenario is far too common: a person makes a decision to follow Christ. Because of subtle pressure from fellow believers to over-emphasize appearance and religious activity, he or she ends up only dealing with the symptoms of sin rather than the roots. Masks and defense mechanisms gradually lose their ability to contain the brokenness of the inner person. Fear of losing control keeps them from being honest with themselves and sometimes a legitimate fear of being rejected by other believers prohibits sharing their pain with anyone who can help.

As the Church, we need to become a safer place for the refuse of our barn to be dealt with, and this can only happen when we are willing to individually clean our own stall (1 Peter 4:17; Matthew 5:20-22; Luke 6:45).

Lord, grant me the willingness to face the unpleasant task of allowing You to expose stuff in my life that needs to be dealt with and purged. I pray with David from Psalm 51, "Create in me a pure heart...."

Dr. Edward Hersh, provides counseling and healing prayer ministry to individuals and families, trains lay counselors here and abroad and helps leaders receive spiritual renewal.

Good News In China

"Jesus looked at them and said, 'With man, this is impossible, but with God all things are possible.'" *Matthew 19:26*

It was a leisurely Sunday afternoon in south central China. A telephone call had let us know that two young teens were coming to visit my hosts for several hours. The decision came that their own children had not seen *The Passion of Christ* and this would be a good time to watch and discuss it. They arrived on time; two fifteen year olds, male and female, intellectually gifted and actively academically consumed. We visited a short time and then all settled to watch the movie.

I sat next to Rebecca (her English name). She was so repulsed at the inhumanity of man to Jesus. At one point she said, "I do not understand some things about your culture." I had a sense that she had questions in her heart. When the movie was over, I simply leaned toward her and asked if she would like to go to my room to talk. She immediately stood up to go. We walked to my room and sat on my bed. I found myself telling Rebecca how she needed to recognize the love in the story. At one point I said, "It is very important for you to understand this. I think I should get someone to interpret for us."

She looked steadily into my eyes and said, "Oh, no Diana, I stay with you. You are speaking slowly and I understand every word you say!"

I said, "God loves you, Rebecca." There was a stunned silence and her small eyes widened in absolute amazement. "GOD loves me?" The good news went forth and was received.

Father, thank you that salvation belongs to You alone. Thank you that the power of Your love and the gift of Jesus not only transcends geography, culture, race, religion and language, but our own weaknesses, inabilities and doubts. Continue to open opportunities to share with others and perform the impossible in whatever way You choose.

Diana Oliphant is a credentialed minister with Teaching The Word Ministries serving with a heart for the region and the nations.

Unity

"...I pray also for those who will believe in me through their message, that all of them may be one, Father, just as you are in me and I am in you." *John 17:20–21*

Within a year's span, my husband and I hosted a child from the Fresh Air Fund, who came from Queens, New York, and a foreign exchange student from Thailand. As you can imagine, the two girls were completely different. They both came from totally different backgrounds and cultures. That meant they each had their own unique personality and also included worshiping God in their own way.

There was a point when we went through a rough time trying to adjust to one of the girls' way of worship. It was completely different than our own. It eventually got all of us frustrated. We came to the conclusion that while she was here living with us, she would attend our church. And when she returned home, she could go back to her own unique way of worshiping God.

All of us were worshipping the same God, but we each had our different ways of doing it. And those little differences caused some friction. But isn't it great to know, that when we get to heaven, all those little differences will disappear. Every one of us will be worshiping the God of all creation in one accord. Praise God!

Lord, continue to make all believers one in You. Help us not to dwell on our denominational differences. May we all serve You together. Amen

Jennifer Paules-Kanode is a DJ for WJTL Radio.

North South East And West

"..that they may be one, just as We are one; I in them and You in Me, that they may be perfected in unity, so that the world may know that You sent Me...." *John 17:22–23*

I n September 2007, hundreds of Christians gathered at the Clipper Stadium for a Weekend of Prayer, to cry out with one voice for the transformation of our region.

Weaving worship and prayer together, we prayed through the very significant themes of 2 Chronicles 7:14, under the leadership of seven different worship teams, prayer leaders and groups of elders and inter- cessors from a variety of churches.

I had the privilege of being the prayer leader on one of the sets and as I cried out for the Wind of the Holy Spirit to blow across our county, I noticed a flag to my right blowing towards the North and at the same time a flag to my left blowing towards the East. With great excitement, I pointed this out to the crowd and prayed through another Scripture. When I looked up again, the flag that had been caught in a Northerly wind was flying Southward and the flag blowing towards the East was now blowing Westward.

I was overjoyed and thanked the Lord, with those gathered, that His Holy Spirit was surly blowing across Lancaster County. Never have I felt such a tangible sense of His presence in my life. It was as if a thick cloud descended upon us.

The Lord longs for us to be one. He wouldn't have prayed for it if it wasn't possible. He was smiling down upon us as we gathered, and I believe there's more to come.

Oh Jesus, this supernatural display of Your presence was the result of us walking together as one, and proclaiming with one voice "You are Lord!" Please lead us into the unity that will let the world know that You were indeed sent. Amen

Kathi Wilson and her husband, Mark, co-authors of *Tired of Playing Church* and co-founders of Body Life Ministries, are members of Ephrata Community Church.

Thorns

"You will show me the way of life..."
Psalm 16:11 (New Living Translation)

Did you ever prune a bush, which has, as a part of its beauty... things called "thorns?" Did you ever wonder why God added them to the structure of each branch? I know that a very steady hand, a good eye, and a good pruning tool is needed whenever you're working with thorns...gloves may be recommended too.

My mother's lingering illness was a thorn that had become a constant reminder of its pricking, piercing nature. Somehow, this thorn wedged itself deeply within my heart of flesh. I had not yet discovered that I needed to know about the right tools.

Small droplets of dismay seeped forth within me. Many new issues, new concerns...new feelings of fear pricked me. I cried out, "Help me, Father, to see with Your eyes into this new garden I'm now tending. Mother has been so warm and gentle...ever rich with gems of truth whenever we would share about You. Her mind is now a garden full of thorns. Help me, Father, to be Your gentle tool of love ever flowing afresh over her mind, body, and spirit. Help me learn to use Your tools wisely, equipping me to attend her garden of thorns now..." and so He did!

As He showed me "the path of life" through Mother's garden, the sunlight of His love healed my woundedness, ever wrapping us in the sweetness of His peace once again.

Lord, Thank you for showing me the path of life. Help me to always walk that path to Your healing and peace.

Elta Seaman is a homemaker, grandmother, and holds a leadership role for Women of Faith, Ono U.M. Church, Ono.

The Spider And The Fly

"Above all things have intense and unfailing love for one another, for love covers a multitude of sins [forgives and disregards the offenses of others]." *1 Peter 4:8 (Amplified Bible)*

Remember the childhood poem of the spider and the fly? "Will you walk into my parlor?" said the spider to the fly; "Tis the prettiest little parlor that ever you may spy. The way into my parlor is up a winding stair, and I have many curious things to show when you are there." "Oh no, no" said the little fly; "to ask me is in vain, for who goes up your winding stair can ne'er come down again."

There is more than a poem here. There is a deep and profound truth. The spider web may signify *offenses*. Offenses ensnare us. Jesus said that it was impossible that "no offenses would come." So shouldn't we be watching?

Trespass is translated *offense*. *Sin* is translated *offense*. In Vine Expository Dictionary, the word "offense" is the Greek word "Skandalon." *Skandalon* refers to the name of the part of a trap to which the bait is attached, hence the trap or snare itself. I read another definition of offense that registered in my spirit (no *offense* to Vine!): *Offense is our emotional response to a real or imaginary injustice or indignation. It is the way we react or respond when we feel we have been unfairly treated.*

Jesus said that in the last days, it would be offenses that cause the hearts of people to turn cold. No matter how much it hurts, no matter what it costs, we had better deal with the offenses in our lives.

In this childhood poem, the fly resists all temptations, but one—flattery ("Come hither, hither, pretty Fly, with the pearl and silver wing")—and goes to her demise.

The spider will invite us several times a day (if not an hour) into its parlor. The only way to avoid the spider's web is to forgive. Let go of the offense.

Jesus, I confess my sin of unforgiveness. I choose to forgive and release those who have hurt me. Above all things, give me an intense and unfailing love for others that will forgive and disregard the offenses of others.

Sharon Weaver serves with Reading DOVE Ministry Center.

Feeding Jesus

"For I was hungry and you gave me something to eat, I was thirsty and you gave me something to drink, I was a stranger and you invited me in, I needed clothes and you clothed me, I was sick and you looked after me, I was in prison and you came to visit me."
Matthew 25:35–36

When fall rolls around so does the season of local fairs and carnivals. Carnival trucks drive into town, and the streets are closed for a week of fun and activities.

Not much thought is given to these carnival folks. Some of them sleep in campgrounds, cheap motels or even in their trucks. They eat mostly fast food and have their own nomadic community. But we don't pay much attention to them. They seem strange and different to choose this kind of life.

Someone in our church decided to reach out to them and to show the love of Jesus in a practical way. A group of carnival workers was staying at a local campground so some women cooked a hot lunch and took it to them. The response was amazingly positive. They sat around the table and talked about their lives and families. They were hungry, not just for food, but for people who would treat them as normal folks and love them. They were open to receive prayer.

These ladies were so blessed they decided to make them another meal late at night, which is their big meal of the day. So at 10:30 they took seventy hot meals to the carnival workers and gave them a taste of the love of Jesus. We fed Jesus that night.

Father, draw us out of our comfort zones and help us see people the way You do. Help us touch their lives and experience Your love in practical ways. Show me someone today whom I can minister Your love to.

Lester Zimmerman is pastor of Petra Christian Fellowship, Apostolic Leader of the Hopewell Network of Churches and council member of the Regional Church of Lancaster County.

Be Still

"Be still and know that I am God...." *Psalm 46:10*

Surgery on my foot forced me to sit more than normal for about two months. The time passed with ease at first as I enjoy reading and watching movies. But after a while, everything annoyed me—the cast, the pain, and the options I did not have at the time.

Then I read this quote from Harold Kushner: "Some blessings will be ours only if we stop chasing after them and let them come to us, like the butterfly that eludes our grasp when we try to catch it, but comes to perch on our shoulder when we stop chasing it and sit still."

I want to catch butterflies of blessings so I pursued learning about being still. I meditated on the writings from centuries ago in the book of Psalms: "Be still and know that I am God.*"* Other translations from the original Hebrew say "Cease striving and know that I am God. Let me and be still, and know [recognize and understand] that I am God."

Cease striving and let be … those words spoke to me. Yes, the time was still long, but I chose to quit allowing the annoyances to rule my days. I quit striving to change what I could not change and instead focused on changing my attitude. I looked for butterflies to catch–more time in prayer, reading to my son, sending cards, making phone calls and long conversations with family and friends. With time, it blessed me to realize I was also catching some other butterflies. Butterflies of truth, of compassion for others, of love and a deeper connection with God.

God, help me to remember to take the time to be still and know that You are God.

Janet Oberholtzer, wife as well as the mother of three teenage boys, serves as associate director for Women of Hope at Hopewell Christian Fellowship.

Glorious Baptism

"For by one Spirit we were all baptized into one body; *whether Blacks or Whites, whether Spanish or English* and have all been made to drink into one Spirit."
(Paraphrased from 1 Corinthians 12:13)

What a glorious sunny afternoon it was as we gathered on the shores of the Schuylkill River in Reading, Pennsylvania. The church of Reading had come to celebrate the baptism of about forty new believers, some fresh off the streets from the RRTN's TRUCE outreach. Twelve pastors entered the river and teamed up to receive the believers, as hundreds stood along the shores to pray, sing, give encouragement, and welcome these new brothers and sisters into God's family.

What a joyous celebration as they came, children to gray-haired men, many nationalities, to receive one Spirit and enter one church! Prayers could be heard in Spanish, English, and heavenly languages as pastors joined together to declare the "old life" ended, and a "new life" in Christ begun. Then it was over, or was it? Someone asked, "Are there any others? Would you like to receive Christ today and be baptized right now?" With tears of joy, we watched as shoes came off, babies were transferred into willing arms, and six people walked into the waters to receive Christ for the first time! What a great privilege for my pastor friend, Angelo, and I to stand with a young woman, leading her in prayer and assuring her of the wondrous truth that her sins and her old life were about to be washed away, and she would rise from these waters a new creation in Christ!

Throughout that afternoon I had linked arms with Black, Spanish, and White pastors, men and women, as we watched hearts transformed before our very eyes! We were one, rejoicing to be a part of the church of Jesus Christ—from all nations!

Heavenly Father, what a privilege it is to be called Your children and be part of the Family of God all over the world!

Lee Ritz serves with the Reading Regional Transformation Network, leaders from all walks of life who worship, pray, and minister together for the glory of Jesus in Reading!

Seeking

"Anyone who comes to him must believe … that he rewards those who earnestly seek him." *Hebrews 11:6*

I walked along the bay when the tide and my energy level were at their lowest. After skipping lunch, I had spent a few hours in quiet reflection. Now, I was tired and having trouble staying focused.

Though my walk was slow, my sneakers sank deep in the exposed, smelly sand. I paused a second after stepping over a dead praying mantis. I realized that though I had seen a praying mantis before, I had never seen a dead one. I brushed gnats off my arm as a straggly plant forced me to walk out nearer to the water's edge. Doing this, I had to step over a water puddle that missed the receding flow of the tide. More loss, as this time a crab lay there dead.

My mind sluggishly talked to God about this. "Why is there so much loss and sadness? Why do I have to keep walking over it?" This felt too familiar…like the recent loss and sadness in my life. I was ready to call it quits, but a speck of resolve pushed me on. I wanted to get through this—both this walk and the unwanted circumstances in my life.

As I rounded a bend, I stopped. There was a burst of life as wild plants rambled through each other in a beautiful unkempt way: iris, hibiscus, and trumpet vine. Butterflies gracefully flitted about and a dragonfly's delicate wings shimmered as he paused on a leaf. Peace filled me as I allowed the beauty and creativity to soak deep within me. I found strength in the truth that continually seeking my Creator brought me to a place where I could see life and beauty around me, even though parts of the walk were difficult.

Spirit of God, help me to always see the life and beauty around me, no matter what my circumstances are.

Janet Oberholtzer, wife as well as the mother of three teenage boys, serves as associate director for Women of Hope at Hopewell Christian Fellowship.

I Don't Have To Be Strong

"Immediately there fell from his eyes something like scales, and he received his sight at once; and he arose and was baptized." *Acts 9:18*

It was an ordinary afternoon. I made a quick run to the post office to mail a present. As I was crossing the street, a distracted elderly woman struck me with her car. I remember flailing on the asphalt in pain crying out, "Lord, help me!" I had no idea just how far He'd take that request.

The doctor's report concluded two fractured vertebrae in my spine. I had to wear a hyperextension brace for three months round the clock. I was given orders not to bend at the waist or pick up anything that weighed more than three pounds. My family had to care for my needs. When the brace was removed, I began physical therapy to strengthen limp muscles. The road to recovery was long and painful.

However, it wasn't the physical pain that upset me as much as the emotional pain. Having been a single mother for a number of years, I was used to being strong and able. My skin was tough as leather and my perspective lofty. God embarked on a new project–deconstructing the high walls I'd built around my heart.

Many people said my accident was a tragedy, but I disagree. To me April 14, 2003, was a triumph. It's my spiritual birthday. For on that day God in His infinite mercy knocked me off my high horse. He removed the scales from my eyes so I could see who He is and who I'm not. No longer do I feel like I have to be strong. I now know when I'm leaning on Him I am most powerful!

Father, thank you for being my strength. You've taken the time to discipline me in my ignorance as You did Paul. Only when I'm humble do I have a glorious view of You. May I be a fully devoted servant in Your hands.

Lynn St.George, an aspiring author, serves as Youth Leader at Glad Tidings Church, West Lawn.

God's Word Became My Lifeline

"The Lord is good. In time of trouble He is the Place to go." *Nahum 1:7*

I felt numb, confused, and at my lowest. I was in a deep pit looking up at the bottom. I had waited at the school where our daughter attended, ready to pick her up, and after a long wait, it finally dawned on me that I was waiting in vain.

So we went home. All the rest of the children huddled together in silence. I don't know how I drove sensibly. I could not talk and had no appetite.

After the rest had gone to bed, I sat alone with my Bible. Looking for some comfort for my weary soul, I opened it at random. My eyes fell on Nahum 1:7. I read it slowly, then read it again. I grabbed onto it as my lifeline! Yes, I would run to Him for help.

And He held me, through that long week until our runaway daughter was found.

Lord, thank You that when we don't know where to turn, You are there. Your presence and strength sustain us. I love You.

Ruth Lehman attends ACTS Fellowship, and she loves God and loves people.

Dive Into His Word

"For God did not give us a spirit of timidity, but a spirit of power, of love and of self-discipline." *2 Timothy 1:7*

Reading the Bible every day has been a challenge for me over these past few years. Sitting down for a time of quiet conversation with God and reading His word takes discipline! I was ashamed of my laziness when God reminded me how eager I am to talk to my husband, how often I seek him out to share my thoughts and ideas, and yet I did not take that kind of time to be with my first love, my Lord and Savior.

But simply reading the words wasn't enough. I wanted *more*. I started writing in a prayer journal, sometimes twice a day. When I delved into word studies, the Bible revealed a depth that flipping through chapters just didn't provide.

I'm often given to fear and worrying so I wanted to see what God had to say about fear. One of my favorite verses is 2 Timothy 1:7. Doing a word study on *timidity*, *power*, *love* and *self-discipline* led me to write the following paraphrase:

For God did not give us a spirit of *cowardice* (an absence of courage or behavior that is cowardly) but a spirit of *mighty ability*, of the *deepest love there is* and of *self-control* (ability to control your own behavior, especially in terms of reactions and impulses).

Wow! God doesn't want me to live my life afraid of tomorrow or what may be just around the corner! He has given me a spirit that is able to do things in a mighty way, to be able to love with the deepest love there is and the ability to control how I react in every situation and circumstance.

God is so good!

Take the time to dig deeper into God's Word and see what He has given *you*, His beloved child.

Lord, thank you for Your word and how it speaks to me. May my relationship with You deepen and become richer every day.

Jennifer Hamilton is a word missionary. She is married to Jason and mother of three beautiful children. She attends Lancaster Evangelical Free Church in Lititz.

Get Your Eyes Fixed

"Therefore we do not lose heart. Though outwardly we are wasting away, yet inwardly we are being renewed day by day. For our light and momentary troubles are achieving for us an eternal glory that far outweighs them all. So we fix our eyes not on what is seen, but on what is unseen. For what is seen is temporary, but what is unseen is eternal." *2 Corinthians 4:16-18*

One day as I was praying, I felt the Lord told me to get my eyes fixed. This made a lot of sense since a few weeks before, I was told that I needed to have cataract surgery on both eyes. I didn't realize that the Lord was telling me; make a shift in my view of life.

A few weeks later, I began a very difficult and dark season of life. My daughter spent a week in the hospital and continued to be very ill for most of a year. In my circle of friends, there was leukemia, anorexia, and suicide. I was terrified, grief stricken, and exhausted. Things that had brought great satisfaction to my life, bible study, prayer, and worship, became joyless activities. Meanwhile I had my surgeries, a major church crisis, and then I broke my leg.

Paul's words to the Corinthians became both my experience and my hope. I knew I was hard pressed, but I trusted that I would not be crushed. I was perplexed, but fought off despair. I felt persecuted, but trusted that God would not abandon me. It was obvious that I was struck down, but I believed I would not be destroyed. I became aware, that in light of eternity, my entire life was "momentary" and "temporary" and I clung to the promise of an eternal glory. I was getting my eyes fixed.

Lord, remind me to look to You, the Author and Finisher of my faith. Help me to set my mind on things above rather than things on the earth.

Karen Boyd, a contributing editor of God Stories, also serves as an intercessor at Teaching the Word Ministries.

Dog Prayers

"...and after the fire a still, small voice."
1 Kings 19:12 (King James Version)

I have a friend who lives in the nation of Suriname, South America, named Jonathan. Recently, he went outside to feed his guard dogs. His newest dog, a Belgian Shepherd, was lying on the ground with its chain wrapped tightly around its neck, choked to death. Jonathan told me the dog was stiff, had flies all over it, was not breathing, and he found no heart beat. With sadness, he went to find his shovel in order to bury this expensive and newly acquired puppy.

Having retrieved the shovel, he heard a voice say, "Jonathan, pray for your dog to live again." Jonathan told himself, "That's crazy; I wouldn't pray for a dog...I have no faith for that." He walked back to his dog and heard the voice again saying, "Jonathan, pray for your dog to live."

He then recounted to me this chain of events, "I laid the shovel down and got on my knees beside the dog, all the while with doubts. I placed both of my hands upon the dog and prayed for life to re-enter this animal. Then, I couldn't believe what happened next. The dog began to shake violently like it was being shocked with electrical impulses. The dog's eyes opened and it began panting for breath. In amazement I leaned back and watched the dog jump up and begin running around my yard barking. And I began running around the yard behind the dog yelling praises to God!"

Hearing that still, small voice from within our spirit is crucial. As you walk through your day today, practice His presence by listening for His voice.

Father, in the midst of all the noise we filter through our minds today, may we discern Your voice clearly.

Steve Prokopchak serves on the apostolic council of DOVE Christian Fellowship International.

We Prayed—The Drought Ends

"If you believe, you will receive whatever you ask for in prayer."
Matthew 21:22

This past year I spent seven months studying at the Hillsong International Leadership College in Sydney, Australia, which is an affiliate of Hillsong Church. It was an incredible experience. Within the first few weeks of my time there, I quickly found out that Australia was and had been in a major drought for 5-8 years. It was a subject of conversation at church quite frequently, especially this past March to May when it got really bad. Hillsong Church decided to hold a "Mega-Prayer Night" to pray for certain pressing needs of the country and the world. So obviously they prayed for rain.

Within 36 hours of the prayer night, it started raining, and it rained at least once a day for the following 2 ½ weeks. It blew us away—although it is really not all that surprising when you consider the awesomeness of the God we serve.

He is the provider of all nations and all people. His love abounds beyond anything we know. Though we may not always understand His timing or His ways, we can stand firm in the promise that He will always do good to those who serve Him.

Lord, help us to pray with true faith, yet also understand that everything is in Your timing, and in Your way.

Jamie Groff is a worship and youth leader at DOVE Christian Fellowship, Westgate Celebration, Ephrata.

Devotion

"Be still and know that I am God…." *Psalm 46:10*

Through the years, I have learned many ways to have my personal devotion time. I was taught to write in my journal, read the Bible in a year, pick a devotional, say prayers and pray scriptures. The list goes on and on. All these are excellent ways of growing deeper in the Lord.

But I find in our busy society, practicing the presence of the Lord is quite hard for me. Recently, I was challenged to sit quietly and sense the presence of the Lord without an agenda. It was so good to clear my mind of all the clutter and feel His peace.

I was reminded of a time when I was in Bible School. The teacher asked us if we would be willing to meet with the Lord, whenever He chooses, even if it was the middle of the night. Not many days later, the Lord woke me saying, "I want to be with you." Unsure it was the Lord, I rolled over and went back to sleep. Twice more, He woke me saying the same thing. The third time, I remember thinking He was not going to wake me again if I go back to sleep. So I pulled myself out of bed, sat on the floor, and listened to Him. I was not disappointed. I remember just sitting there and drinking in God's love for me. It was a sweet time of fellowship.

So my challenge for us today is to still ourselves for a few minutes, sense the presence of the Lord, and enjoy Him. Then take that presence into our workday. Isn't it a privilege to be a child of God?

Dear Jesus, You are always with us whether we know it or not. Today we want to know Your Holy Spirit is with us each second of the day. We thank You Heavenly Daddy, for desiring to have a relationship with us.

Donna Van Scyoc serves on the leadership team of the School of Global Transformation, and attends DOVE Christian Fellowship, Westgate Celebration in Ephrata, PA.

A Dream

"...The days are at hand and the fulfillment of every vision."
Ezekiel 12:23 (Amplified Bible)

Early in my Christian walk, I began having a repetitive dream about my dream house. In the earlier dreams, the house was nothing more than a dilapidated mansion, filled with rooms in disrepair, with timbers, broken walls and tiles strewn across each living space. Yet each room also held a treasure of architectural possibilities. The grounds were immense, but overgrown and jungle-like.

As the years passed, marked by many challenges, disappointments, and some wonderful accomplishments, so did the construction and location of the house. Sometimes the changes departed sharply from the original vision!

The one thing that remained constant, however, was that in spite of all my efforts, I was never able to "close the deal." Each time I awoke from the dream frustrated, wondering what God was trying to tell me.

One day this year, the dream changed. Everything in the house was as it should be. Even the construction remaining was simply for growth. Each colorful room contained its own wonders. A grand veranda surrounded the house. As I signed the contract, the owner smiled and pointed out the window saying, "See, even the river is open and is flowing alongside the house again."

I awoke from the dream with a start. I knew the dream was finally over. That day we signed a contract on our church building, concluding a long and difficult search.

My dream spanned nearly thirty years of ministry and personal growth. It ended with the fulfilling of a personal dream and ministry vision. Some dreams take longer than expected to develop! God's timing is always perfect.

Lord, we thank You for finishing the good work that You have begun in us. Give us the courage to stand when our dreams and visions fade. Help us to see Your grace in all aspects of our lives.

Mary J. Buch is Senior Pastor of Breakout Ministries and serves on the Regional Council of the Regional Church of Lancaster County.

SEPTEMBER 25

Ask

"...how much more will your Father who is in heaven give good things to those who ask Him!" *Matthew 7:11*

"...You do not have, because you do not ask." *James 4:2*

We had just had a new dishwasher installed, replacing a failed one, and three weeks later our oven followed suit, flashing a fatal error code. The manual advised turning it off at the breaker box and then contacting a service center. I fooled with it trying everything I thought might get it working. My wife and I knew the drill–the service man comes out, pronounces it dead, and charges us eighty dollars. Then it would be off to shop for a new one. Hundreds of dollars later, we would be back to normal.

Since our house church meets on Thursday evenings, we often spend part of our Sunday mornings discussing the Bible and/or praying together. This Sunday we prayed for direction regarding this fresh challenge to our finances. As we prayed in the Spirit, I heard the Lord say, "Lay hands on it and I will direct you," so we knelt and did so. We prayed, "Lord this is Your oven. All we have is Yours." We asked Him to set it in order and declared that nothing is too hard for Him.

As we finished, I received clear directions to go to the breaker and turn it back on. As I returned I heard it beeping, and it displayed the same code as before. I reset it and then after a few seconds it began again. I sensed the Lord saying, "After the seventh reset, turn it on." I did and it started working as it had in the past. Hallelujah! How cool is that?

Father, we know from Your word that You care for even the small concerns of our lives and that You want us to bring our concerns to You. You have blessed us again, and we thank You sincerely for it. You are so kind Lord.

John Hughes serves as worship leader and elder, Gates of Praise House Church Network.

Boy, You Have Ugly Feet!

"As it is written, 'How beautiful are the feet of those who bring good news!'" *Romans 10:15b*

I used to attend a singles ministry called SCOPE (Single Christians in Outreach, Prayer and Encouragement) in Lancaster. While I was on the leadership team, it was suggested that we go on a short term mission trip. So, we went to Miami, Florida, to minister for a week with a missionary, Bill Iverson. He had a Christian Study Center in the heart of the Little Havana neighborhood. It was a great week of prayer and ministry as we learned, from Bill, about evangelism.

Part of the team stayed in the Iverson home during the week. We all ate meals together there as well. One rule for the home was that you had to remove your shoes at the door. One morning, while still a bit groggy, during breakfast, Bill came up to me as I waited in line to grab some cereal and said to me, "Kevin, you have some of the ugliest feet I have ever seen!" I am 6' 1" with size 12 feet, so I figured that Bill had a great grasp of the obvious. Then he added, "But you are here bringing the Good News to the people of Miami and that makes them the most beautiful feet in the world." I recognized that he was right.

How do your feet look? Are they old, tired, ugly and smelly? Or are you using them to carry you to share the Good News of Jesus Christ to those around you, or around the world. If so, they are prize winningly beautiful!

Lord, help my feet take me to where You want me to go and share what You want me to share in a lost and dying world.

Kevin Kirkpatrick is the pastor of Berean Bible Fellowship Church in Terre Hill, and a former street evangelist with the Pocket Testament League.

Divine Appointment In Darfur

"…be prepared to give an answer to everyone who asks you to give the reason for the hope that you have." *1 Peter 3:15*

My friend, Ibrahim, was privileged to visit a war-torn region of Sudan, "tagging along" with a humanitarian organization. The outcome of this trip, however, was quite different from what he expected.

From the capital city of Khartoum, they took a small aircraft to Darfur, then a UN helicopter into a Sudan Liberation Army-held territory. The SLA allows only UN aircrafts in their airspace, and the Sudanese army had cut off all road access into this region, so a UN helicopter was their only option for entry.

During an unexpected but divine appointment with the Islamic Sultan, the leader of the region, Ibrahim learned that he was sick and using medication. Before he was asked to pray for the Sultan, one of his men explained that they were reconsidering their relationship with the Arabs and with Islam as a religion. They would want a religion that respected their culture and did not look down on their dark skin.

Ibrahim asked the Sultan if he could lay hands on him and use the name of Jesus in prayer. He was in agreement. Ibrahim then prayed for his healing and the healing of the whole tribe.

The next morning as they were getting ready to board the helicopter, Ibrahim heard someone shouting his name: "Ibrahim, Ibrahim" He turned and saw the Sultan on horseback, galloping toward them. Ibrahim ran back just as he jumped off the horse.

He gave Ibrahim a big hug and then started stretching his legs and arms while shouting, "I am healed, I am healed."

You never know when you may meet another person and have an opportunity to pray with them a prayer that is specifically and unmistakably ordered by God. That's what a divine appointment is! Take the risk today that comes with walking by faith and become aware that God is setting up divine appointments with the people you meet today.

Lord, I don't want to miss one divine appointment You have for me today. Help me to be ready and willing to pray for others when You prompt me.

Larry Kreider is the International Director of DOVE Christian Fellowship International, Lititz, PA.

God Will Make A Way

"'For My thoughts are not your thoughts, neither are your ways My ways,' declares the Lord." *Isaiah 55:8*

In July 2003, my employer needed some volunteers to go and work in England for a month. When my manager asked me whether I wanted to go, I said I would not be able to since I was a single mom with two teenage children.

After my manager left my desk, I kept thinking about this offer. I really wanted to go. Then the thought went through my head, "If God wants me to go, He would work it out." So I went and added my name to the list. Needless to say, God wanted me to go. I did not even have a passport. God worked everything out. I found out on Tuesday that I was leaving the following Sunday. Everything was in order in time.

But when I found out who was in my group to go to England, I was not a happy camper. One particular woman really worked on my nerves. Four weeks in England meant being around her seven days a week. However, God knew what He was doing. Being with her for that much time, I got to know her better. I also better understood why she reacted the way she did. After we got back from England, we actually became friends and began doing things outside of work together.

This trip was a lot of firsts for me. Flying in a plane, riding a train and subway, and being out of the country were all first-time experiences. The last Sunday we were in England, we took the Eurostar and went to Paris for the day. I even got a ten-year passport for free. God sure blessed me while I was doing my employer a favor.

Lord, I'm so glad that Your ways and thoughts are not my ways and thoughts. You see the big picture and respond accordingly. Thank you for not always doing as I ask.

Julie Gehman serves on the Prayer and Ministry teams at Ephrata Community Church.

The Secret Weapon

"And we pray this in order that you may live a life worthy of the Lord and may please him in every way: bearing fruit in every good work, growing in the knowledge of God." *Colossians 1:10*

Some time back I had a deep concern for a friend who was spending time with the wrong crowd. So I gathered a few friends together who were willing to use a "secret weapon" to influence my friend to find good friends to hang out with. Within a short period of time of persistently using the weapon, the dubious friends moved on and my friend began to develop a whole new set of friends. He never even knew what had happened! Coincidental, you may ask? No, it was a direct result of the secret weapon.

Some years ago, I had the privilege of spending time in Korea and seeing 80,000 people in a stadium simultaneously using this "weapon" and changing their nation by its power. You guessed it! It is the mighty weapon of *prayer.*

We need to constantly pray and read the instruction manual, the Bible, and use the weapon according to its instruction. Prayerfully pour over the manual as though your life depends on it, for it truly does!

During the past few years, I have taken various trips to Brazil where thousands are coming to Christ. One Brazilian pastor told me that 10,000 new believers were baptized in one day. They are using their secret weapon of prayer. Prayer has changed their nation. Prayer will change us and our communities if we use this vital weapon the Lord has made available to us. Let's get serious about using the secret weapon of prayer!

Lord, teach me to use the secret weapon of prayer and to get to know the instruction manual for life—the Holy scriptures. My life depends on it!

Larry Kreider, author and speaker, serves on the executive team of the Regional Church of Lancaster County and as the International Director of DOVE Christian Fellowship International.

Strength For The Race

"The race is not to the swift, nor the battle to the strong…."
Ecclesiates 9:11

Some people feel the need to test their limits. I'm not one of them. I'm somewhat lazy by nature. So when a friend, a marathon runner, talked me into running a "little" 5K race with her, I surprised myself by saying, "Yes." After all, it was for a wonderful cause—a women's run for breast cancer.

But I must admit the immediate picture that flashed through my mind was of the possibility of losing about ten pounds and gaining well-formed athletic legs as I trained. Realistically, I'm of a certain age that actually physically obtaining that airbrushed-swim-suit-model-look is over for me, so I quickly abandoned that notion.

On my first week of training in muggy 100 degree summer weather, I almost gave up. The only aerobic activity I wanted at that point was the exercise of lifting a heavy book from the bookshelf, pacing myself as I walked over to a soft chair and plopping down in it carefully so I was in no danger of "hitting the wall." I could exercise my mind and receive a reader's high of secreted endorphins. How important, really, was it to experience a "runner's high?"

As of the time of this writing, I have three more weeks of training. I've worked up to running two and a half miles without fainting or throwing up, so I think I will make it without unduly taxing my respiratory and cardiovascular system.

Today's scripture encourages me. Not all races are won by strength or swiftness. God gives strength to the weak, and they, too, can take the prize. I have no confidence in myself, but with God…!

Lord, help me not to be hindered by obstacles or limits I impose in my life. You alone give me the strength for the victory in any area of my life.

Karen Ruiz is the editor of House to House Publications in Lititz.

October

A Quiet Nudge From The Lord

"To those who have been called, who are loved by God the Father and kept by Jesus Christ: mercy, peace and love be yours in abundance." *Jude 1:1-2*

One morning, I felt a strong urge to go look under the eaves of my attic bedroom. I was sitting at my desk enjoying time in the Word. I thought to myself, "I don't think I am just being distracted, I think this really is the Lord speaking to me. Besides, I've just showered and getting on my hands and knees to crawl into the dusty attic space is not something I would think to do myself!"

I decided to be obedient to this nudge, and discovered a large china set I had forgotten about. I decided to give it to my aunt who was looking for more dishes for her growing family. The timing was perfect.

My aunt had just written in her journal to God the day before about how hard it was giving up pretty things like dishes because of the twenty years she and her husband had spent on the mission field. When she heard that she would get a lovely set of dishes, she trembled with joy at hearing God speak in this specific way.

God loves to encourage us and affirm that He cares about the details of our lives. Not only was I encouraged to listen and hear further from God during my quiet times, God answered my aunt's hearts desire by showing her that He really does care.

Father, we thank you for caring for us. Open our ears to hear and eyes to see more ways to pass on those blessings and serve others in our family and community.

Sarah Sauder works as a graphic designer and serves as a small group leader at DOVE Christian Fellowship Westgate.

Precious Is His Blood

"He will rescue them from oppression and violence, for precious is their blood in his sight." *Psalm 72:14*

Upon being discharged from the military and a brand new husband, I was surprised to find out that I had failed an employment physical. At first I was told that I had a low red blood cell count. "No worries," I thought, "I'll just rest, take vitamins and eat well." Later, a lab technician informed me that it was not a red cell count problem, it was white cell depletion. Something was attacking my white cells and winning. With each blood test came more disheartening news—my count was getting lower and lower.

I was having trouble staying awake at work and simply had no energy. While only 21 years old, I felt like I was 100. My new bride, being a registered nurse, was very concerned. She knew, although she did not share with me, that this condition could be very serious and life-threatening.

Finally, the doctors determined that I was in need of a bone marrow test. The night before this test was to occur, I went forward for prayer at our local church in Virginia. The elders anointed me with oil (James 5:14) and prayed for healing. They prayed that the blood of Jesus would cleanse my blood.

The next day I endured the dreaded bone marrow test and awaited the results. With an anxious heart, my wife prayed in the waiting room. Praise God, the marrow was clean, and from that point each blood test revealed that my white cell count was steadily improving. While the blood disorder was never diagnosed, I was healed.

Do you need a miracle today? His blood was shed for your healing.

Father, thank you for Your Son and His shed blood. It not only purchased my salvation, but my healing as well.

Steve Prokopchak serves on DOVE Christian Fellowship International's Apostolic Council and is team leader for the DCFI Caribbean churches.

Consistent Christian Living

"For the unbelieving husband has been sanctified through his wife and the unbelieving wife has been sanctified through her believing husband. Otherwise your children would be unclean, but as it is, they are holy." *1 Corinthians 7:14*

This verse seems mysterious, since the entire force of the Gospel message tells us no person is saved merely by marriage to a Christian spouse, nor can children enter the Kingdom merely because a parent knows the Lord. God has no grandchildren.

But the key words 'sanctified' and 'holy' used here do not mean 'saved.' They mean *set apart* – placed in a position of privilege and special advantage. Family members of Christians dwell right at the threshold of the Kingdom of God. They are so close to a source of spiritual radioactivity, it is no surprise when they do absorb Christ-radiation in their souls!

In our congregation, a Jewish-born husband was married to a Christian wife for many years. He did not practice his Judaism. When he encountered a deep personal crisis, he turned to our pastors and Christian counselors for help. He soon made a very strong profession of faith in Christ.

Another man had long held the church at arms' length. His wife's quiet Christian witness was combined with remarkable evidence of Christ at work in their two zealous sons: one went to the mission field and the other was called to seminary. The father finally came to humbly seek Christ, stating that he was stunned to realize there was a crucial something he did not share with his beloved sons and wife.

Never discount the power of consistent Christian living within your family. Never stop praying for your unsaved relative. They may dwell right at the threshold of grace.

Thank You, Lord, by Your grace we stand for those in our homes who may not yet know You. Please lead them into Your family.

Dr. Michael A. Rogers is senior pastor at Westminster Presbyterian Church, Lancaster, and is heard on WDAC-FM's *The Westminster Pulpit*.

When God Cries Out

"A voice says, 'Cry out.' And I said, 'What shall I cry?'"
Isaiah 40:6

L isa knew she needed to talk to her co-worker, Kim. Every time, though, seemed like the wrong moment to approach the subject of faith. But, then again, Kim was just getting out of a messy divorce, and had told Lisa how depressed it had left her. Uncomfortable thoughts flashed through Lisa's head, "What if I say the wrong thing and make it worse?" "Should she leave it alone and trust God would provide someone else to meet Kim's need?"

The prophet, Isaiah, was faced with a similar situation. God told him to "cry out" to the Israelites. However, Isaiah was at a loss as to what to say. He replied, "What shall I cry?" The story goes on to describe how the Lord filled Isaiah's mouth with words.

God wanted someone to cry out, to have a voice for His people; someone to show them His heart. Likewise, the Lord wants us to "cry out" to the people He brings into our lives for a purpose. How many times have you heard Jesus telling you to "cry out"? Do we reason that voice away? Isaiah did not, and trusted that the Lord would provide him with every word He wanted him to say. It is the same for us. When our hearts are open, Christ will fill it with His voice.

Dear Lord, thank you for always being with me wherever I am. The best way I know how; my heart is open to Your purposes, ready and willing to be used for Your glory. Your love for me is perfect. Give me the words to say to show others Your matchless love. Amen

Mandy Satta is a student at Lancaster Bible College and Graduate School.

292   *God Stories 3*

The Narrow Gate And Path

"Enter through the narrow gate. For wide is the gate and broad is the road that leads to destruction, and many enter through it. But small is the gate and narrow the road that leads to life, and only a few find it."
Matthew 7:13-14

Recently, while waiting for a flight to Brazil at the Miami International Airport, I had plenty of time to watch people. The airport was filled with long security lines, and people hurrying everywhere to catch their flights to some destination. Faces seemed etched with varying degrees of anxiety and weariness as each traveler found their way through the maze of lines, counters, shuttle buses and boarding gates.

My focus shifted to the narrow security gate that carefully screened everyone wishing to board a plane, and I thought of the scripture about the narrow gate and path and the contrast between the two. It seems that the security gate at the airport, although narrow, comes with a constant long line of people while the gate in the Jesus story has few who utilize it.

Suddenly, it seemed so ironic that the heavily used gate leads to so many earthly destinations while the little used gate leads to an eternal destination. Suddenly, my heart was full of gratitude that I had found the narrow gate with an eternal destiny years ago.

I realized all over again how important it is that we who have found it, and point the way for others to find it also. Quietly I prayed, "Lord, use me to point others to the gate." A few days later, while preaching through a translator in a large city in Brazil, I was prompted to teach on the meaning of the narrow gate and path. And then as I had prayed, two young men found the gate and walked through it declaring, "I will follow Jesus." God had answered my prayer but also renewed my desire to work near the gate to bring others to Jesus.

Lord, use me today to point the way so that someone may find You and enter through the narrow gate that leads to life.

Glen Yoder is the pastor of Oasis Fellowship, Akron, and Director of Home Fellowship Leaders Int'l.

God's Plans Give Us Hope

"For I know the plans I have for you," declares the Lord, "plans to prosper you and not to harm you, plans to give you hope and a future." *Jeremiah 29:11*

My husband, Bill, and I sat in the cold doctor's office while the July sun baked the California earth outside. The doctor met my eyes and spoke the unthinkable: "The tumor is malignant." Stunned, I tried to imagine how cancer fit into the big plans we had made only two weeks prior—big, life-changing plans. And they were God's plans, too; I was certain of it. I stammered, "But…but we're moving to North Dakota in three weeks. My husband was accepted into a Ph.D. program there." The doctor congratulated Bill and scheduled my surgery for that Monday.

By itself, Bill's acceptance had been a shock. He had applied a year earlier and I had dismissed it as one of his quirky moments. After he phoned me at work to tell me the news, I drove home through the familiar California hills in a daze. Leave California? Bill wanted to earn his Ph.D. Was this my heavenly Father opening a door? "But…North Dakota, Lord! *North Dakota?*" I asked the blue expanse of sky outside my windshield. His answer came swiftly. A feeling of peace, profound and sure, settled over my spirit. "Okay, Lord. We'll go," I thought with a *gulp* and started a mental "To Do" list for the move.

"Go through cancer" was not on my list. But God's hand was in every circumstance. First, I sailed through major surgery, even with my diabetes. Then the doctors decided chemo wasn't needed. We were free to go! Home after surgery, I looked about weakly and wondered how we could be packed in one week. Early on moving day, friends came to help finish the packing and clean the house. By noon, our things were neatly stored in the U-Haul truck, with our car on a trailer behind. We left, amazed at what God had done.

Thank you for Your loving plan for me, Lord. Help me through the difficult times on the way.

Robin Archibald is a freelance writer who attends Grace Baptist Church of Millersville.

The Roasting Pan

"But the fruit of the Spirit is love, joy, peace, patience, kindness, goodness, faithfulness, gentleness and self-control...."
Galatians 5:22–23

In 1972, we bought Mom's birthday gifts early that year because she was sick with cancer. I still remember the store my dad took me to and exactly where I found her present. My dad pointed to a large black roasting pan on the bottom shelf and asked, "Do you think she'd like that one?" I excitedly picked it up because I knew without a doubt that it was exactly what she wanted. But eight days before her thirty-ninth birthday my mom died. I was devastated. In my nine-year-old mind I could only believe that she thought we'd forgotten her birthday and had not bought her anything. No one could convince me otherwise. Time went on, and my dad remarried a wonderful lady.

In 1985, I was engaged and was attending my third bridal shower! My second mother had come to each one and had given me very special gifts - never store-bought. She gave me my parents' wedding china at one shower and a boxful of memories at another. I was, therefore, somewhat surprised when I opened what I perceived to be a brand-new roasting pan. But then she shared the story about my mom. I had completely forgotten about the pan after thirteen years and was completely overwhelmed by her love and generosity at such a special time in my life.

I bought a gift for someone who would never receive it, and it was passed on to someone who would never use it, but who, instead, lovingly saved it and returned it to me. It is, by far, my favorite and most memorable gift. I look forward to one day passing it on to my daughter, Hannah.

Thank you, Lord, for giving me the privilege of being dearly loved by two mothers. I praise You that they both truly demonstrated the fruit of the Spirit in their lives.

Stephanie Eshleman serves with her husband, Kevin, at Ephrata Community Church.

OCTOBER 8

Being The Light And Sound Of The World

"In the same way, let your light shine before men, that they may see your good deeds and praise your Father in heaven." *Matthew 5:16*

Often times we talk about being a light in a world of darkness, and I have never felt this so literally until a few Sundays ago. It was a typical Sunday evening here in Fortaleza, Brazil, where my husband and I have been serving as DOVE missionaries for the past two years. We set up chairs on our outdoor basketball court under the stars of the night sky, when it's not in the heat of the day. We had just finished our first worship song when poof —all the lights, sound system, keyboard, everything went out. It was easy to see that the whole neighborhood was out of electricity. But that didn't stop us. We still had the guitar and drums. In the quietness of the night when people would normally have their TVs on to watch the soccer game or be at the bar drinking and listening to music, we filled the air with praises to God. What better way to spend 30 minutes without electricity!

What ways does Satan try to stop you from being a light or sound in the world? Does he try to "pull the plug" on you? Do you stand out from those around you because you have chosen to follow Christ? You can look for small, simple ways to let your light shine just like we did with our singing the night the lights went out in Fortaleza. Maybe that night nobody gave their life to Christ because of our singing, but the presence of God that night under the stars, gave all of us more power to do our Kingdom work.

Lord, help us to recognize the small ways we can be a light in the world. Don't let the electricity go out in my life today. Help me to be different than those around me.

Lyndell Thiessen has been serving with her husband, Bruce, in Fortaleza, Brazil, since September, 2005. Before moving to Brazil, they lived in Akron, and attended DOVE Westgate. Lyndell currently is involved in teaching English, leading groups of teenage girls, and playing on the worship team.

Mighty Warrior

"When the angel of the Lord appeared to Gideon, he said, 'The Lord is with you, mighty warrior.'" *Judges 6:12*

A t the time Gideon heard these words, he was not a mighty warrior. He was hiding from his enemies in a hole in the ground. But you see, God always looks at His children for what they will be, not what they are now. His biggest job is convincing them of what He already sees in them. God had already seen Gideon as a leader of others, not just some guy hiding in a hole in the ground.

I recall a time in my own life when I was attending a retreat for the men of the church I attended. I felt the Lord had impressed upon me that we should have an invitation for men to respond to. I went to the leader of the retreat and submitted to him what I believed God was speaking to me, asking him to consider an invitation. His response was as quick as it was startling. He said "I confirm that; I think that's a great idea. When I am finished speaking, I'll call you up and you can share what God has laid on your heart. Then you can pray for those that respond."

That wasn't exactly what I had in mind. I thought if the leader confirmed what I was sensing he would handle it. But God was saying, "The Lord is with you, mighty warrior." I did ask the men to respond and several did. God moved in an awesome way and men's lives were changed forever as a result. God used my feeble efforts and obedience to see some awesome things happen. In doing so, He built faith in me, beginning the call to ministry that He had placed upon my life.

God is looking at you today and He sees a mighty warrior. If you could see what He sees in you, you would be amazed.

God, grant me the faith to see myself through Your eyes and to take steps of faith, beyond my own abilities, so that Your glory will shine through me.

Deryl Hurst serves as an Executive Pastor at DOVE Westgate Celebration, Ephrata.

Jesus Loves The Little Children

"Let the little children come to me, and do not hinder them, for the Kingdom of God belongs to such as these." *Mark 10:14b*

The church I pastor has been ministering to children through our day camp program for forty years. When I arrived seven years ago, I immediately jumped in and helped as the teacher of the sixth grade class. During the week, I also make a Gospel presentation to the entire group of children from grades one through six. At the end of these presentations, I encourage the children who have followed along with the prayer of salvation to speak to their teachers or helpers so that we can follow up with them. In the past, we have seen anywhere from one or two to twenty responses to receive Jesus as their Savior.

This year was no different. Following the message, I again gave an invitation. Later, I asked our director if she knew of any responses. She had heard of two or three children who responded, but didn't know their names. The next day, I was privileged to speak to one of them.

I was eating lunch in the pavilion with some staff and a few sixth graders, when a little boy from the second grade class came up and asked to talk to me.

When I responded, "Sure, what do you want?" he proceeded to tell me that the day before, he had asked Jesus into his heart. My feet didn't touch the ground the rest of the day. That's what it's all about. I encourage all children's workers who tirelessly teach our children week after week to not grow weary in doing good. Because once one of these precious little ones tells you that, it makes your year. Don't think the ministry to children is a waste of time. It may pay dividends in the future.

Dear Lord, thank you for those precious little ones You find so special. Thank you for allowing us to lead them to our Savior.

Kevin Kirkpatrick is pastor of Berean Bible Fellowship Church in Terre Hill. He is the husband of Diane and sits on the Regional Church leadership council.

Forgive

"...forgiving one another, even as God in Christ forgave you."
Ephesians 4:32

In 1974, I married a man from Chile, South America. Two years later, our daughter was born in New York. In 1977, the three of us went to Chile to meet my in-laws and introduce our 14-month-old daughter. When our vacation was over, my husband remained in Chile without my consent. He never came back. In 1983, I received Jesus Christ as my personal Savior, and I remember forgiving my husband for abandoning me.

In 1997, twenty years later, while I was pastoring a church in Medellin, Colombia, a group of 34 pastors from Chile came to our city to participate in an international seminar for pastors and leaders. I hosted 14 of them in my house. On the second day, the Holy Spirit spoke to my spirit: "Marta, ask the pastors for forgiveness, because you hate Chilean men." I answered: "Holy Spirit, just open the opportunity to ask them for forgiveness."

That evening in September 1997, the pastors asked me to share my testimony. My heart started beating faster. I knew this was the opportunity to obey the Lord. In my testimony I got to the point where I knelt at their feet, and in the midst of the 14 pastors, said: "Pastors, the Holy Spirit has convicted me of sin against you. I hate Chilean men. Would you please forgive me for my sin?"

After prolonged silence, one of the pastors finally answered: "Marta, we Chilean men forgive you, but we also ask you to forgive us because we have hurt you too." They helped me stand, and all of them embraced me. We all wept. The Holy Spirit's presence was so thick and His anointing so strong that no words can describe that moment. I was filled with joy and great laughter filled the room. I was forgiven.

Lord Jesus, thank you for forgiving our sins.

Marta Estrada is an author, founder and director of Restoration of the Nations (a ministry under Harvest Field Ministries) and member of Petra Christian Fellowship in New Holland.

Mike

"Do not grow weary in doing good." *2 Thessalonians 3:13*

'll never forget the day that I went back to visit the institution for the mentally retarded—this time armed with an attorney so that I would be allowed to look at their records. (When the fellows were released into my care, almost no records accompanied them. I had no idea if they had any allergies to any foods or medications. I had little knowledge as to their family backgrounds—but knew that most of the fellows in my home were abandoned by their families.)

Finally, we were granted permission to look at the records of those I took into my group home—but only in the presence of the institutional record-keeping staff. We were not allowed to look at any papers unless *they* knew exactly what we were looking at. If we wanted to have copies, we'd be charged the ridiculous figure of $2.00 per page.

Mike was one of the last fellows that came to my home. He was twenty-one years old, and had been institutionalized most of his life. He was Deaf, legally blind, and stubborn! I imagine the institutional staff were glad to get rid of him. He had a knack for getting on one's nerves! He had an uncanny talent for flooding our upstairs kitchen when he became angry. He would "forget" to turn off the water faucet in the sink. But, back to the original story...

I always kind of wondered why Mike was so stubborn. In reading his records, I began to find out why. Not much was known about Mike's childhood, but what we found out was shocking. His parents split up, and eventually the courts had him committed to the institution. At the time he was committed, at about age six, Mike was still not toilet trained, nor could he walk. He was treated like some kind of animal—records indicated that he was fed under the table like a dog.

Attorneys at times can become hardened to life's situations. The attorney I asked to help me was different—I never saw an attorney cry before—right in the middle of reading Mike's records is when I saw big tears fall from the attorney's eyes and wash down his cheeks.

Mike is still in the group home—and doing well.

Lord, thank you that even "hardened attorneys" can be touched with compassion—because You have compassion.

Jim Schneck is a free-lance interpreter for the Deaf.

How Does A Jesus Follower Grow?

"I write to you, dear children, because your sins have been forgiven on account of His name. I write to you, fathers, because you have known Him who is from the beginning. I write to you, young men, because you have overcome the evil one. I write to you, dear children, because you have known the Father. I write to you, fathers, because you have known Him who is from the beginning. I write to you, young men, because you are strong, and the Word of God lives in you, and you have overcome the evil one." *1 John 2:13-14*

The apostle John identifies three levels of growth, maturity, understanding and experience within the lives of Jesus' followers: children who have come into the experience and revelation of forgiveness and have encountered the Father and the Son; young adults who are overcoming the devil and becoming strong in God's Word; mature adults who know their Heavenly Father and endeavor to help make the way clear for others to encounter Him and enter into His Kingdom.

At nineteen, I stopped running from God. I stopped believing the lie that God was going to wreck my life. I discovered that God will guide us into three levels of assurance. First, He is *for* us; second, He is *in* us; and third, He works *through* us. After receiving Jesus by faith, I started choosing to follow His way instead of going my way. As I detached myself from the world, I was led into consecration and sanctification. This does not happen overnight but is a long process.

The key is in discovering the root of our being. We begin to see not who we are, but who we are not. Only with Christ as the center of our lives can we become His true followers. He is our total righteousness. We are complete in Him.

Lord, I pray that You continue to lead me in the path of righteousness for Your name's sake.

Patrick Glennon is the Director of the National Christian Conference Center in Valley Forge.

Thank You!

"Rejoice always, pray without ceasing, in everything give thanks; for this is the will of God in Christ Jesus for you,"
1 Thessalonians 5:16-18

The year 2007 was a milestone year for my parents. They each turned seventy years old and were married for fifty years. Since they didn't want a party, I decided to surprise them with a "card shower" - informing people to visit, call, and/or send cards. I made several phone calls to solicit help.

A friend from their church responded, "Oh, I would feel honored to do this. Your parents are very special people." My Aunt Betty drove to some unlisted residences to obtain addresses.

A classmate of theirs said, "I'm so glad you're doing this shower. Giving you a list of names is the least I could do for your wonderful parents."

I called Dad's former workplace. The secretary emphasized, "*Please* make sure you include me!"

A lady with whom Mom played pinochle for almost fifty years responded, "Your parents mean so much to me! Your mom helped me through my divorce!"

My heart was thrilled to hear all these tributes to their generous character and reputation. These testimonies reminded me of Ray Boltz' song, *Thank You,* but thankfully they wouldn't have to wait until heaven to know how they have touched so many lives.

I thought of numerous times when other people took the time to listen to me, prepared a meal, gave me a hug of reassurance, offered words of encouragement, or gave a gift. Somehow the list of my "thank yous" in response falls far short. Don't let today go by without calling or writing someone to say, "thank you" for what they have done for you.

Heavenly Father, help me to continually have an "attitude of gratitude" and to offer my thanks to You, the giver of all gifts, and to others, the bearers of good gifts.

Tamalyn Jo (Heinbaugh) Heim, of Willow Street, is thankful to the Lord for her parents: for their legacy of giving her a good name and giving her the gift of caring for other people.

God Remembers Us

"To the One who remembered us in our low estate, His love endures forever." *Psalm 136:23*

"Mommy, mommy, mommy come see the rainbow!" Exclaimed my seven year old daughter as she excitedly ran into the house. When we went out to admire the sight together, we were amazed to find not one, but two rainbows adorning the sky.

Nine years later, on October 26, 2005 my daughter again ran into the house exclaiming with that same childlike enthusiasm, "mommy, mommy, mommy you have to come out and see this!" We ran back outside together and there it was, an arch of color adorning the blue sky with no hint of rain anywhere in sight. Once again, we stood in awe of God's handiwork.

Since this second occasion was around the same time of the year, I curiously looked back through my journal to find the exact date of the first. The following entry, dated October 26, 1996 was written three weeks after the death of my first husband and five days after the birth of our third child: *...You know how difficult it is to be opening sympathy cards along with congratulations cards and I thank You for the sign You gave me today that You will keep Your promises to me and that You are a faithful God. Lord, seeing two rainbows without any rain has given me the complete comfort in knowing You will provide for our needs and You truly will never leave us nor forsake us.*

It was nine years to the day! It was as though God was telling us, "I remember you."

He doesn't always give us rainbows but God is a God who sees us and remembers us. He remembers our times spent in the valley and those on the mountain top and through both He desires that we remember Him.

Father, we praise You for being a God who remembers. Lord, help us to remember You through both the good times and the bad.

Chris McNamara is the Director/Mentor Coordinator of New Mornings Reentry Services, an initiative of Life Transforming Ministries in Coatesville.

Am I A Blessing To My Boss?

"Everyone must submit himself to the governing authorities…Consequently, he who rebels against the authority is rebelling against what God has instituted, and those who do so will bring judgment on themselves." *Romans 13:1-2*

Going into this year's men's retreat, I felt I had complete victory in the weekend's subject: "Authority." I had read the books, listened to messages, and experienced church as well as business leadership. I considered myself the model servant at both work and church. I respected those in authority and was always open for correction and constructive criticism whenever necessary.

As God can only do, He found one area that I hadn't given over to Him. I had failed to look deep inside my heart where there was a part of me that was still a mess.

God brought back memories of me listening to the other employees bad mouth the boss and criticize him. I started agreeing with them, adding my own jabs. Why did I allow myself to gossip and criticize? Why had I never prayed for my boss or the success of his business? Right then I asked for prayer. When one of the other men prayed for me, I felt a release from condemnation and fear of others.

I've learned a valuable lesson—not to be proud of my victories, but to be proud of Him who has won the victory, as I humble myself before Him. I must always remember I am the Potter's work in progress, and He's not yet finished with this lump of clay.

Lord, help this lump of clay to be moldable to Your image. When I am proud, rebuke me. When I speak ill of someone, remind me to remove the log in my own eye first. Remind me that authority is from You; when I speak of authority, I speak of You. Bless my boss today and guide his steps each and every day. Bless all in authority and may they listen to Your voice and make wise decisions.

Rod Redcay, DOVE Westgate Celebration, Ephrata.

Follow The Master's Footsteps

"Greater love has no one than this, that one lay down his life for his friends." *John 15:13*

The idea of laying down my life is great in theory, but its certainly not my natural tendency. Human nature screams, "Save yourself!" But when Jesus taught about true discipleship, He said, "Whoever wishes to save his life shall lose it; but whoever loses his life for My sake shall find it" (Matthew 16:25).

I love His clarity! Recognizing the weakness of our flesh, He "spells out" the cost of discipleship so that it flies in the face of self-preservation. Just to begin this journey of discipleship, we must say "no" to ourselves. In a culture that says, "if it feels good, do it!" and "look out for number one!" the practice of denying ourselves is no small accomplishment.

We simply cannot do what He asks us to do without His influence upon our hearts. Without His empowering, we can't even attempt to follow in the master's footsteps.

This business of Jesus increasing and us decreasing is at the core of it all. Too often we think we've "got it' when we really only have the idea in our head. When the reality of God living His life through us renders us dead, it is no longer a theory but a truth indeed.

Realistically speaking, do we deny ourselves? Ever?

My heart longs to be made more like His. Am I able to say with joy, "not my will but Yours be done?" Have I ever tasted Gethsemane?

Oh Lord, I am tired of living my life in theory. Given to my natural inclinations I will choose to save myself—but Lord, I ask You to help me daily choose to deny my flesh and live only for You. Help me, my precious Savior. Thank you for Your patient instruction and constant care. For Your Kingdom and for Your glory, Amen.

Kathi Wilson and her husband, Mark, co-authors of *Tired of Playing Church* and co-founders of Body Life Ministries, are members of Ephrata Community Church.

You Can Teach An Old Dog New Tricks!

"And we, who with unveiled faces all reflect the Lord's glory, are being transformed into his likeness...." *2 Corinthians 3:18*

My parents divorced when I was just four, and until the late 1980s I rarely had contact with my father, Buddy Varner. Then in 1996, my 77-year-old dad, an avid motorcycle and race car fan, came roaring into my life. My dad was a rebel most of his days, and I am strong-willed, so to say that "sparks flew" is putting it mildly.

My dad was very volatile and critical; therefore, I never knew how he would react from one moment to the next. However, it is said that what is in us will come out when we're "bumped," and I found things coming out of me that were not pleasing to the Lord. So, God used my dad to show me areas in my life that needed repentance and change.

While God was working in my life to change me, He was also moving on my dad's heart. My home group had been praying for my dad for quite some time, and as soon as he moved to this area, they began to lovingly reach out to him. He soon began attending our small group and made a profession of faith.

On his birthday in 2006, I gave him a One-Year-Bible, and for the first time he showed a genuine interest in listening to the Bible. I read it to him in the evenings and personally witnessed God's Word transform his life. He became a humble, kind-hearted man who genuinely wanted to please others.

We finished reading the Bible at the end of October 2006, and Dad went home to be with the Lord two weeks later on November 14, 2006.

While changing my dad, God also changed me in many areas of my life. So two old dogs learned new tricks!

Thank you, Lord, for changing every one of us more and more into Your likeness each day.

Sandy Kirkpatrick attends DOVE Christian Fellowship Westgate, Ephrata.

Exceedingly Abundantly

"Now unto Him that is able to do exceedingly abundantly above all that we ask or imagine according to the power that is at work within us. Unto Him be the glory in the church by Christ Jesus throughout all ages, world without end." *Ephesians 3:20-21*

Thirteen years ago my husband, Jay, and I eagerly anticipated the birth of our first child. Within minutes of Natasha's birth, we were told that she had Down syndrome. We dedicated her to the Lord and claimed the above verse for her life. We thanked God for our large supportive families and our wonderful church. The years followed with early intervention and later, elementary school. Last spring the educational team voiced concern about transition to middle school. Our daughter was very shy in larger settings and spoke very little or very quietly. I was very anxious and mentioned this to a friend. She asked if I didn't have supportive people that I could ask to pray about this.

You know how it is easier to pray for someone else than to ask for prayer yourself? Well, I humbled myself and sent out an extensive email letter requesting prayer and a miracle that Natasha would not only transition well to a new school, but become more social.

The school year started, and over the first weeks of school, we were told by classmates and teachers who knew her in elementary school that she was talking more loudly, was more social and she told us that she loved middle school.

Our middle child commented recently that it's like a miracle how much more outgoing her sister is. We know that we have many challenges ahead, but we want to give God credit when we clearly see His hand in our situations.

God, thank you for others who can walk with us through life's challenges. Help us to be quick to ask for prayer and support and quick to thank you for Your faithfulness in our lives.

Gloria Martin, of Ephrata, is a mother of three and part-time Registered Nurse. She and her family attend Lancaster Evangelical Free Church.

OCTOBER 20

Great is Thy Faithfulness

"Surely goodness and love will follow me all the days of my life, and I will dwell in the house of the Lord forever." *Psalm 23:6*

"**A**re you a Christian?" she asked a bit tentatively. Not too surprising a question, really, considering the previous ten minutes of our conversation regarding my total frustration. My mom had flown 3,000 miles to be present at my wedding. Not a monumental feat for most people, but for her, critically ill with lung and liver cancer, this was indeed a major feat. Greeting her at the Philadelphia airport, her frailness had been painfully evident. Now just two weeks later, she lay close to death. During her last days she moved quickly from brief periods of awareness to long conversations with her sister who had passed on 15 years earlier. "Esther, stop nagging! I'll come when I'm good and ready!" Occasionally she would sing a line or two from *Take Me Out to the Ballgame*. That still makes me smile.

This young hospice nurse and I were standing on either side of Mom's bed, discussing the dark cloth I had carefully tucked over the curtain rod. Mom's arm was thrown across her eyes as if blinded by the mere shadows now edging the window. "She keeps shielding her eyes from the sunlight no matter how dark I make the window," I sighed.

The nurse began sharing experiences she had with other Christians who were anticipating their journey into Eternity. "That light is His light; it's not the sun that is lighting her world now. He's beckoning her forward with His light, and Esther is with Him to encourage your mom to join them." The nurse's visit ended with her encouraging us to tell Mom that she was "free to go and be with Esther," that we would be "OK." Within hours, Mom quietly left her earthly home to be with her Savior.

How amazingly wonderful that God, in His infinite love and understanding, sent just the right nurse to our home to ease not only my mom's *forward journey*, but to ease our journey of *letting go*. What magnificent gifts He imparted to my family—the gift of knowledge, the gift of certainty, the gift of peace that only He can give. Our view of death was forever changed that day!

Great is thy faithfulness, O God my Father. Amen!

Janet Medrow Assistant to the Director, National Christian Conference Center, Valley Forge. Deacon, Great Valley Presbyterian Church, Malvern.

Be Like Jesus

"The Word became flesh and made his dwelling among us…"
John 1:14

I knew with one glance that Charles was not himself today. He had been here at the Mission for almost eight months—highly articulate, educated, lost everything in a series of inappropriate relationships. I often thought of Charles as a non-traditional resident. And yet not. He's trying to find God's purpose for his life like all of us. He's broken. Angry. Needs to find his worth in God alone. So today I thought of walking by him, but found myself sitting down curbside with him. "Do you want to talk?" I asked.

"It won't help," he said. "This place is nuts. Everyone is walking around here like a freaking zombie! And I have to wipe their backsides!"

Charles was agitated, but I was not uncomfortable with his authenticity. I was grateful he was being transparent.

The following words came quickly to me. "Charles…Jesus basically wiped peoples' backsides. He washed their feet. He lived among dirty people. Living in community is messy. All He requires is that we be like Him."

I said it as much for him as for myself. I was reminding myself to be like Jesus. I knew Charles's pride was getting in his way. (Mine does too.) I knew he was feeling sorry for himself. (I do too.) I knew he didn't feel like being like Jesus this morning. (I can be a reluctant servant.)

At that moment there was no breakthrough. No life-changing moment. Not even any tears. But communion in the body of Christ was taking place. The Homeless One was ministering to me. Curbside.

Jesus, the Homeless One, help me to be a servant. Help me to remember that everyone is equal at Your Cross. Help me to live my life in Your name. And Your way."

Debbi Miller is the Assistant to the President at the Water Street Rescue Mission, on the Leadership Board at Manheim BIC, married, and a Mom to four great teenagers in Lititz.

From My Head To My Heart

"And behold, the Lord passed by...but the Lord was not in the wind...not in the earthquake...not in the fire...(but) a still small voice." *1 Kings 19:11-12 (New King James Version)*

I retired from the retail family business at the age of 65 and wondered what I would do with the rest of my life. Now, thirteen years later, I find there are ways to share my life with others.

God dwells with His people. An example of this happens when tempted in actions or thoughts, I notice words of a song or a bible verse present in my mind, a still small voice.

When reflecting on it, I became aware of the blessings of thinking on good things. I am grateful that I was encouraged to memorize scripture when attending summer and winter bible schools, and that I learned meaningful songs in Sunday school and worship services, beginning when I was a child.

Life has many phases, or seasons in which to share spiritual Christian truths. We have an awesome responsibility and privilege to nurture and to relate to people, sharing the values we've learned. It is a joy to sit with people who are hungry for a word of encouragement and hope, and then find the answers in the words of our Lord. New translations of the scriptures in modern day language help to communicate the message.

All of us need encouragement and a feeling of self-worth. Other people helped me to be a listener when communicating with others speaking to God. When I pray and make a request, I need to take the time to listen for the answer. My spirituality needs to go from my head to my heart.

Dear God, thank you for sending the Holy Spirit after Jesus left planet Earth. I claim the promise that He has arrived and communicates with us.
I quote Jesus' words recorded in John 16:13, "When the Spirit of truth comes, He will guide you into all truth" (NLT).

Jay R. Oberholtzer, retired from a retail business and a church deacon, now shares his faith in contemplative spiritual relationship with seekers.

Is My Heart Soft?

"... today, if you hear his voice, do not harden your hearts...."
Psalm 95:7-8 (New American Standard Bible)

Lately I have been meditating on whether it really is difficult today to hear the voice of God. While it is true our culture provides many clamoring voices from television, radio, movies, music, or videos that can crowd out hearing the voice of God, He still speaks loud and clear. My conviction is that I just need to lean in, put aside distractions, and really listen.

Because of a congenitally caused hearing loss, I wear hearing aids in each ear, and still I struggle to hear. Lately, I've come to see that my disability helps me better understand what it means to listen for the voice of God.

The most difficult times for me to hear are situations where many people are talking at the same time like in a restaurant or at a party. At those times, I have to lean in toward the person I am speaking with and tune out the other voices. My attention must be totally focused on the other person, or I just don't hear. It seems to me that I might hear God better were I to focus on listening for His voice with that same attention.

At the same time, I realize that part of hearing from God means considering the condition of my heart—is my heart hard or soft? A hard heart is not open to doing what it has heard, and God's words are like rain running off a well-built roof. There is no penetration. A soft heart by contrast is porous and allows the message to soak in. When our hearts are soft, we can be formed by God's words. We are willing to change. At bottom, I believe what the psalmist is communicating is that we need to lean in to God and listen closely for His word. If we listen well for God's word, that word will soften us and empower us to be transformed.

Today, let us listen for God's voice, welcome it with joy, and hasten to do His will.

Jim Owens is an ordained deacon in the Roman Catholic Church and serves as the Associate to the Director of the Office for Permanent Deacons in the Archdiocese of Philadelphia. He works as an attorney in private practice in West Chester.

Yield To God

"For I know the plans I have for you, declares the Lord, plans to prosper you and not to harm you." *Jeremiah 29:11*

What next, Lord? God clearly pointed the way during a Susquehanna Valley Pregnancy Services banquet. As a sonographer, I could use the vital tool of ultrasound to help in the raging battle for life at a crisis pregnancy center.

As the pieces fell into place to pursue the education I would need, it became clear that obedience to this call would come with a price. Personal attacks, both great and small, came from all directions. Graduation was a great victory! Then, a job shortage created a desperate situation for a new sonographer who needed to maintain skill.

Finally, I began to work in a large hospital. Time passed and it became evident that this was not the place for me. Overwhelmed, I left my job and new career. I began to struggle with confusion and doubt. Hadn't I heard God clearly? What about the fight for life?

I began to cry out to Him in prayer and worship. At times I held out my hands, as the tears streamed down my face, offering back to God ultrasound, the gift I thought He had given me to serve Him. Months passed, and I learned about yielding, trusting, and waiting.

Then one day, I received a call from the Executive Director of SVPS. I tearfully explained my story. She listened intently, and then asked me to consider applying for the open sonographer position. The plan God revealed to me more than four years ago would come to pass! Within weeks, God gave me back what I had yielded to Him!

It is now my joy and privilege to use this special gift of ultrasound to reveal the truth and the wonder of life at its earliest stages.

Lord, help me to yield to You, to obey, and to trust in Your promise that You have wonderful plans for me!

Linda Page serves as the sonographer for SVPS. She and her husband, Tom, are members of Lancaster Evangelical Free Church.

The Chasm

"As Solomon grew old, his wives turned his heart after other gods, and his heart was not fully devoted to the Lord his God, as the heart of David his father had been." *1 Kings 11:4*

Sixteen inches generally isn't considered a great distance, but it can be a major chasm in our walk with the Lord. I didn't come to Christ until my late thirties, in part due to an analytical mind that, like Thomas, relied upon physical and visual evidence. And, even after I accepted the Lord as my Savior and I saw the many ways that God worked in situations around me, much of my understanding of Him resided in my head.

In recent years, however, as I have undertaken more prayer and focus on "what is it You are trying to show me, Lord" and "help me to be faithful in carrying it out" that I really have been able to experience God at work in both good times and those that are less enjoyable.

That sixteen inches is the distance between my brain and my heart (being analytical, I have measured it, of course). The difference between head knowledge and heart knowledge remained the Great Divide in my life for many years, causing me to miss experiencing and fully appreciating the many blessings that God was providing every day in situations all around me.

The Merriam-Webster Dictionary describes "experience" in the noun form as "practical knowledge, skill, or practice derived from direct observation of or participation in events or in a particular activity." The verb, however, is "something personally encountered, undergone, or lived through."

Will your experience with the Lord today be a noun or a verb?

Please help us to experience You more fully, Lord, not just in our minds, but in our hearts and all around us. Amen

Casey Jones, an organization management and grants advisor, resides in Parkesburg. He also focuses on family ministries and those that come alongside the hurting.

The Protector

"O Lord, you will keep us safe and protect us...." *Psalm 12:7*

Recently, my wife and I took a short trip to celebrate our anniversary. On a small winding road, a speeding car came at us head on and at the last minute swerved – missing us by inches. We were deeply shaken and thanked the Lord for His protection.

I'm sure there are many times we are not even aware of danger, and God activates His angels to protect us. In Hebrews 1:14, angels are called ministering spirits sent to serve those who will inherit salvation.

While living in inner city Baltimore, we sensed God's supernatural protection many times as we went into places considered high drug and violence areas. We went because that is where Jesus would go. We used wisdom but trusted God for His protection.

One day while standing in our home by our front window a drug fight broke out on the street. One guy pulled a gun and shot. The bullet came crashing through our window, missing my head by inches. Another time I got in the middle of two guys in a knife fight and was able to break it up without getting cut up.

Yes, God's protection is very real in our lives. You may not always be aware of it but His angels are dispatched on your behalf. Take a moment right now to thank God for His protection in your life and take a moment to pray God's protection over your family and friends today.

Father, thank you so much for Your hand of protection over me and over those I love. Protect me today and protect my family and friends. Thank you for Your ministering angels in my life.

Lester Zimmerman is pastor of Petra Christian Fellowship, Apostolic Leader of the Hopewell Network of Churches and council member of the Regional Church of Lancaster County.

Eyes of Faith

"Trust in the Lord…lean not on your own understanding…" *Proverbs 3:5 (New King James Version)*

During our mission trip to Fiji, we were invited to go snorkeling. I was excited to experience the island off of the mission compound. Although I had never snorkeled before, I greatly anticipated it.

The boat took us away from the island and stopped the engines. After instructions to the group of us, fins and masks were handed out. I stood at the end of the line, watching each diver swim away from the boat. As I entered the water to put my face under, I panicked in a way I had never before experienced. I could not convince my mind to go against reason and experience. How can I actually breathe underwater through the provision of the little air tube? I understood the logic of it, but every time I attempted, I would freeze up. This is ridiculous! I didn't come all the way out here to just sit in the boat!

"Lord, please help me – You've promised me the mind of Christ and eyes of faith, but I'm stuck on 'leaning on my own understanding,' which feels more like bondage right now. Free me to trust You."

Graciously and patiently He calmed me enough to trust Him for the outcome. And great was my reward when I placed my trust in Him and my head under the water! I was totally smitten by the beauty of the reef and the creativity of all the colorful life I could see. Such splendor I would have missed! Not only was I breathing underwater, I began to spontaneously praise God and literally laugh "out loud" as I was privy to delighting in the glory of this otherwise hidden aspect of God's creation.

Thank You that through faith our eyes are opened to many things otherwise hidden, both in the natural and in the spiritual realm.

Cindy Riker, contributing editor, a mother of four, is involved with her husband at Teaching the Word Ministries and also teaches at Change of Pace.

The Kindness Of God

"Until now you have asked nothing in my name. Ask, and you will receive, that your joy may be full."
John 16:24 (New King James Version)

Recently, I had an assignment to conduct a training seminar in Philadelphia. It required that I drive into the city four times within nine days, two times at night. Although I was familiar with the area, my husband and I both felt it was not wise to drive into that particular neighborhood alone, especially at night. I had put out a call for assistance weeks before and it looked like all bases were covered. The day before I started, all the plans fell through. I did not want my husband to have to cancel his plans to accompany me, so we prayed for direction. "Sometimes we don't have what we want or need just because we don't ask," he reminded me.

Late at night, I sent out emails to two fellowship groups I attend, as well as to staff at the pregnancy center. By 8:00 the next morning, a friend called and asked me what time she should pick me up! She not only wanted to take me, she wanted to drive me there. For a not very adventurous driver, this was more than I could even hope. In addition, four other people responded, trying to see what they could arrange. Three of us went in that first night, with my friend deftly and patiently navigating excessive traffic and detouring around accidents. I arrived on time and refreshed for the teaching task ahead.

Lord, thank you for reminding me of Your kindness and care in all situations. Help me to remember to call on You without hesitation and ask You first for help. You have magnificent ways of providing care.

Joan Boydell serves as the Senior Director of Amnion Crisis Pregnancy Centers, as a consultant with Care Net, and with her husband, Bruce, inLifespan®,

Have It Your Way

"…Mary has chosen what is better and, it will not be taken away from her." *Luke 10:42*

No doubt about it, we are a consumer-oriented society. We can have it our way. My wife, Mary, noticed the new Burger King in town was open. It was a bit of an unusual Burger King, however. First of all, we were greeted by the new manager offering free champagne. That was different! After we declined, we went to order our food.

"Everything on the menu tonight is free," blurted out the bright and cheery teenager taking our order.

"Wow," we thought, "let's call the boys, they'll show them what *free* is all about" (referencing our two eating-machines we call *sons*).

"Free?" my wife asked again.

"Yes, it's all free, even the Reese's frozen pie. Would you like one?"

"No," I replied, "just a Whopper, please."

While I found a seat in the crowded dining room, my wife went to the drink fountain. "Can you believe all the food is free? This is a great grand opening," she confessed aloud to the gentleman beside her.

"Of course it's free," was his response. "It's a test run for our children who will be employed here, and we as the families were invited," he declared with a big satisfying smile on his face.

Mary ran back to me with a look of horror on her face. "We gotta get outta here…this is for employees and their families…if they find out we're neither employees nor family, we're in big trouble!"

"Mary, settle down, slow down, it's okay…let's not *look* guilty."

"But we *are* guilty, and further we may know some of these people," Mary exclaimed!

"Look, let's eat quickly, and not attract any attention," I remarked.

We still laugh about this memory-making moment. I want to be like Mary in the Bible and sit at His feet without demanding it my way. I don't want to have anything to do with consumer Christianity, but I do want to be a Christian who is consumed by His presence.

Lord, consume me.

Steve Prokopchak serves on DOVE Christian Fellowship International's Apostolic Council and is team leader for the DCFI Caribbean churches.

The Dress

"Now that I've put you there on a hilltop on a light stand—SHINE!"
Matthew 5:15–16 (The Message)

I pulled it over my head and smiled—"fabulous." Its colors were wild and triumphant, a dancing mixture of orange, brown and turquoise, swirling and twirling about in unabashed happiness across the draping fabric. Suddenly, voices from my childhood converged. "You don't want to wear anything too bright. Big prints will make you look bigger. You don't want to stand out. Fit in. Conform. Hide your colors. Apologize for your essence and make yourself as small as possible. Quiet the laugh. Dumb down the talent—people might notice you."

How can one lead by blending with the crowd? When does dismissing one's talent make the world a better place? Where did this idea come from that Christians are doing a SERVICE by spending their energy on maintaining the status quo? I wonder if perhaps, instead, it is a direct affront to God and the wisdom of His creation. If I mold myself into what I perceive others want me to be, then what is left of me to carry out God's purpose? If God created me to stride in pinks and greens, then who am I to decide that it is my duty to skulk about in drab shades.

As God gives me the courage to live vibrantly, I find my soul moving toward a new level of peace. I have and will face people who scoff at my exuberance and smirk at my authenticity. On the other hand, I have this priceless confidence that comes from the knowledge that my Father delights in me. So today, the dress twirls, the strappy sandals dance, and I am happy. I have not covered my lamp. I am still salty (and sour and sweet). God looks down and smiles. He likes the dress.

Dear God, Thank you for creating me in color and vibrant ones at that. Help me not to hide, so that my radiance can bring You glory.

Tricia Groff, M.S. is a counselor at Crossroads Counseling Center, Lancaster.

Nothing To Lose

"...My grace is sufficient for you, for my power is made perfect in weakness...." *2 Corinthians 12:9*

I was petrified. *God, I can't do this!* I thought as the Father's Heart soup kitchen rapidly filled with people. The room bustled with activity as hungry people filed in and took their places at the long tables. Most of them were older, many appeared to be recent immigrants, befitting New York City's claim as an international melting pot.

Somehow I'd been recruited to walk around and offer to pray with people as they finished their meals. I was not at a good place with God at the time yet I found myself lifting up a desperate plea. *"God,"* I silently prayed, *"I have nothing to give; it is going to have to be all You."* Never before and never since have I felt such an urgency for the Holy Spirit to work. And He did! He took my "I can't" and turned it to a "but I can." He directed me to the right individuals and gave me the words to say. Even though I wasn't walking with Him as I should have been, because I was willing to admit my own inability and seek His ability, He filled me with a power I have rarely experienced. God doesn't want us working out of our own strength. It is often when we are weakest that His strength is most evident.

Are you trying to work out of your own strength? Can you admit your inabilities and allow God to take over? There is a risk involved. We have to step out in obedience and believe that God will provide us with the grace and power to face whatever lies before us. But when we are at the point where we truly have nothing and it all has to be God, well, we really have nothing to lose!

God, help me to come to You when I'm weak and seek Your strength.

Marisa Barnett is a recent graduate of the School of Global Transformation and is a youth leader at DOVE Christian Fellowship Elizabethtown.

my fury;
I will gasp and pant like a
woman giving birth.
I will level the mountains and
hills
and bring a blight on all their
greenery.
I will turn the rivers into dry
land
and will dry up all the pools.
I will lead blind Israel down a
new path,
guiding them along an
unfamiliar way.
I will make the darkness bright
before them
and smooth out the ... head
of them.

lowed Israel to be robbed...
Was it not the LORD? It wa...
whom we sinned again...
people would not go wh...
them, nor would they ob...
That is why he poure...
fury on them and destroy...
battle. They were set o...
burned, but they still
understand.

The Savior of Israel

43 But now, O Isra...
who created yo...
not be afraid, for I hav...
you. I have called you b...
are mine. When you...
deep waters and great...
be with you. When yo...
rivers of difficulty, ...
dr...! When you wal...
f... oppression, yo...
...; the flames...
For I am th...
One...
Egypt...
for y...

We're On A Pilgrimage

"Blessed are those whose strength is in You, who have set their hearts on pilgrimage." *Psalm 84:7*

My car shook as the angry marchers pounded on it. Having blonde features easily identified me as an American, an unenviable position given that I had inadvertently found myself in the middle of an anti-NATO demonstration. The Spanish suburb where I lived housed an American air force base, and anti-American sentiment was high. It was my tenth year of missionary service there but the past months had been some of the most difficult. A postal employee was stealing our mail, so no communication reached us, making me feel totally cut off from loved ones back home. I had just suffered the miscarriage of a baby I'd long hoped for, and prior to the demonstration, had attended my first church service since the loss. No one mentioned the baby or extended sympathy, which only deepened my sense of isolation. The angry faces of the marchers seemed to confirm the rejection which was all too real for me in those days. *I don't belong here. I'm just a foreigner who's not wanted. God, why is it so difficult if this is the place You've called me?*

God protected me that day and provided a safe exit from the angry crowd, yet my sense of not belonging persisted. But in the year that followed, God confirmed to my heart the truth that as Christians, we are all on a pilgrimage which will ultimately lead us to an eternity with Him. I can be "at home" with Him wherever He has placed me, because it's His companionship on my journey that gives security and purpose. Are you struggling today, longing to be somewhere else—to have a change of location or circumstances or friends? Pursue friendship with Him and find your "true home" in the only safe place.

Father, thank you for where You have placed me. Help me to enjoy Your companionship and see You glorified in this season of my journey.

Nancy Barnett serves with her husband, Tom, in pastoring DOVE Christian Fellowship Elizabethtown.

Do You Want To Be Reconciled?

"Now all things are of God, who has reconciled us to Himself through Jesus Christ, and has given us the ministry of reconciliation."
2 Corinthians 5:18-19 (New King James Version)

It was the end of a long day, and it was late. I was sitting in a room with another leader in another nation. We were discussing the events of the day and communication that had taken place between the two of us. He was presenting his point of view of what took place, and I was trying to communicate my heart on the issue. We were at a stalemate and not making any progress. In fact, we were beginning to acquire some uncomfortable feelings toward each other. I was convinced that he did not understand what I was saying because when he repeated back to me what he understood me to say, it was not what I was trying to communicate. He was convinced that I did not understand him as well. I was frustrated.

All of a sudden, the Lord whispered to my heart, "Do you want to be right, or do you want to be reconciled?"

It hit me like a rock. "Lord, I want to be reconciled."

"Then accept the wrong," the Holy Spirit said.

I turned to the individual. "I am so sorry. Somehow today I have offended you, and that was not in my heart to do so. I apologize for what I have said and ask you for forgiveness. Please forgive me. I have embarrassed you in front of some of your leaders, and I will ask them for forgiveness tomorrow."

You could literally feel the pressure leave the room. His response was, "Well, I haven't been responding properly toward you either. Please forgive me." The Lord brought about a sweet healing between us. If you have a broken relationship in your life, maybe the question the Lord asked me fits your situation?

Lord, You have reconciled us to Yourself and have given us the ministry of reconciliation. Grant us the grace to desire to be reconciled that is above the desire to be right. In Jesus' precious name, Amen.

Ron Myer serves as assistant director of DOVE Christian Fellowship International.

Overflow

"The good man brings good things out of the good stored up in his heart, and the evil man brings evil things out of the evil stored up in his heart. For out of the overflow of his heart the mouth speaks."
Luke 6.45

I love baseball! I will buy a newspaper just to read the box scores. My computer gives me access to a multitude of details about batting average, pitch counts, etc., and I thrive on them. Once on vacation on Chincoteague Island, I got "lost" at a little league game played between strangers. (Dianne told my daughters, "Daddy needed a baseball fix.") Football may have become America's game, but baseball is still its national pastime. There are few more pleasant ways for me to "pass the time" than in a ballpark watching a well-contested game. *And I can talk about baseball any time all the time.*

Jesus said that what we focus our lives upon—that which we cherish in our hearts—multiplies and grows, ultimately producing an overflow in our words. If baseball is stored up in your heart, then we will talk baseball. If politics is stored up there, then conversations about political candidates will pour forth. If we harbor corrupt thoughts, corrupt words will flow out. If we accumulate evil and deceit, evil and falsehood will cascade out of our lips. If we cherish God and His love in those hearts, then the abundance overflows with Godly wisdom and loving praise. We will glorify God.

Is the cultivation of Christ's life within us our true pastime? "Out of the abundance of our heart, the mouth speaks." What do your words reveal about what you cherish in your heart?

Fill my heart with Your goodness, Lord, to overflowing.

Dr. Stephen Dunn is the lead pastor for the Church of God of Landisville and a faithful fan of the Detroit Tigers.

Never Abandoned

"...I will never leave you nor forsake you." *Joshua 1:5*

For the past eight years, I've struggled in the area of abandonment and rejection. At the young age of eleven, I was abandoned by my mother and then at the age of thirteen came the beginning of rejection from my step-mother and my father.

Then I would feel guilty for being so torn apart by the fact I was abandoned and rejected, because I saw how so many other kids who were going through the same things I was, had it even worse than I did. Still this did not fix the emptiness and hurt in my heart. It just became an endless pursuit of longing to love and actually be loved and wanted in return.

On July 28th, 2007 in the midst of being in Liberia, Africa, I had a revelation of the Father's love for me. I realized it when I picked up a five month old crying orphan, named Martin, in Acres of Hope Orphanage. I just began to love on him by covering him with kisses. I sang an African song over him... "No matter what they say, what they say, you are always a winner! No matter what they do, what they do, you are always a winner!"

It was at that moment I realized Martin, too, was abandoned and rejected. He was longing to be loved and desired. Like I sang over him and lavished him with kisses, this is what my Heavenly Father is doing to me. He's jealous for me. He desires me. Man may abandon and reject me, but My Heavenly Father never will!

Thank you Lord for desiring and longing for Your children. Help me to help others realize Your great love.

Tonya Hess, serves as an intern at the Gateway House of Prayer and attends Ephrata Community Church.

Healing The Wounded

"He heals the brokenhearted and binds up their wounds."
Psalm 147:3

I was intrigued when I heard that my church was sponsoring a mission trip to a Navajo Indian School in Arizona. As I decided to join the mission team, I became excited about personally reaching out to children who live in a different culture far-removed from my everyday existence. The mission school was located close to the border of the Navajo Indian Reservation in northeastern Arizona.

When we reached our destination, we were greeted enthusiastically by staff and students. My heart was touched as the children eagerly crowded around and greeted us with open arms. There were many tasks to be accomplished by our team, including replacing a roof on a school building, office/billing work, and assisting teachers.

Three large crosses had been erected on the school property in a quiet area where students could meditate and pray. As I walked toward the crosses one afternoon, a group of seven and eight-year-old girls gathered around me and grabbed my hands. As I became acquainted with them, they began pouring out their hearts to me. One of them described how she had been taken from her home because her parents abused her. She showed me her scars. Another told me she has nightmares because her brother had taken his life and she saw him do it. Tears came to my eyes as I listened to their stories and their pain. They invited me to their dorm room and I spent the afternoon with them, giving lots of hugs and encouragement. We talked about Jesus and how much He loves each one of them.

That mission trip left a lasting impression on my life. My eyes were opened to the great needs of the Navajo people and the love of God as He provides a compassionate mission school for hurting children.

Thank you, Lord, for Your love and healing power toward the wounded and brokenhearted.

Sharon McCamant, Director of the SVPS Lebanon Pregnancy Clinic, also serves as a ministry leader at the Ephrata Church of the Nazarene Celebrate Recovery ministry.

We Can Never Go Where He Is Not

"The earth is the Lord's...." *Psalm 24:1*

There were no stars to guide nor to cheer me. The night was very cold but still. All I could see were the tall saplings they placed in the guardrail posts to show where the snow-buried road was cut into the side of the steep mountain. My headlights picked up one sapling at a time as I gingerly rode my snowmobile on the deep snow. My husband, Lewis, followed, the light from his headlights bouncing along beside me, assuring me he was still back there. I sang loudly to myself, "This is my Father's world, I rest me in the thought."

We stood on the left running board with our right knees on the seat so if the snow got so steep or unstable that the sleds started to roll, we could jump off. "He shines in all that's fair, He speaks to me everywhere," I sang over and over. It was scary, but the kind of adventure we thrived on.

The rest of our group of a dozen or so were back on the trail somewhere huddled together as one by one they ran out of gas until my hubby and I were the only ones with gas. The guide had gas buried at places in the snow but they had used all of it.

I knew the way. The road led from West Yellowstone on the west side of the Yellowstone Park, across the park to outside the east gate to Pahaska Teepee, the summer resort that had been Buffalo Bill Cody's hunting camp in the early 1900's. The year before, Lewis and I were in the first group the guide had ever led across the ungroomed trails to this place where we were treated to a great western feast and warm fireplace as we talked into the night with our company-starved hosts. In the morning daylight, we would make the trip back.

Our sleds kept going and eventually the lights of the camp broke the darkness. We rode right up to their gas pumps and turned off the sleds. As I looked into the gas tank with my flashlight, all I saw were the dry drain groves in the bottom of the tank. We were running on fumes or plain supernatural fuel!

Thank you so much, Lord, for allowing us to see Your great creation, and for keeping us safe and well.

Jackie Bowser attends DOVE Westgate Celebration.

Rebuilding Ruins

"Your ancient ruins shall be rebuilt; you shall raise up the foundations of many generations; you shall be called the repairer of the breach, the restorer of streets to dwell in."
Isaiah 58:12 (English Standard Version)

In mid-1975, the Lord radically redirected my wife and me. We sold our nice suburban home. I resigned my position at a well-known Philadelphia institution. We left our friends and comfortable surroundings and moved by U-Haul truck with our two young children to help establish a ministry on 100 beautiful acres of land in the Endless Mountains of Pennsylvania. Our mission: To provide a place where hurting and wandering people could meet Christ and begin a new life in a Christian family environment. We poured our hearts, time and fortune into this ministry. Five years later, God redirected us again and, with much pain and concern, left the work. While our minds and bodies occasionally returned, we ceased to be involved. God was faithful to provide for us and open new opportunities.

In August of 2007, we received word that this ministry had virtually shut down, and the current Board had plans to give the assets away. My wife and I, along with others, began to pray and felt led to submit a proposal to re-create this ministry. While the story is still unfolding as I write, I am reminded that the plans of God and the dreams He inspires in our hearts often move to the backburner or off the stove altogether, sometimes for a long time. Things fall into disrepair, become derailed, or even turn to ruins. Just when we think it's really over, God begins to move in restorative and re-creative ways. I am reminded that His plans, ways and thoughts are different than mine.

Lord, I thank You that You are not only Creator, but Re-creator—that You delight to rehabilitate disappointed dreams and broken lives and rebuild them as testimonies of Your glory and just love.

Bruce Boydell serves emerging leaders, businesses, and ministry organizations through Lifespan® Consulting and Coaching Services.

November 8

"'...no matter how deep the stain of your sins, I can take it out and make you as clean as freshly fallen snow. Even if you are stained as red as crimson, I can make you white as wool!'"
Isaiah 1:18-19 (The Living Bible)

I remember it like it was yesterday. I was separated from my husband, dealing with my own struggles, and realizing that mentally I was in pretty bad shape. For the first time, I decided to seek counseling for myself and stop focusing on my husband and the help "I" felt he needed. I was raised Catholic. I knew about God, but I didn't "know" Him. A friend of mine told me about Rest Ministries in Coatesville.

After several weeks of learning about the Bible, God, and myself, I was ushered into the most wonderful experience of my life. As I learned about forgiveness, I realized I had some of my own issues that I thought God Himself would never forgive. On November 8th 2002, as I sat alone in the dark of my living room, ready to give up, I heard a voice tell me to look up forgiveness in the Bible.

Along with the verse above, I read Isaiah 43:25, "I, yes, I alone am the One who blots out your sins for My own sake and will never think of them again." I knew and finally understood what the cross meant for the first time in my life. I was forgiven and loved. I accepted the work that Jesus did for me that night and I knew I was forgiven and that I would spend eternity with my heavenly Father.

Thank you Father for Your undying love and forgiveness on the cross. I pray that many more will come to the same understanding that I did, that it is by Your blood alone that we are truly forgiven and that we will walk with You again in heaven.

Eileen Christiansen, serves as a leader and youth leader in Celebrate Recovery, a 12 Step Christ center recovery program at Kingsway Church in Sadsburyville.

The Quiet Teachers

"Teach these great truths to trustworthy people who will, in turn, pass them on to others." *2 Timothy 2:2b (New Living Translation)*

Reflecting over names like Billy Graham, Jerry Falwell, some talk show hosts, and others, men who declared truth boldly without apology, I have always appreciated them. They have had a great influence on my life.

But I'm reminded of some of my quiet teachers, like two of my Sunday school teachers. Each Sunday morning they taught us from the Word of God without a lot of fanfare, but we knew they cared. They cared by taking us to Crystal Cave and Roadside America.

A ten year old at Roadside America thought he was having a foretaste of heaven! It is fifty plus years later, but I will never forget those outings. Even though I can't remember specific things they taught us, I know the Word through them left a deep impact on my life, largely because I knew they loved us and prayed for us.

Let us never become too busy to kneel down to the level of a little one and let them know they are important, and that God desires to be directing the rest of their lives.

Heavenly Father, keep us older men faithful teachers to the end. With Your wisdom, may we help raise up many youth to replace us. In Jesus' Name, Amen.

LaMarr Sensenig serves as an elder at Lancaster Evangelical Free Church.

God Knows What To Do With It

"Look at the birds of the air, that they do not sow, nor reap nor gather into barns, and yet your heavenly Father feeds them. Are you not worth much more than they?" *Matthew 6:26*

My dear friend, Arnie, and I shared many laughs and tears, but staying in touch became difficult after my family moved away some twenty years ago.

I decided to write my friend and a reply soon came. Arnie had been diagnosed with breast cancer four years ago and it had metastasized. But in her letter were no words of regret or anger … rather a savoring of each day and a peace concerning the fullness of the Lord.

I arranged a visit and the years vanished as soon as we saw one another. Her sense of humor, always quick, remained intact, as did her love for others. Over a cup of tea she shared this wonderful story: Arnie had begun chemo for the second time. She woke one morning to find that she had been sleeping on a mohair pillow. "There was more hair on the pillow than on my head!" She asked her husband and son to come on the deck with her and shave her hair off. The fall breeze was taking the hair away and her son asked if she would like to save some. "No, God knows what to do with it."

The following spring Arnie and her husband went on vacation. Shortly before their return, a storm littered branches and other debris in the yard of their country home. Her son, wanting to have things cleaned up before his parents' return, enlisted the aid of a friend. As they worked, something caught his friend's eye. Gently he placed a small bird's nest in his hand and carried it over to Arnie's son. The nest was made entirely of human hair—Arnie's hair. God knew what to do with it.

Thank you Lord that even the hairs on our head are of value to You.

Kathy Zubik serves as director of client services for Susquehanna Valley Pregnancy Services.

Evidences Of God's Protection

"[Jesus said,] 'My prayer is not that you take them out of the world but that you protect them from the evil one.'" *John 17:15*

I decided to take a photo of our home and walked across the street to get the best possible view. The developed and printed photograph was beautiful. The added blessing was that the photograph revealed brilliant rays of the sun covering our home. It was as if the Lord was revealing His protection with the very clear and beautiful light rays just above our home.

There are many evidences of how the Lord protects us. From the time we open our eyes until we close them, we should count our blessings! The book of Proverbs says, "Your insight and understanding will protect you, and prevent you from doing anything wrong." And verse 12 states: "It is the Lord who gives wisdom. Knowledge and understanding comes from him. He provides help and protection for righteous, honest men" (Proverbs 2:11-12 from Today's English Version).

The Lord is our protector. He guides us when we travel, when we are at home, when we choose our friends, and His wisdom is freely given (James 1:5-6). He guides us to serve and protects us as we balance life's priorities.

Lord Jesus, protect us from the evil one. Help us to keep our eyes open and listen and hear Your Word for us. We thank you for Your wisdom, Your knowledge, understanding, and insight.

Bob Burns is pastor and shepherd of Spiritual Growth Ministries, a guiding ministry to church leaders in areas of spiritual growth, and serves on the advisory board of The Potter's House (an after-prison care ministry).

The Right Thing To Do

"Then a poor widow came and dropped in two pennies. He called his disciples to him and said, 'I assure you, this poor widow has given more than all the others have given. For they gave a tiny part of their surplus, but she, poor as she is, has given everything she has."
Mark 12:42–43

It is a treasure to see a spiritual gift birthed in your very own child. I have two very different children, one very vivacious and spirited daughter and one very quiet and thoughtful son. It has been delightful to watch how each of them discover and use their different spiritual gifts.

My son, Jordan, was in the sixth grade and reveling in all the A's he had on his report card. It was his first semester of middle school, so making the honor roll was a pretty big deal. He could not wait until his dad and I saw it; he reveled in the praise he received. As he shared the news with his grandfather, he received a twenty-dollar bill as a reward. His faced beamed as we told him to do whatever he wanted with it.

The next morning as we sat in church, the pastor gave a small talk on tithing – nothing pushy, just heartfelt. The next thing I knew, as the offering plate passed by Jordan, I saw him slip in the twenty-dollar bill. My heart swelled, sang, and tears rolled down my face (even now as I recall the tender moment). I hugged him tightly and told him that God saw that act as mighty and beautiful. He smiled at me, very humbly and said, "It was the right thing to do."

Father, thank you for reminding me how beautiful tithing is in Your sight. Thank you for moving our hearts to return to You what is rightfully Yours with an attitude of humble obedience. Help me to give as Jordan did, with a thankful and precious heart.

Wendy Reasner, formerly from Susquehanna Valley Pregnancy Services, is a supervisor at Caron Treatment Centers in Wernersville.

Faith to Believe

"Delight yourself in the Lord, and He will give you the desires of your heart. Commit your way to the Lord, Trust also in Him, and He will do it." *Psalm 37:4–5*

S ome time ago, while praying about some urgent situation and seeking answers from the Lord concerning the matter, the words came to me, "Delight yourself in the Lord, and He will give you the desires of your heart."

At that moment I knew it was God speaking to me, and faith to believe and receive the answer from Him arose in me. He said, "Commit your way to the Lord, trust also in Him, and He will do it." I knew He was telling me that as I pressed into Him and delighted in worshiping and committing everything to Him, He would be faithful to answer my prayers. He said I needed to trust also in Him, and He would do it. God was even using this urgent and difficult situation to cause me to trust in Him and delight in Him, and He would then be faithful to answer my prayer according to His will.

God is so good and so faithful, even in difficulties. He draws us closer to Him.

Lord, Thank you for Your Word that causes faith to rise up in me and for the promises You give to us, Your people. Thank you for Your answer to the earnest, desperate prayer of my heart that is according to Your will. Thank you that we, Your people, can completely trust You and Your goodness. You are faithful, trustworthy and so good! I commit the difficult situations to You, and I know You are faithful to hear, answer and see me through. Thank You, Father. Let this day and the rest of my life be a testimony of Your goodness! Amen

Cheryl Wissler and her husband, Barry, have been pastors of Ephrata Community Church for the past thirty years.

You Are My Rock

"And He will be the stability of your times, a wealth of salvation, wisdom, and knowledge; the fear of the Lord is his treasure."
Isaiah 33:6 (New American Standard Bible)

After 20 plus years on the mission field in Jamaica, our family returned for a sabbatical to Lancaster County, my husband's childhood home. God has been faithful to provide for our needs: the provision of a furnished home, a second car to use for the year, free membership at a local gym, even the desires of my 12 year old daughter who wanted a kitten!

There are many differences from our life in Jamaica where we serve as volunteer missionaries with Youth With A Mission. The biggest one I noticed right away was the peace and safety I felt as a woman, walking and driving around our neighborhood. There is a high crime rate in Jamaica and as a result, we have fences, bars on our windows and guard dogs on our campus. What a wonderful change to move about in peace and not have to be vigilant for my safety or that of my children. Another wonderful blessing is the presence and involvement of men in the churches, schools, and homes. It was a pleasant surprise to see so many daddies walking their children to school the first day or waiting on the corner for them after school. In our culture, the family is so broken, it is normal to grow up without knowing your father, let alone having a relationship with him.

No matter where we live, I am learning that God is the same God. His grace is sufficient for us in whatever challenges we face. It is a fresh reminder for me to see God meet the needs of our family, and to prove Himself faithful in this new adventure.

Jesus, thank you that You are a strong rock and tower to run to. I thank You that You are always with us. Please help us to remember that Your grace is sufficient for whatever we are going through. In Jesus' name, Amen.

Val Landis, a missionary on a year-long sabbatical, lives in Lancaster County with her husband, Bill, and three children.

Jesus Can Relate

"Because he himself suffered when he was tempted, he is able to help those who are being tempted." *Hebrews 2:18*

As a young person, I, like many other people, thought that leadership was something that was full of ego, gratification and glory. Boy was I in for a surprise. I was eager to be involved in helping people, so I took a position as the leader of a youth group. It didn't take long for someone to question my motives and even my sincerity. You mean everyone doesn't agree with the direction I feel we should go? You mean people think I have a personal agenda? These experiences early in my life brought some reality to my expectations as I learned to serve in areas of leadership in the church and the marketplace.

Leadership is not for the faint of heart. It can be one of the most rewarding and yet the most challenging endeavors, sometimes at the same time. I remember one particularly challenging occasion where I felt I had been mistreated by others as I was involved in a leadership position. I felt hurt. I felt misunderstood. I felt rejected. I felt betrayed. I felt judged. I was having a particularly dreary pity party one day when I sensed the Lord wanted me to write down how I felt. I came up with the list that I just gave you. As I looked at this list, I realized that these were all things that Jesus had gone through and must have felt. He was rejected. He was betrayed.

In a moment, I realized that He could help me through these things. As I opened my heart to him, I felt him release me from these burdens. He set me free.

Jesus...thank you that You have gone before us. Thank you that we can open our hearts to You and receive freedom and cleansing from life's experiences that have injured us or burdened us down.

Brian Sauder serves on DCFI's apostolic council and is the director of the Church Planting and Leadership Training School.

What's In Your Hand?

"...[He] said that something should be given her to eat."
Mark 5:43 (New King James Version)

Usually one looks in their rear view mirror to pull out to pass. I confess I was looking in mine that day to finish my make-up on the way to work as I sat in traffic. Little did I realize with one glance I would be face to face with the living Lord!

I am used to dreaming dreams, but here it was daytime and suddenly I was seeing Jesus in my rear view mirror intimately inviting me into the room as He spoke "Talitha Kum!" to Jairus's daughter. "Little girl, I say to you arise!"

In this vision He immediately turned to me, handed me a large heavy loaf of bread, and said "feed her something." Next, I saw myself on a platform breaking the bread before multitudes of black faces with hungry eyes. Hands were reaching for the bread, and it was feeding endless mouths. I somehow felt it was for 5,000.

Arriving at my desk that morning, I began to write quickly the sermon that had been given for the body of Christ. Surely as the Lord does the miraculous, we need to be accompanying Him and available to disciple with the Bread of Life and the Living Word.

I clicked on the computer keys and sent the revelation in an e-mail to my pastor friend in Kampala, Uganda. By Sunday, he had preached it to 5,000! Little did I know that day, that five months later I would be in Africa teaching this lesson to children at an orphanage in Mbale, Uganda. When we speak to a child, we never know the true size of the audience we are affecting. And when we share our testimony of times with Jesus, we never know how the bread will multiply. What is in your hand to share?

Lord, teach us to be ready to feed those You raise up to new life!

Nancy Clegg, mother and grandmother, is a worshiper and Kingdom mobilizer in Chester County and the nations.

Set Free

"...He rescued me, because He delighted in me."
Psalm 18:19 (New American Standard)

As David said in this Psalm, the cords of death encompassed me, I was in the pit of destruction. But who would have known that the attack would come from within?

For most of my life, from the age of five, I struggled with self-condemnation, depression, and internal suicidal threats. It was my own secret battle, until one day when it was no longer empty threats, but a chilling promise.

I was lost in the vortex of guilt and shame, pushing me to pay for my transgression with one and one thing only—my life. I've never felt so completely helpless. It wasn't just an option anymore, it was a decree. I tried to stop it, to make it all go away, but I no longer had control.

Rocking to stop what seemed to be my own thoughts, I suddenly understood that I couldn't save myself. Out of the darkness I cried out for my life, desperation lacing my plea. Suddenly, there was stillness in my being. The voices of accusation had been silenced, and I knew that He saved me.

It has almost been a year since that day when I walked through the valley of the shadow of death. I have been free from depression and suicidal thoughts since then.

I was just one of thousands in my generation who have struggled with being suicidal, and my heart is to see those who cannot save themselves set free. I have no doubt in my mind that He was with me through every second of my trial, longing for me to cry out for Him to save me. He rescued me. He rescued me because He delights in me!

Jesus, save those who cannot save themselves, that they might know that You delight in them. Father, rescue Your children!

Hadassah Wilson serves as an intern at the Gateway House of Prayer, is a part of Body Life Ministries, and attends Ephrata Community Church.

The Light Came On

"...at all times they ought to pray and not lose heart." *Luke 18:1*

The speaker from the main stage said, "And you on the hill, under the lights, come down." I sat on the hill and turned to look behind me. The lights that illuminated the huge, grassy arena were shining in my eyes, almost blinding me. I knew that Someone was talking to me. I stood and made the walk to the front of the stage where hundreds had gathered to invite this "Someone" to change them.

I gave my life to the Lord that night in 1985 at Creation Festival in Mount Union, PA. Honestly, I didn't understand what I had just done, but I knew that I had found the Truth!

I was raised in the Church, but stopped attending at age 17. Worldly pleasures were my focus as a teenager and young adult. Church life held no place for me, but God's Word is faithful and the prayers of my mother and others were heard!

How God drew me to Him still amazes me. I knew nothing of being born again, saved, washed in the blood, whatever phrase you want to use.

None of that made sense to me. I didn't know the Bible, yet God directed my steps and took me out of a deep pit. He moved my feet that night and supernaturally brought me to Him. No one went to that stage with me except Jesus.

I hope my story brings you encouragement. Maybe you've been praying for a child, friend or relative for a long time. The "light doesn't seem to be going on." Their heart still seems cold, but God is working! Don't give up! Keep praying. God is faithful to hear your prayers and can work in any heart. I am proof of that reality.

Thank You, Lord for hearing our prayers and being faithful to answer.

Nancy Aument serves with Youth with a Mission, Lebanon and is an intern with Gateway House of Prayer, Ephrata.

Desire Of Your Heart

"Delight yourself in the Lord and he will give you the desires of your heart." *Psalm 37:4*

My husband, Attila, and I had been married twenty-five years when we purchased our very first home in June 2006. It shouldn't have happened. We couldn't afford it and we didn't have a down payment. Attila was on disability, suffering from end-stage renal disease and recovering from a failed kidney transplant and quadruple bypass. I was working part-time as a Controller. We plunged ahead only because my mother needed to sell the home we had been renting from her for the previous twelve years. We needed a new nest and we knew how awesome it would be if it was one we could own. But how?

Through a series of God-incidences, we miraculously pulled together the money for closing costs. I was offered a full-time Controller position that qualified us for a 100% mortgage, and a house that was perfect for us dropped into our price range (a little over didly-squat) at exactly the right time.

Soon after settlement, I found myself writing in freehand with a paint-pen around the top of our parlor walls: *"Delight yourself in the Lord and He will give you the desires of your heart - Psalm 37:4."* The lurching script looks like a hippie on Quaaludes penned it, but the thought was pure and my heart was true! The Lord had provided the desire of my heart in the most incredible and detailed way.

Attila and I continue to feel joy every time we turn the key in the lock of our home. It blows my mind that God not only *knows* the desires of my heart, but as I delight myself in Him, He delights in providing them to me.

Oh Lord, You bless me in so many ways. Thank you for knowing me, and help me to continue to know You better!

Kristin Williams Balla is a member of the Praise Team of Upper Octorara Presbyterian Church in Parkesburg.

Ok God...You got me!

"Wealth is worthless in the day of wrath, but righteousness delivers from death." *Proverbs 11:4*

About eight months ago, I was at an evening church service in Guatemala, listening to the pastor speak about the importance of material possessions. He posed the questions to us, "Is your level of happiness and contentment directly affected by your earthly possessions? If they were all taken away tomorrow, would you still exalt the name of the Lord?" Sitting up straight and proud, I responded with an affirmative, "Yes, of course I would!"

The very next day I had items, including my laptop, camera, some money, and important documents stolen from me. Boy was I upset! How unfair, right? Here I am in Guatemala doing the Lord's work, and I get robbed. I thought God was supposed to bless those who are following His will. As I went to bed that night, deeply mourning the loss of years worth of photographs that I had failed to back up on CD, God spoke to me. He spoke using that small voice which comes from within. He didn't sympathize or mourn with me like I might have expected. Instead, He spoke one simple sentence which I will never forget. "I thought you said you didn't put your joy in material possessions." That comment sure put me in my proper place!

I now realize that God wasn't trying to hurt me, or punish me. On the contrary, He was really helping me. The circumstance brought out a fault of mine I didn't know existed. Material possessions aren't at all wrong, but putting our joy in them is. At times, God uses painful situations to help mold us into the people He wants us to become.

Heavenly Father, I acknowledge that I am human, and therefore a sinner. I get caught up with the wealth and ways of the world. Forgive me. Help me to realize that earthly possessions come and go, but You are eternal. I want my joy to be solely in You Lord. You choose to give, and You choose to take away. Through it all, I will still bless Your name!

Chelsey Bollinger, served in Guatemala with Luzy Vida Ministries for the year of 2007, member of DOVE Westgate.

Fervent Prayers

"...The effectual and fervent prayer of a righteous one avails much."
James 5:16

The Lord has been showing me a lot on prayer recently. The main aspect of prayer that I am learning right now is that prayer is so vital in fighting off the attacks of the enemy.

For example, when my boyfriend, Calvin and I were on a five hour drive back home, I found myself being attacked severely in my mind. Thoughts of fear and anxiety about various circumstances happening in my life at that point were flooding my mind. It was so intense that I felt like I was about to scream or have a panic attack. I could not still my mind and it was really affecting me physically. Calvin could see my face and saw that something was wrong. I saw him look over at me and then, literally in a split second, the thoughts just ceased and my mind and heart were at complete peace. I looked over at Calvin and the Lord put the impression on my heart that he had been praying. I asked him if he had been and he said yes. I told him what happened, and then I was fine for about an hour.

Then after an hour, the attack came on me again. Calvin knew something was up, so he prayed silently once again. The thoughts ceased another time and peace flooded my mind once again. I asked him if he had been praying again and he said yes. At this point, he began to pray aloud casting away any influence of the enemy that may have had hold of my mind and thoughts. Because of his continual and fervent prayer, the attacks were gone. The Lord is so faithful to answer the fervent cry of His children!

Jesus, give us the revelation of Your power in prayer. We thank You that You are quick to answer and save us out of the path of the enemy. Praise You, Lord!

Bethany Daly, intern at Gateway House of Prayer in Ephrata, PA.

Faith To Move A Tornado

"He makes His sun rise on the evil and the good, and sends rain on the just and unjust." *Matthew 5:45*

One summer in the late 1990's, a storm was coming in to the area with a tornado watch. As my co-workers and I listened to the weather report, I realized the tornado was predicted to go across my backyard.

Faith rose up and prayer went out asking God to move the tornado. Finishing the prayer with asking God to keep the people safe and that the storm would not cause any harm to the other homes.

As one of my co-workers was driving me home, we heard on the car radio the weather man report the tornado turned and was going in another direction. This time it was going in the direction of her home. She became fearful of what would happen to her home. God led me to pray for her. His peace came over her. Later, she called and said the tornado went down the middle of the street and not one home on her street was damaged.

Thinking about this later, I saw God show Himself to this co-worker, who was not a believer. She was touched by God's concern for her. This act of love showed His love and care for her, it was evident as her countenance changed. His love continued to minister to her whenever she shared the event.

She has told that story to many people, each time she gives God glory.

Awesome God, what a wonder You are, thank you for Your love, power and mercy that continues to show us Your gentle way of drawing man unto Yourself. May we catch the bigger picture of Your heart for the lost and not limit how You would use any situation to show Your love to the world. In Jesus' Name, Amen.

Debbie Davenport, wife, spiritual mother, serves on the leadership team at Living Truth Fellowship and intercessor for the Hopewell Network of Churches.

I Will Praise You

"Though the fig tree does not bud…yet I will rejoice in the Lord."
Habakkuk 3:17

I tapped the brakes. The first rain in six months was turning the Los Angeles Freeway into a slippery trap—as treacherous as black ice. It was Thanksgiving evening 1976 and the traffic was bumper to bumper.

When my car didn't slow, I braked again. My speed dropped but my big-block Chevy engine roared in protest. The engine revved, straining against the brakes.

Like native Californians, I avoided street travel except in the case of fog and rain. This was no time to be driving seventy miles an hour so I took the next exit. But every traffic light became a contest of wills—I would plant both feet on the brake and brace myself against the seat to bring the car to a stop. Finally I reached my apartment.

When I turned it off, the car continued to run…and backfire. Neighbors all hit the floor, thinking there was a gun battle in the parking lot. Long minutes later the car quit. One man, venturing out to count the bodies and finding my wheezing car, told me my engine was ruined.

In the middle of my first semester of graduate school, I had no money for minor repairs let alone a major engine replacement. My family and friends lived a continent away on the east coast.

With adrenaline at floodtide and my imagination mass-producing horror movies, I didn't even try to sleep. Crying and praying I began to read the Word and found Habakkuk's declaration: "though (all manner of disasters befall me) yet I will praise the Lord." I made his choice mine…and, after praising Him with tears dripping off my chin, I fell into a peaceful slumber.

Three days later, God brought a retired mechanic who checked my engine, adjusted the carburetor and charged me ten dollars. My car was back to her high-performance self.

Father, though the problems come, yet I will praise You.

Ruth Morris is a small group leader at The Worship Center and writer for Loving & Caring, Inc.

Get To Israel

"Righteousness shall go before Him and shall set us in the way of His steps" *Psalm 85:13 (King James Version)*

Stepping off the plane in Tel-Aviv, Israel was special. For my wife, Suzie, it was a fulfillment of prophesies the Lord had spoken years ago: "You must get to Israel." The Lord did not disappoint, it was as if He put out the welcome mat for us! The very first person we met was a Christian Arab Pastor who escorted us through baggage, customs, and even to our rental car! We had come to visit our daughter who was with a mission team working as a Teacher's Aide, and stayed with a Messianic couple she had met. As our daughter took us to the different holy sites around the Sea of Galilee, we remembered the words someone had spoken to us about "walking where Jesus walked."

It was at the Mt. of Beatitudes that the Lord emphasized a particular truth. While walking those ancient paths where Jesus walked, I sensed the Lord telling me to step off the macadam. As I did, I had a vision of His footprints in the dirt and the command to step into those footprints. When I did, Jesus spoke: "It's more important to walk where I am walking now." A couple days later, as we were traveling to the Dead Sea, Jesus again emphasized this truth to me as we watched sheep following their shepherd single file, walking right on his footsteps.

Later on, towards the end of our trip, we went to visit the Arab Pastor who met us at the airport, and were blessed to witness places Jesus is walking today, as his congregation ministered to orphan children, many of them Muslim, many from dire circumstances. There Messianic Jews and believing Arabs worshipped together, fellowshipping in love. We left Israel with a new calling to walk where Jesus is walking today, and not one step to the right or the left.

Father, true obedience is walking where You walk. We desire to step into only what You're stepping into. May we all find grace to do this. Amen

Val and Sue DeLuca are Elders at Hampden Mennonite Church in Reading.

$5.00 Lunch

"Although He was a son, he learned obedience through the things which He suffered." *Hebrews 5:12 (New Living Translation)*

I t was a period in our lives when finances were extremely tight. I was attending an evangelism conference in Virginia and sitting in the morning session when an offering was taken. I knew the Lord was asking me to put everything in my wallet in the collection basket. At 10:00 in the morning, it was easy for me to be obedient but as we approached the time for our $5.00 lunch, I began to fret and worry.

As I stood waiting in line to pay (having already emptied my wallet), I wondered what I was going to do. The *'Money Lady'* announced, due to time constraints, that we should proceed inside because the servers were waiting to feed us and if we hadn't paid we could make our way to her during lunch. Relieved for the moment, I went on in but could not eat knowing that now I was eating the 'Money Ladies' $5.00 lunch for which I had no way of paying.

Finally, having suffered enough, I just had to go and explain my situation. As I walked, very nervously, across the room toward the 'Money Lady' someone walked up next to me and asked, "You don't have any money for lunch, do you?" I admitted that I didn't and immediately this person offered to pay for my lunch as well as give me some extra money for the trip home. There was no explanation required, they just gave me the money. God had provided in a unique way as a result of my obedience to His voice earlier that morning.

Lord, teach us what Saul didn't know; "Obedience is better than..."

Frank Ferrari, along with his wife, Sue, serve as the directors of Transformation Ministries. Working in both Lancaster County and Central America, their desire is to see the church equipped and walking in Godly freedom living a transformed life.

Jumping With Joy

"And we know that in all things God works for the good of those who love him, who have been called according to his purpose."
Romans 8:28

I ts all fun until someone gets hurt, or so the saying goes. We were having a great time destroying old furniture, chopping it up into small pieces so we could throw it into the junk pile, when one unprecedented moment proved that saying true. The axe bounced off the cabinet we were breaking and hit my friend, Brandon, square on his ankle. Thankfully it was the blunt end of the axe head, but it still bruised the bone so badly that he was unable to walk without using crutches. Going into the last week of our time together, it was really a disappointment for him to not be able to walk. Little did we know that God had other ideas, beyond what we could see at the time.

That night during a time of prayer and worship, God asked me to go over and pray for Brandon's ankle to be healed. I was not at all confident, but decided to obey. When I walked over to him, I found him removing the sock and shoe from his foot. God had told him to remove his sock and shoe as an act of faith for being healed. At this point we were both pretty sure that something was up, so we prayed together for his ankle. A few seconds later, he was jumping up and down with joy, totally healed! What had seemed to be a depressing and painful day had been turned into one of praise and thankfulness by the goodness and power of God.

Thank you Lord for Your goodness, help us to walk in obedience to Your words, overwhelm us with a revelation of Your character.

Matthew Gehman, S.E.E.R. Intern at Gateway House of Prayer.

Coming Alongside

"A friend loves at all times, and a brother is born for adversity."
Proverbs 17:17

We sat next to each other at a Thanksgiving eve church service, responding to the pastor's call to share a blessing in our lives. My pew neighbor shared excitement about a friend in the throes of divorce getting together for dinner with her husband the next day. My new acquaintance had been providing encouragement and prayer support for her friend for many long months, with no apparent results. She recognized this as a breakthrough, with praise to the Lord.

Having experienced divorce, little did I know that this would be a preview of what I would see over the next several months. No less than a half dozen marriages, some only days away from separation or divorce, stabilized when one spouse turned to or renewed his or her focus upon the Lord.

Satan would have us adopt the world view that breakups of rocky marriages are a "good thing for everybody." Some "friends" even offer advice on how to end a marriage quickly and move on to a new relationship. However, statistics indicate there is as much as a 50% greater chance of failure in second marriages as new trials and compounded baggage develop for spouses and children.

The positive differences in these reversals were prayer and support from friends who provided hope in Him and inserted His Truth into difficult times. A change in perspective by one spouse resulted in new attitudes in the entire family, displacing prior feelings of despair, shame and isolation.

Lord, please remind me each day of the many blessings You provide.
Help me to encourage others in crisis, rather than backing away
when I see someone in pain who needs someone to come alongside.
Amen

Casey Jones, an organization management and grants advisor, resides in Parkesburg. He also focuses on family ministries and those that come alongside the hurting.

I'll Do The Best I Can

"The one who calls you is faithful and he will do it."
1 Thessalonians 5:24

I was a teacher's aide in a federal program for teaching institutionalized deaf mentally-retarded people. Fred was the very first deaf mentally-retarded student I ever worked with. He was full of energy—and got into everything. Fifteen year old Fred hated to go back to his ward because it was a horrible place. It housed about 50 other mentally retarded youngsters—in diapers. There were no toys on his ward—the others would trash them or eat them.

Fred was diagnosed as being profoundly mentally retarded because he couldn't communicate. (I strongly believe to this day that Fred was not retarded, but because of his misdiagnosis, placement in the institution, and subsequent lack of stimulation, functioned as a mentally retarded person and even copied the behavior of the mentally retarded youngsters around him.)

Fred's world began to change as he began to learn sign language. He became excited when he discovered that things had names and that he had a name! But, he hated going back to his ward. We had to drag him back to his building and lock the gate behind him. Frequently, he would scream and shake the gate until he would fall exhausted onto the ground.

I pitied him. I remember crying out, "Oh God, please change things for Fred. He should be in a better place." I remember a still, small voice asking me, "Are you willing to be part of this change?" I stopped for a moment and then answered, "Yes, with Your help, I'll do the best I can."

Four years later, I remembered that promise I made. And then, I remembered how far Fred had progressed. I had to teach him how to behave socially and even how to eat using silverware, (he was accustomed to using only his hands). I remembered how far he had come—and I began to realize how *I* had grown through this experience, too. We'd all come a long way, and I could draw strength for each day from God—one day at a time.

Lord, You are faithful! How often do we need to be reminded?

Jim Schneck is a free-lance interpreter for the deaf.

Don't Walk Away

"The Lord hurled a great wind on the sea and there was a great storm on the sea so that the ship was about to break up." *Jonah 1:4*

Love is often inconvenient and serving God takes precious time. I don't know about you but I often find myself too busy with life to allow any interruption to serve.

One evening, as my wife and I were on our way to our favorite restaurant, we came to a stalled mini-van on a busy highway. Relieved that I could still squeeze in the entrance to the restaurant I overlooked the two women and a man standing behind the van in busy rush hour traffic. As we slipped into the entrance, we were confronted by yet another obstacle that totally blocked our path to our "savory meal." A small child had opened the door of an SUV and was unwilling to close it. I sat in frustration thinking, where are the child's parents and why doesn't someone come and help us by closing the door?

I looked in frustration in my rear view mirror to see if someone saw our dilemma. That's when I noticed the people, who were out in traffic, trying to push their mini-van to safety in the parking lot.

Finally, I realized I was being called to serve and not to be served in this case. So I ran and assisted them in getting to safety. God will do whatever it takes to help His people learn to care for those around them who are in need. For me it was blocking my path to a restaurant so I could help someone to safety, for Jonah it was a fish (Jonah 2:10) to carry him back to a people in deep need (Proverbs 3:27 *Msg)*. Never walk away from someone who deserves help; your hand is God's hand for that person.

Loving Father, please forgive us for being too busy to serve and thank you for blocking our busy paths so we can become Your hand to touch our neighbors in need in the name of Jesus, Amen.

Ken Keim is pastor of Living Connections Ministries house church network & Chaplain of the Community Support Foundation in Ephrata.

Stunned And Thankful

"...We do not know what to do, but our eyes are on you."
2 Chronicles 20:12

Our family was living in Israel as we were in the process of immigrating as Jews. The rent was due...and for one year in advance at that! This was normal for Israel but not something we were used to in the USA. We were unable to work as our immigration status was still not completed.

Oh, Lord, what will we do but trust in and wait on You? What miracle would He do on our behalf this time? Helpless in ourselves and shakily trusting, we waited.

Suddenly, word came from a dear friend that worked at the Christian Embassy in Jerusalem! Money had come! An elderly widow, from the midwest of the United States, had written them having received their name and address from God. She had been awakened in the middle of the night, being instructed by God to send the $10,000 she had set aside for living the rest of her years, to three couples in Israel in need. She then sovereignly received all of our names AND the name and address of the Christian Embassy in Jerusalem to use as a means to get the money to us. She asked that she remain anonymous.

We each received over $3000 *just in time to pay the rent*! Stunned and thankful we praised God! We could not thank her personally so we blessed her for her obedience and her gracious gift!

Oh, Lord, You answer before our cries are out of our mouths. You use the most unlikely people to show forth Your wonder and kindness. I love You!

Vanyanna Rickie Kendall is a Christian counselor and life mentor in the greater Lancaster County area.

Photo by Linda Page

December

Our Poverty Mentality

"But I will not drive them out in a single year, because the land would become desolate and the wild animals too numerous for you. Little by little I will drive them out before you, until you have increased enough to take possession of the land." *Exodus 23:29-30*

During the first half of my spiritual journey with the Lord, I had a "victim" or poverty mentality. I expected the Lord to perform wonderful acts and give me my spiritual inheritance. I wandered through my spiritual life wondering when God was going to wave His mighty hand and all things would be given to me.

About ten years ago, the Lord began the process of changing my thinking and understanding. The biggest lesson I had to learn was that at the moment I was born again I walked into my inheritance, but I was too small to possess it.

Discipleship is the process of the Lord enlarging us so that we may possess our inheritance, little by little. He puts us through exercises, through experiences; He takes us by ways that will bring about our spiritual expansion until we occupy the larger place.

God didn't hand over the Promised Land to the Israelites. They still had battles to fight, and each battle made them stronger and more prepared for the next. God uses the circumstances of our lives to strengthen us and prepare us for the future. He doesn't just hand it over; we must be actively involved in the process.

Ask God to break you out of the poverty mentality and show you how He's been enlarging you to possess your inheritance.

Lord, please open my eyes to see where You're enlarging me, so that I can partner with You in that process.

Jim Herbert is senior pastor at Emmanuel Christian Fellowship, a nondenominational church in East York. He has been actively involved in the transformation movement in York County. Pastor Jim is married with two children.

His Name Alone Is Exalted

"People of all the earth, men and women, both young and old, praise and exalt the name of the Lord, for His name alone is exalted and supreme, His Glory and Majesty are above the Earth and the Heavens." *Psalm 148:11-13 (my paraphrase)*

This past year I studied at Hillsong International Leadership College in Sydney, Australia. Within a few days of being there, I realized that the nick-name "the church that never sleeps" was quite true. Being a church of about 25,000 people, there was always something going on. Hillsong is definitely doing something incredible for the Kingdom, and I counted myself privileged to be able to be a part of it for a few months.

One event that took place while I was there was their annual worship album recording. I got to be on stage in the choir, which was great, but honestly the best part about being on stage was the view. Looking up into the balconies and viewing 17,000 people worshiping our Lord and Savior was something I will never forget. This was not 17,000 people who came out to a concert, or to hear a big name speaker; it was a church getting together to worship our most awesome God.

To me it was a taste of what heaven is going to be like, worshiping with thousands upon thousands of people, from all different backgrounds and races.

Lord, You alone are worthy of all our praise from all tongues. Give us a fresh revelation of Your holiness so we can give You the honor You are due.

Jamie Groff is a worship and youth leader at DOVE Christian Fellowship, Westgate Celebration, Ephrata.

Help From Above

"I will lift up my eyes to the hills, where does my help come from?
My help comes from the Lord, Maker of heaven and earth."
Psalm 121:1-2

My three children and I were flying to Nebraska for Christmas. Our plane was two hours late leaving Philadelphia due to delays, so we missed our connecting flight. An airline agent was trying to find us another flight but they were all full. By this time it was 3:45 p.m., and she said we would be on standby for an 8:50 p.m. flight.

However, the possibility of getting a standby flight, let alone four seats, was next to impossible. She kept looking for about 20 minutes and then said that if we didn't make the standby flight, the next possibility (not guarantee) would be a 7:00 p.m. flight the next evening! By this time the children were almost in tears and I was getting discouraged myself. My children asked, "What are we going to do?"

I looked at the kids and said, "We need to pray and ask God to give us a flight; there is nothing else we can do." So we all continued to pray silently and ask the Lord for a flight. The agent had pretty much given up when all of a sudden with an astonished look on her face she said, "The plane you were to be on is coming back because of mechanical problems." The plane came back, they acquired a different plane and gave us our seats back that they had given to someone else—a rare occurrence! We left within an hour and ended up getting to our final destination only an hour late. Having a plane turn around and come back is a very rare occasion. I believe the Lord turned that plane around for us, at the request of my children and me.

Thank you Lord for providing for us, for being our help and for taking care of us.

Becky Mellinger, mother and homemaker, attends DOVE Rivers of Life, Refton.

Confident In The Lord's Goodness

"I am still confident of this: I will see the goodness of the Lord in the land of the living. Wait for the Lord; be strong and take heart and wait for the Lord." *Psalm 27:13-14*

The first time I heard this scripture it latched onto my spirit. I began to rejoice and praise the Lord for His promise to show us His goodness. I have always been confident that I will one day see the Lord in all of His beauty and might when I reach heaven, but this passage increased my faith to see the Lord in a greater way here on earth.

David's declarations of faith in the Lord's goodness in verse 13 and 14 are encouraging to read by themselves, but I began to gain a greater appreciation for David's faith when I read all of Psalm 27 and considered his treacherous position. War had broken out against him (v. 3), his enemies had besieged him (v. 3), and evil men were slandering his name (Psalm 27:2). Despite these difficult situations, in verse three he declares that he will still be confident in the Lord.

David declares that the Lord will keep him safe (v. 5), provide a safe shelter for him (v. 5), set him in a high rock (v. 5), be merciful (v. 7), hear his prayer (v. 7), be his helper (v. 9), and provide a safe place when he has no where to go (v 10). In the midst of hardship, David chose to take heart and stand strong while he waited for the Lord to reveal His goodness in his current circumstances.

We do not need to wait until we have passed from the land of the living, before we are able to see the Lord. Can we believe that the Lord wants to show His mighty power here on earth by pouring out miracles, signs and wonders? Can we take heart and expect Him to redeem lives, mend families, and restore relationships?

What areas in your life do you desire to see and experience the goodness of the Lord? May faith rise up in us and may we stand confidently until we see the Lord's goodness here in the land of the living!

Lord, reveal Yourself to us and demonstrate Your goodness. Lord, increase our faith to believe that You are good through out every circumstance that comes our way!

Konrad Martin is a member of ELANCO DOVE Christian Fellowship and a S.E.E.R Intern at Gateway House of Prayer.

In God's Lap

"...I have loved you with an everlasting love. I have drawn you with loving kindness." Jeremiah 31:3

It was a couple weeks before Christmas. I got up that morning with my agenda—clean the house, wash a pile of laundry, do the ironing, go for groceries, work on Mom's scrapbook so I could send it to Alabama on time for Christmas—on and on the list went. My day started off with "bless MY list today," and I started running.

A couple of hours into the day, I felt the Lord speaking to me, "Take time for Me." I ignored the voice. My list was way too long to take the time off. I started working on my scrapbook and the creative juices started flowing. The pages were looking great.

Again I heard God's voice, "Come spend some time with Me." I just didn't have the time, and besides I was on a roll. About the fourth time I heard His voice, I finally said, "Okay, Lord, fine, I'll stop what I'm doing because I'm sure this is going to be good."

I was thinking of all kinds of awesome things the Lord was going to say to me. I thought maybe He had a great prophetic word for me or a word for me to give to someone.

As I quieted myself before the Lord, I said, "I'm listening, what is it that is so exciting You have to tell me?" I heard Him say, "Nothing really, I just wanted to hold you in my lap."

God loves us so much. He longs to spend time with each and every one of His children.

Daddy, thank you that You love us so much and You want to spend time with each of Your children.

Brenda Boll serves as an elder, along with her husband, Steve, at Newport DOVE. She is on staff at House to House Publications.

God's Calling

"Do not neglect your gift, which was given you through a prophetic message when the body of elders laid their hands on you."
1 Timothy 4:14

When I was around fifteen years old, I was lying in bed one night when I felt that God began to speak to me about my life. I felt this strong impression that He was calling me to some kind of pastoral ministry. I remember feeling excited yet somewhat overwhelmed as I fell asleep that night. I often thought about this experience over the next couple of years as I finished high school and considered the big decision as to what I should do after graduation.

After spending a year or so working in construction, I was led to attend a short-term missions program which took me on a two month trip to Thailand. It was here that God spoke to me clearly again. Over a one week period during this outreach, I had two different people who had never met me before suggest that I should consider pursuing pastoral ministry when I return home to the United States. Even more important was the personal scripture that I came across during that week through which the voice of God came so clearly to me that this was part of what He was calling me to do with my life.

Since returning home from this time in missions back in 1997, I have taken steps of obedience to be able to live out this call that God has placed on my life. It has been through a number of different churches and ministries that I have had the privilege to use the gifts that God has been so gracious to give me. Now, when facing the challenges that come with Christian leadership, it is so precious to me to know how clearly God has led me to the place that I am!

Father, help me to never neglect the gifts that You have given me to serve Your church.

Mike Stoltzfus serves with the Lancaster Micro Church Network.

I Passed The Test

"For the righteous God tests the hearts and minds." *Psalm 7:9*

God knows His children have desires. He is a good God that wants to bless us with things here on earth, but not when those things invade and control our hearts. I faced this particular test at a time of need in my life.

My husband and I had a car that was breaking down constantly, so some good friends loaned us their car. Now, I happened to think this car was very cool. So before I knew it, I was driving down the road in my borrowed car and I stopped at a red light. All of the sudden, I recognized pride and feelings of "I've arrived" bubbling up in my heart and mind. As I entertained these feelings for a moment, I began to discern the state of my heart and confessed the truth; that this is just a car to get me around and this is not who I am. A few days later, the owners of the car felt led to sell us the vehicle for a dollar. I was shocked when I found out, because I immediately realized the time when I was at the stop light, God was testing my heart to see if I could handle the thing He was desiring to give me. I passed the test.

I think of Abraham and others like him in the Bible who were tested because of God's great love and jealousy for them. They were tested and allowed to keep the desire of their heart because they desired God more. God will come and test us. He is a great Father desiring to pour out His gifts on His children. But we must pass the "first love" test. Our identity is not in things but God!

Father, You have entrusted us with things here on earth. May I be found loving You with all my heart, mind, strength and soul.

Lydia Nimon is the mother of five children and serves on a worship team in Gateway House of Prayer.

Dinner with Dr. and Mrs. Dolittle

"Do not neglect hospitality, for through it some have unknowingly entertained angels." *Hebrews 13:2*

It was after the last mass of the weekend. The shadows stretched clear across Fifth Street and a light breeze caressed the faithful exiting the church. As I bid farewell to the last parishioner, I saw a middle-aged woman—a stranger—lingering curiously. "Father," she said, "We are on our way home to Florida and we need some help."

She told me that she and her husband were vacationing in Maine. Their resources were running out, and they figured they could find more generous hearts along the smaller highways—or at church.

"I wish I could help you," I replied, "but just yesterday we took a father of five to shop for food, and we've no money to give for gas."

"Actually, we're just really hungry. By the way, my name is Ruby."

Then I remembered the bowl of ziti that Mrs. Colon brought to the side door earlier that afternoon. Extra sauce. Bread, too. "Well...would you and your husband join me for supper?"

Ruby and I quickly set the table on the side porch, put the ziti in the oven, and went to meet her husband. In the church parking lot, a faded van sat alone. Reclining in the driver's seat, baseball cap over his eyes, was Ruby's husband Bob—with a *skunk* lying across his chest!

"Is that a...!?" "Yeah, but acts more like a cat. We call her Boots. Bob, this is Father Wuslak. He's invited us to dinner." Bob sat up quickly, spooking Boots. *I hope she's not loaded.*

"I'll bring Henry," Ruby said. "He's our prairie dog." She pulled the critter from the van, as we walked toward the porch. Soon the five of us were sitting at the table, asking God's blessing. Boots paced the porch while Henry seemed content to be held by Bob. Our conversation was interesting—and my guests were genuinely appreciative of the meal. When the time came to see them off, they packed up their "family" as I reflected on the surprisingly wonderful evening.

"Good night," I bid them. "If you're ever in the area again, be sure to stop in." I meant it.

Father, may we have a true spirit of welcome for any person who shows up at our doors.

Rev. Thomas Orsulak is pastor of St. Peter the Apostle Parish, Reading.

Contending For A Miracle

"Ask and it will be given to you...for everyone who asks receives."
Luke 11:9–10

The doctors were almost certain my mother's polyp was cancerous so they'd scheduled her for major surgery. When I heard her diagnosis, John 10:10 came to mind: *"The thief comes only to steal and kill and destroy."* It felt very much like a thief was attempting to rob my mother of vitality during her "golden years." She had asked me why these things happen to us, and I had answered that sometimes God allows difficult situations in our lives so that He can demonstrate His love for us. We prayed together, binding the spirit of cancer and forbidding its presence in her body. Others in our church fellowship were also praying.

But in the days before her surgery doubts filled my mind. "Why should I expect God to answer our prayers for healing, when so many others have to go through cancer treatments?" In one moment of great doubt, I simply stopped and walked into the throne room in heaven. "Lord Jesus, I am not backing down. I am asking You for a *MIRACLE:* I am asking You to heal my mother!" I picked up the phone and called Mom. "Mom, I am asking God for a miracle!" She answered, "I agree!" and faith rose as we agreed together.

In her post-op hospital room, through the haze of anesthesia, Mom groggily told me there had been *no* surgery. We had received our MIRACLE! First, God had instructed the doctor to "examine again, *before* he operated" (not common procedure). Second, there was no polyp, only scar tissue where the polyp had been!

Today, my octogenarian mother golfs, bowls, visits her grandchildren in Wisconsin, and is growing in her faith in a weekly Bible study. God is giving her golden years!

God, You are the God of miracles. Thank you. Build our faith to see more!

Janet Richards and her husband, Rusty, pray for the healing of European nations through their ministry, *PRAY BIG!* She also writes, acts and paints.

An Awesome God

"...and without faith it is impossible to please God...." *Hebrews 11:6*

Several years ago, I began asking God to give my husband and me a way to serve him when we reached retirement age. After taking an early retirement offered by his company, my husband starting working a part-time job. Then Katrina hit the Gulf coast.

We were in a group of 21 from our church who went to New Orleans in March of 2006. Our eyes saw devastation our eyes could not comprehend. It was there God answered my prayer and did an awesome thing! He gave my husband a heart for the people of New Orleans.

Even before we left for home he knew God wanted us to return to help with the recovery. That meant some big things had to change.

The biggest being a job that would allow my husband the time off. We also wanted to downsize our home, being empty nesters.

So buying and selling a home was on the list. Big list. But God is bigger! He doesn't call you to serve Him without making a way.

However it was a test of our faith and patience. The job came first. God closed the door on one and opened it on another in a different department (it was offered to my husband without his asking!) It required him to work 3 months, have off 3 months, work 3 months, have off 3 months. Perfect! He got the job in July, we found our "answer to prayer" home in August, and sold our home and moved in October.

New Orleans here we come! And by January 2007 that's exactly what we did - for 6 weeks! And we returned for another 5 weeks in July and August. God provided finances and some real "God story" experiences - but that will have to wait for another time.

Father, I thank and praise You for Your faithfulness and for building faith in Your children as they obey You.

Saundra Rineer serves as a volunteer and intercessor for Susquehanna Valley Pregnancy Services and Sanctuary.

Love In Action

"May you experience the love of Christ, though it is so great you will never fully understand it." *Ephesians 3:19 (New Living Translation)*

One day while I was out running, I began asking God about how he wanted me to reach out to the teens in Terre Hill. Many of them are skateboarders who really need someone to love and encourage them. God told me to take my small grill with some hotdogs and hamburgers and cook a meal for them at the skate park near our community park. I began meeting with them on Monday nights to bless them and build relationships.

The teens received me well and many wanted to know why I brought them food and drinks. This opened the door for me to share with them the love of Jesus Christ. As we eat and talk together, I have opportunities to discuss such things as school, current events, family life, pray for those who are not feeling well, and most importantly, encourage them to give their lives to Jesus and live the glorious life they were created to live. *God has a plan for them...Jeremiah 29:11.*

We currently meet Monday evenings on our back deck, since the skate park was recently closed. I'm praying that these teens would experience the love of Christ and that the seeds that are planted would fall on fertile ground and bear much fruit. God loves these kids and wants to transform their lives!

God, grant to us Your wisdom and creativity to reach the lost and hurting in our communities. Fill us with Your love so that we can share that love with them, for we desire to see Your Kingdom advance here on earth. Amen

Craig Sensenig works at the Ephrata Hospital as an electrician, is a member of ELANCO DOVE, in Terre Hill, and previously served as youth pastor at Groffdale Mennonite Church.

Smoothing The Rough Edges

"All Your waves and billows have gone over me." *Psalm 42:7*

Many years ago, while walking along the Delaware River's edge, I found a piece of broken green glass. What caught my attention was the glass seemed to be broken from a bottle yet the misshaped piece had no sharp edges, it was perfectly smooth. I wondered how many years it took being under the waves and billows to become so smooth.

It was at that moment the God of the universe spoke and said, "I do the same with My body." He calls us deeper and then allows His waves and billows to come over us, preparing us for His good work, smoothing off the rough edges from the brokenness caused by sin. I could see the Master fashioning His body into a piece of mosaic artwork, removing sharp edges that cause pain and hurt to one another, carefully fitting us together. When He is finished, we reflect the *Son* – revealing His Glory.

I often wonder why, on that day, did the God of the universe plan that a piece of green glass would wash up on the river's edge to be found, and that He would speak His design for His body into the heart of a new believer. Perhaps the answer is found in *Psalm 42:8*: "The Lord will command His loving kindness in the daytime, and in the night His song shall be with me." A prayer to God for my life.

God, You call deep unto deep and we hear the call to come to the rivers edge, thank you that Your waves and billows cover over us. May we hear Your heart and live our lives as a prayer unto You, reflecting Your glory unto the world. Amen

Debbie Davenport, wife and spiritual mother, serves on the leadership team at Living Truth Fellowship, is an intercessor for the Hopewell Network of Churches and is the executive director at Cornerstone Pregnancy Care Services.

God is Faithful

"God who has called you into fellowship with his Son Jesus Christ our Lord, is faithful." *1 Corinthians 1:9*

Back in the mid-seventies, God and I established the first group for the Deaf multi-disabled in the state of Ohio. The beginning days of the home's founding were exhausting. For the first seven months, I was in charge of the boys seven days a week, 24 hours a day. Funding did not permit the hiring of any other staff. Though the work was exhausting, it was rewarding—and I never had a dull moment!

After the first week, I got tired of washing dishes, so I came up with the bright idea of teaching the fellows how to do it. In the midst of our first lesson, the phone rang. After a five minute conversation, I returned to the kitchen—and saw soap bubbles all the way up to the ceiling! I guess the guys felt that they needed more soap, so they used up the entire bottle! I couldn't get mad, since they never washed dishes before.

Christmas was approaching. Although the state of Ohio officials promised to send a check, it did not come. After several calls, I found out that no money would be coming until sometime next year. In the meantime, how was I to pay the rent, utilities and food? I had already spent all of my personal savings in order to operate the home.

A few days passed. A local newspaper reporter wanted to do a story on our group home. Soon after, a nice article about our home appeared in the paper. I requested no appeal for money or assistance in the article, since I did not want to appear to be "begging" for funds.

One week before Christmas, there was a knock on the door. I opened the door to discover a family of five bearing a tree, food and Christmas presents! "We read about you in the paper," they said, "and decided to adopt you for Christmas!"

I'll never forget that act of kindness. It was amazing—they knew all our names and had gifts for everyone—including me! I never heard from or saw that family again. I can't even remember their names... maybe they were angels.

Lord, thank you for those "angels" among us!

Jim Schneck is a free-lance interpreter for the Deaf.

Anticipating Christmas

"Thanks be to God for his indescribable gift!" *2 Corinthians 9:15*

I love anticipating Christmas. I love the feeling of love expressed by sending and receiving cards and letters. I love the beauty of decorating my home, of putting fresh greenery and lights on the stairway banister and mantle, and candles in the windows. I love hanging ornaments on a real Christmas tree. I find the smell of freshly baked cookies and breads irresistible. I love sharing hand-dipped candies and colorful wrapped gifts topped with bows. I love the laughter shared at gatherings. I love the season's music—classical, traditional, or contemporary. One of my most treasured family traditions is reading short stories from our favorite anthology to my children each year.

Christmas may be a favorite holiday for a variety of reasons. However busy our calendars become or how frequently we repeat the greeting "Merry Christmas" to another, let's remember to worship God's most precious gift to us—Jesus Christ. Come, let us adore Him: Christ the Lord.

Father, help me to focus on exalting Christ in my thoughts and activities throughout this busy season.

Nancy Leatherman, an administrative assistant at Teaching The Word Ministries, is anticipating her daughter's December wedding.

Absolutely Perfect Night

"...God's kindness [goodness] is meant to lead you to repentance."
Romans 2:4 (Revised Standard Version)

We invited an unbeliever along on a fishing trip in Florida. An evening with "believers"...fishing with no alcohol, a night out with no women? Then he finds out I'm a preacher—he wasn't impressed! But when God orchestrates the events of the evening, everything changes.

What a gorgeous night out on the bay. As we stopped the engine and allowed the boat to drift, everyone immediately started catching fish. We drifted by a line of pelicans doing equally as well; they were floating quietly in the shadow of a bridge catching fish that were in the light from the road above. After some tremendous fishing, our friend said, "what a great night, all that would make this better would be seeing some dolphins." No sooner said and four or five dolphins swam by the boat jumping out of the water putting on a spectacular show.

Having caught plenty of fish, watched the pelicans stealthy hunting skills and enjoyed a dolphin show, I set our course to travel back across the bay. Our friend said, "I kinda wanted to go watch the space shuttle take off, you know tonight is the first night launch." Looking toward the east, we saw what appeared to be an extra bright street light but it climbed above the others and angled south. We quickly recognized the shuttle as it climbed out of the lights on the ground and became brighter and easier to see. We could actually see its shape and followed its path up until the solid boosters burned out and separated. At that he said, "this has been an absolutely perfect night."

No dirty jokes, no alcohol and no women, just hanging out with a few believers and a preacher! But in his own words, an absolutely perfect night.

Father, thank you for showing Your goodness to unbelievers as we show them life without the sinful attractions of this world.

Captain Clair Stauffer, founder of Refreshing Leaders Ministry.

Light Of The World

"[Jesus] said, 'I am the light of the world.'" *John 8:12*

Scientists tell us that light travels over 182,000 miles per second. Microwaves and lasers use light as energy. Rainbows use light through droplets of water to create colorful wonders. Plants and animals need light to exist. We as humans need the vitamin D that light provides to us—important for bone mass. Even this morning, the light of dawn appeared at your place in the world. But, who can explain or even understand the existence of light?

The infant Jesus was found by the Wise Men navigating their way via starlight. Paul, the apostle, ran into a blinding light on the road to Damascus. Characteristically, the closer you come to light, the brighter it is. Light reveals darkness (hidden things). Light reflects more clearly on clean surfaces. When someone walks away from light, they walk in a shadow. Light and darkness have no fellowship together. When light is present, darkness has to flee. Lights are plentiful at Christmas to remind us of the hope we have in the One who is the light of the world.

We are called to walk in the light as He is in the light (1 John 1:7). The blind do not appreciate the light; they can't see the light. John 3:19–21 tells us that men love darkness instead of light because of their evil behavior. The scripture then states, "But whoever lives by the truth comes into the light, so that it may be seen plainly that what he has done has been done through God."

As incomprehensible as light is, God, the Creator of light, determined His life was to dwell in us and that through us He would be "the light of men (John 1:4)."

Father, when we see light may we see You and be reminded of Your life in us.

Steve Prokopchak serves on DOVE Christian Fellowship International's Apostolic Council.

Fight The Good Fight

"And this command we have from Him, that the one who loves God should love his brother also." *1 John 4:21 (Amplified Bible)*

Laura was a young (17-year-old) girl with a slight hearing loss, mental retardation, and severe behavior problems. She was unable to speak with her voice, but began to learn sign language in order to communicate. I had the "joy" of working with her. Most of the other teachers couldn't stand her! She was dirty, smelled bad, and pinched. Laura's favorite disgusting habit was to eat cigarette butts—and to spit on you when she was angry.

One day during a summer class, I was determined that Laura was going to go through the entire lesson completely without spitting on me. Every time she spat, I would start at the very beginning of the lesson and repeat it. After one hour, my shirt was soaked, but we got through the lesson!

Laura was so needy. Although I dreaded working with her, I was determined to *not* show her I didn't like her. I acted like I was so happy to see her, when in reality, I wished she was sick at home. In time, Laura began to respond and began to behave. I found that I also had changed and actually *was* glad to see her.

I thought she would never learn her name. Everyday for one and one-half years, I worked with her *daily* to get her to respond to her name and to learn how to spell it. For awhile, I thought it was hopeless—she would never master it. Then one day, she spelled her name perfectly and even went on to spell her last name, which was very long.

By the time I was done working with her, Laura had learned over 800 signs and could communicate some things very well. She actually became one of my favorite students. Don't ever, ever give up!

Lord, thank you for Your faithfulness! You didn't give up on us—help us not to give up on others.

Jim Schneck is a free-lance interpreter for the deaf.

Hunger And Thirst

"…You have anointed my head with oil; My cup overflows."
Psalm 23:5

I remember this moment so clearly. I was listening to a *Watermark* CD and one of the lines in the chorus swept over me like a water fall. "Oh Lord, if only I could make my road look like Your road… if I could love the way You love…if Your Word in my heart was the only thing I used to fill me up." I landed on my living room floor and was undone for several minutes.

We hunger and thirst, but we don't always know what for. We are always looking for something to fill us. I can say "we" with confidence because I'm sure you, too, have looked for love, identity and value in all the wrong places. Not that loving our mate or our children is "wrong" —but when we look to anything other than God to fill our cup, we're simply not satisfied.

Each one of us has a hunger and a thirst that can only be fulfilled through that which is eternal. Jesus, the Word who became flesh, is our only offer of Eternity and the only answer to our deepest longing. Only the Lord Himself can adequately fill us.

And fill us He does. Not just partially, but to "overflowing!" Why do we settle for less? Why do we even look elsewhere?

I want to be found singing the song, "My cup is full and running over, running over, running over!" How about you?

Lord, You know how quickly I forget what I learn and You know that I will probably try to get my fill some other way, but I cry out to You to stop me from such futility. You are the only answer to this longing. Please don't allow me to settle for anything less, Sweet Jesus. Truly, You are my all in all. Amen

Kathi Wilson and her husband, Mark, co-authors of *Tired of Playing Church* and co-founders of Body Life Ministries, are members of Ephrata Community Church.

Forgive As Christ Forgave You

"Therefore, as God's chosen people, holy and dearly loved, clothe yourselves with compassion, kindness, humility, gentleness and patience. Bear with each other and forgive whatever grievances you may have against one another. Forgive as the Lord forgave you. And over all these virtues put on love, which binds them all together in perfect unity." *Colossians 3:12-14*

The author of Colossians connects several dots in these verses. First, those "dearly loved" are "God's chosen people" because "the Lord forgave" their sins through an act of sovereign grace. Secondly, without the clothing of the virtues mentioned, we are naked, and our nature tends toward making us want to run and hide just like Adam and Eve hid from God as a result of the original sin. Thirdly, it is assumed here that grievances against other people is a common and ordinary experience in life. Finally, we are challenged to "put on love" which is the expression of "perfect unity," and the key to make forgiveness accomplish its purpose.

Somehow those of us who have been Christians for any length of time hold out the hope that forgiveness will become easier to practice as we get closer to God and experience more of the depths of His love towards us. Perhaps in some respect this is true, but for me, every time I am faced with the pain of a wrong done to me, I am freshly tempted to grab my "dirty clothes" of pride, bitterness, resentment, impatience and everything opposite of the clothes I am told to "put on." Then I remember what Christ did for me in extending the gift of forgiveness and taking all my transgressions to the cross at Calvary. I release my right to secure justice and yield to His finished work. I do not have to be a victim and allow someone else's transgression to hold me captive in "dirty clothes." I can choose to walk in the love Christ has lavished upon me and give the gift of that love to others who need it.

Lord, help me to put on love when I am tempted to hate. Give me the grace to work through the hurts caused by wrongs done against me and be able to receive Your healing as provided in the cross at Calvary. Help me to forgive others as You have already forgiven me.

Dr. Edward Hersh, provides counseling and healing prayer ministry to individuals and families, trains lay counselors here and abroad and helps leaders receive spiritual renewal.

Why Not Ask God First?

"Some trust in chariots, and some in horses; but we will remember the name of the Lord our God." *Psalm 20:7*

Early in my Christian life I experienced a head injury that caused me to have ongoing issues with headaches. For someone like myself, who rarely gets sick at all, this was a real challenge to deal with this daily, sometimes almost debilitating, pain. After many doctor visits and a number of tests, my doctor finally announced that there was nothing that he could do for me. I would just need to be patient and hopefully the headaches would diminish and pass over time.

At that point, after exhausting all other options, I finally went to the Lord and asked Him for healing and was instantly delivered from headaches to the point where I have rarely suffered from them at all since then.

As I saw God at work in this way, my first response to myself was "Why didn't I ask Him for healing long ago?" As a new Christian, I was literally unaware that God so desired to heal me, and I was embarrassed that it was only after nothing else worked that I sought Him for healing.

I now realize that God is always the source of the healing I need. Regardless of whether the healing comes through the care of a medical doctor, a change in lifestyle, or by a miracle from Him, He is always the source of my health and healing.

In 2 Chronicles 16:12, King Asa became diseased in his feet, but did not seek the Lord, only physicians. I am grateful for those who serve in the medical field. The way they minister healing is an awesome blessing! But I never again desire to fall into the trap that King Asa did. The Lord is the source of my health and healing.

Father, I thank You for those who serve our region in the medical profession. They are a blessing to many. I also recognize You, Lord, as the source of my health and healing and the sustainer of my very life.

Kevin Eshleman serves as executive pastor of Ephrata Community Church.

DECEMBER 21

Seeking God First

"But seek ye first his Kingdom and his righteousness; and all these
things shall be added unto you."
Matthew 6:33 (American Standard Version)

We had a Christmas tradition in our home to invite those we
knew with no family or place to be to join us for Christmas
breakfast. Earlier that year, Ken and I had responded to
God's call to trust Him with our needs and give ourselves to full-time
ministry, giving up our business. With joy, we entered into a divine
orchestration of events that left us no doubt that God was leading. Ken
felt as though he and God had an understanding that he was willing to
work bi-vocationally, but as long as God supplied, we would work in
full-time ministry.

The problem was, we were now behind on a garage bill and had no
money for gifts or groceries for Christmas breakfast. I remember walking through my living room and a thought flitting through my mind: "I
wish I had some homemade jelly left for Christmas breakfast."

That Friday, a pastor from another congregation stopped by and
held out a nicely decorated box. My mouth fell open as I saw that
it contained two jars of homemade jelly, one of them my favorite
(raspberry). God heard my wish and even knew what kind I forgot to
request. He then handed us a check, enough to pay the garage bill. That
Christmas we were able to celebrate the goodness of our God, and His
absolute faithfulness. When December 29 came, the garage we had owed
money sent us a check. They chose to contribute locally rather than
abroad and gave us a generous gift. We were overwhelmed at how God
added all these things unto us.

*God, let me never forget how You delight to give good gifts, even to
the flavor of jelly we like. I want to seek Your Kingdom first today
and always.*

Betty Eberly is a homemaker and grandmother, serving in Behold Your God
Ministries and on the leadership team with Hampden Mennonite alongside
husband, Ken (eighteen years).

This Far And No More

"God is our refuge and strength, an ever-present help in trouble, Therefore we will not fear… though its waters roar and foam and the mountains quake with their surging…" *Psalm 46:1-3*

The swollen waters of the Schuylkill River were already above flood stage on that Wednesday in June 2006, as our prayer team from the Reading House of Prayer held its weekly noontime Worship and Intercession vigil for the blessing of God over our City.

At 12:30 pm, the call came for us to evacuate because the flood waters were projected to rise six more feet by evening. Already ravaging the lowest lying areas of Reading, they were threatening to move inward toward the center of town.

As I had the privilege of leading the prayer team, we paused to ask the Father for instructions. A word was spoken from one of the intercessors: "You have Authority…" In the silence that followed, I began to see a faint vision of the flooded Schuylkill River; before it, with His back to me, stood a lone figure whom I perceived to be Jesus. I knew the Lord was saying that if we spoke the word, He would restrain the floodwaters. Boldness rose up within our Spirits as we began once again to worship, declaring in song and voice: "This far and no more" to the water. The room filled with the power of the presence of God and we stayed, interceding for the remainder of the two hour set. I could literally feel the hand of God holding back the river's rising tide.

The news later reported that at 1:45 pm the river had crested below what was predicted earlier, not rising beyond the point it was at the time we prayed!

Awesome God seated on the throne, stir our faith to take our place with You in heavenly realms, declaring Your blessing over our regions, for nothing is impossible with You!

Lee Ritz is pastor of Hampden Mennonite Church in Reading and serves on the leadership team of Reading House of Prayer.

Angels Among Us

"Do not forget to entertain strangers, for by so doing some people have entertained angels without knowing it." *Hebrews 13:2*

A young man was seeking God's will for his life. He loved fly-fishing the waters in the west, and was offered a summer job on a guest ranch in Wyoming to take guests fly-fishing. He accepted, while still being perplexed about God's will for his future. The ranch was owned by Christians and all the staff had to have a personal relationship with the Lord in order to be employed. The Christian staff had many opportunities to touch the hearts of the unsaved guests with the message of the Gospel as they visited the ranch.

One day a lady surgeon and her son arrived at the ranch. The young man guided the lady and her son on a day of fishing. While in the stillness of the day, the lady asked the young man a question. "When I arrived at this ranch, a white brilliant light approached me. I haven't seen that light since I was in a coma as a child. Do you know what it was?" she asked.

The young man told her of the power of the Holy Spirit who lives in Christians, and that God was inviting her to give her heart to Him so she could experience that brilliant light forever. She was very receptive.

The young man decided to go to seminary and become a pastor, all because of his summer experience.

May we be an aura of light for others to find the Lord.

Oh God, opportunities are everywhere. Sometimes You bring them as angels among us. May we never ignore the opportunity to tell others about You. Amen

Dona L. Fisher is Chairman of the local National Day of Prayer, director of Change of Pace Bible Studies and a free lance writer for Lancaster Sunday Newspaper.

The Wonder Of Christmas

"Glory to God in the highest, and on earth peace to men on whom his favor rests." *Luke 2:14*

On a cold Sunday evening I joined a group who went caroling in one of the communities in Lebanon City. Teens and a few youth leaders sang songs of the Christmas season. As we sang the familiar verses, I had an unusual experience. I sensed angels were there with us in the village. They were talking together about the first Christmas. I couldn't even begin to tell you what they said. What held my attention was *how* they talked. They exchanged details of the story like someone who has just seen a close win by their favorite football team—unmatched enthusiasm as they poured out all the details of how it happened.

It made me realize how weak and dull my view of Christmas really was. I saw the event as a quaint, old story, instead of the earth-shaking event it really is. When I thought of Christmas, what came to my mind were the things that surround it, not what it really is about—*God coming near*. When I remember the experience, I am again reminded of the tremendous joy of the season. It's not just excitement about family gatherings, cookies and presents. It's about a Savior who came to change the course of human history. He came to change *my* history!

Now *that* is something for which to throw a party and celebrate!

Father, Christmas reminds us of how You remembered us and our need of a Savior. We are grateful for Your gift to us. Thank you so much for sending us our redeemer. Amen

Sarah Sauder works as a graphic designer and serves on the youth leadership team with DOVE Christian Fellowship International.

A Star Is Born, And Is Here To Stay!

"After Jesus was born in Bethlehem in Judea, during the time of King Herod, Magi from the east came to Jerusalem and asked, 'Where is the one who has been born king of the Jews? We saw his star in the east and have come to worship him.' When King Herod heard this he was disturbed…." *Matthew 2:1-3*

It was December 23, 1976 on a cold winter's night in the small town of Lititz. A manger scene was given and dedicated to the Lititz Borough Council by a Lititz resident for the town square.

In a small town called Bethlehem the world's first manger scene unfolded where a babe born of a virgin would forever change our lives.

As in the day in Bethlehem when King Herod tried to eradicate the events that unfolded in history, so it was in Lititz that the ACLU tried to remove the long standing crèche in Lititz. Like King Herod, they were unsuccessful. It was there to stay after becoming a hotspot for controversy. It turned out that this manger scene on the small corner of the town square was not on public property, but instead owned privately by the Moravian church. In light of this, the ACLU could not remove it.

There are people, governments and activities that try to take Jesus out of our lives. But there are just some things that government cannot shake. Let's celebrate today the birth of our King on this Christmas Day. Merry Christmas!

Father, make our life adventurous just as You made Your Son's life adventurous that we too would make the kings and queens of the earth shake for Your glory. Amen

Jeff Burkholder is on the Elizabeth Township Board of Supervisors.

A photo of the Lititz crèche appears on page 351.

Hands-On

"Humble yourselves, therefore, under God's mighty hand, that he may lift you up in due time." *1 Peter 5:6*

I enjoyed a restful 2005 Labor Day weekend in Ocean City, New Jersey, under sunny skies and in front of a gentle ocean. Yet, the images of Hurricane Katrina were everywhere. I began to pray for the Lord to open up an opportunity for me to help in a "hands-on" way.

It was not too long after I began to pray that an opportunity presented itself. I inquired about the specifics and was told that volunteers with administrative skills were immediately needed to help out in the shelters in Houston, Texas. I would need to provide my own transportation there and back, as well as my own lodging and food. It was not quite what I had been hoping for, but I was thankful and excited, nonetheless.

While it seemed the Lord had answered my prayer, I was disappointed when, after reviewing my budget and work obligations, I had to decline the offer to go.

Just a few weeks later, a door opened for me to accompany a group from my church to drive to Waveland, Mississippi, as Samaritan's Purse volunteers. The trip did not cost me anything, as we used a church van and stayed at the Bayou Talla Fellowship Church. The trip was also planned for January 2006, which was a much better time for me to go. We spent the entire week "mudding-out" flooded homes, ministering and witnessing to the homeowners, sharing testimony and making new friends with the other volunteers, the congregation of Bayou Talla, and the Samaritan's Purse staff.

It was very "hands-on" and more wonderful and life changing than I could have even imagined!

Thank you, Father, that when we humble ourselves before You, You lift us up in the most perfect and wonderful ways!

Lorena Patricia Keely is a member of Glad Tidings Assembly of God in Sinking Spring, where she is active in several ministries, including the writing of the yearly VBS program and a Bible Study tool available on the church's website.

God's Prompting

"You can be sure that God will take care of everything you need, his generosity exceeding even yours in the glory that pours from Jesus."
Philippians 4:19 (The Message)

The little phrase "Quit your job" seemed to echo in my ears again and again. Could it really be the Lord speaking to me, I wondered. How could I possibly stop working my part-time job when we had college bills over our heads and a brand-new mortgage payment?

But the Lord seemed to gently prompt me again: "Devote your working hours to Me. Trust Me. I will take care of all your needs. I want to teach you My ways."

After praying about it with my husband, Brent, and seeking the counsel of a few close friends, it seemed to be the right decision (even though it really didn't make sense). We worked and reworked our budget, but it still looked impossible. We finally concluded that we didn't want to risk the consequences of disobeying. So, the following week, I scooped up my mustard seed faith and handed in my resignation.

Then just ten days later a most amazing thing happened! One of the senior managers at Brent's workplace approached him saying that he wanted to reduce his own salary in order to give Brent an increase in pay. Brent explained that it really wasn't necessary, but the man insisted, saying that he knew the company was unable to spend more for raises and felt he deserved it!

We were awestruck at the goodness of God as we worked out the numbers that night, realizing that this man (who was not even a believer) gave us exactly the amount of money that I would have earned at my part-time job that year!

Father, we marvel at Your ways! Teach us to trust You even when it doesn't make sense. Increase our faith to believe You even when it looks impossible. Thank you for Your faithfulness, goodness, and generosity in our lives.

Bonita Keener helps with prayer in the region and serves as an elder alongside her husband, Brent, at New Life Fellowship in Ephrata. They have four precious children.

Worthy

"In a loud voice they sang: 'Worthy is the Lamb, who was slain, to receive power and wealth and wisdom and strength and honor and glory and praise!'" *Revelation 5:12*

I was just worshipping the other day and came across a line in a song that said, "You are worthy" (referring to God). That really stuck out to me and made me think for a while. I feel dumb telling God He is worthy. It is so painfully obvious that I am embarrassed. Who am I, the clay, to tell the potter of His worth? I am not worthy to call Him worthy! So, I had to wait for God to explain it to me. And, He did, as He seems to do a lot these days, with an illustration from my more consuming occupation of parenthood.

My baby daughter does not speak words yet. She babbles pretty well, and we can usually get a nice string of "dadadadada" in various inflections. I even caught her with some "mamamama's" the other day. But since she is not associating these sounds with anything yet, they are not really words. They sound sweet, yet mean nothing. I am so excited for the day when she looks at me and says, "mama," unmistakably addressing me. Why? I know I am her mother. But I want to know she knows. Then I will understand she knows who I am. Obviously, the God of the universe knows He is worthy. But He created us with free will to be able to show Him our love and respect for Him. We need to praise Him and let Him know we know who He really is.

Dear God, You are worthy! I recognize that. I give You all of my being to worship You. Amen

Tracy Slonaker is a wife and mother of three. She is also the Director of Christian Education at Harvest Fellowship of Colebrookdale in Boyertown.

Ponder These Things

"But Mary treasured up all these things and pondered them in her heart." *Luke 2:19*

My future husband lived in Reading, PA. He had a lovely home and a good job, so I knew we would be living there a while. One night while talking with my heavenly Father, I expressed my gratefulness for His provision, but I didn't really like the idea of living in Reading because none of my family were in the area. "Be patient because in two years you will be back in Lancaster County," was God's response.

"Wow, how was that going to happen," I thought. I knew that I needed to ponder that in my heart and wait to see how God was going to work it out.

After a year of discontentment at his job and God's leading to make a change, Scott began looking for another venue to practice medicine. During this time I said nothing about my conversation with God. I was waiting for the perfect time.

After several interviews, Scott landed a job in Ephrata, PA. When he needed to give a six month notice at his job, I sensed he needed a confirmation. I then told Scott how God had spoken to me that we would move to Lancaster County in two years. It was five days before our second anniversary when we moved to Ephrata. God is so good and His timing is perfect!

God has a plan for each of our lives that can be fulfilling, but we need to hear His heart and walk in His perfect plan for our lives. "'For I know the plans I have for you,' declares the Lord, 'plans to prosper you and not to harm you, plans to give you hope and a future' (Jeremiah 29:11)."

Thank you, Father, for listening to and answering our prayers.

Karen Jackson serves on the eldership team at Oasis Fellowship, Akron.

Inspire Someone!

"Similarly, encourage the young men to be self-controlled. In everything set them an example by doing what is good...." *Titus 2:6–7*

Several summers ago I started jogging early in the morning, several days a week. It was difficult at first with many periods of walking mixed in, but I slowly improved. During this process, God used a few very brief and simple encounters to help me understand something better.

Since I would run at basically the same time in the morning, I began noticing other "regulars." One such person was a woman I'd see fairly regularly, and we'd say hello as we passed. One morning I happened to be jogging up a hill when we passed and she said, "I can never jog up this hill, I need to walk." As I passed, I called back something like, "Sure you can, I couldn't at first either."

A week or two later, I passed her again in the same area, and she called out, "You inspired me, I can jog up this hill now!"

The word "inspired" caught my attention as God strengthened this understanding: You *encourage* by what you say, but you *inspire* by what you do. Encouraging her with "you can jog up this hill" would have been very empty if I were also walking up the hill.

In Titus 2, Paul is instructing Timothy on what should be taught to various groups/ages in the church. When he comes to young men, you might think this list would be long, but Paul only mentions one thing: self-control. But then he adds, "in everything, set them an example." Wasn't Paul teaching that "showing" was as important as "saying"?

Who can you inspire today? Your words are so important, but your actions add inspiration to your encouragement! No matter how new you are in your faith, there is always someone who can be inspired by you.

Father, use me today to inspire others to greater levels of faithfulness and service.

Ron Ressler is the senior pastor at Living Hope Community Church, west of Lancaster City. Ron is married to Molly, and they have two children.

Keeping Faith

"Open the gates that the righteous nation may enter, the nation that keeps faith." *Isaiah 26:2*

This summer we spent a weekend as a family at a mountain cabin. I was very much looking forward to a nice four-day weekend. The first day was very relaxing and my spirit was feeling the refreshment.

On the second day, a deer decided to run out in front of our van. We hit it head-on and it crunched the hood and split the radiator. The van was older, but I had just recently refreshed all of the systems in hopes that we could get several good years from it before laying it to rest. The course of our weekend changed abruptly, and I knew that the challenges wouldn't end there.

Early the next morning I whined my prayers to the Lord and sought His insight on how to respond. A scripture came to mind: "Thou will keep in perfect peace him whose mind is stayed on Thee." I looked it up in my Bible and discovered the above verse connected with it. I sensed the Lord's call to "keep faith." I shared later that morning with my family that I had chosen to be a man who keeps faith, and we would one day testify to God's faithfulness.

The details of God's abundant provision are too much to tell here, but they are nothing short of miraculous to me, and should you see me, I would be happy to share. This call to keep faith has been a theme in my life over the past two years and when my mind has "stayed on Him," I have witnessed His faithfulness.

Would you take up the call to join me to keep faith this day? Should the Son of God return today, He will find faith.

God, grant me this day the strength to keep faith. I will trust in Your promise to keep me in perfect peace as I fix my attention on You. I look forward to one day giving testimony to Your faithfulness.

Barry Stoner serves as an associate minister at Teaching The Word Ministries in Leola.

A Celebration of Partnership

The following regional networks within South Central Pennsylvania partnered in publishing this volume of devotionals. We invite you to contact them to learn more about how God is at work to bring transformation in your local region.

The Regional Church of Lancaster County

Keith Yoder, Chair, and Kevin Eshleman, Assistant Chair
Box 311, Leola, PA 17540
Phone: (717) 625-3034   www.theregionalchurch.com

Our mission is to build relationships and ministry partnerships which position us for the answer to Christ's prayer that all God's people be one in a way that transforms the region. Our strategies are to

PRAY To blanket the region with continual prayer and worship
WITNESS To saturate the region with the gospel witness of Jesus Christ
TRANSFORM To mobilize initiatives to transform our communities with God's love
GUARD To guard the well-being of the church through reconciliation, relationship, accountability, intercession and spiritual discernment
Many partnerships; one mission: Lancaster County transformed by the Kingdom of God

Reading Regional Transformation Network

Craig Nanna, Director
P.O. Box 8188, Reading, PA 19603
Phone: (610) 371-8386   Email: craignanna@readingdove.org

Reading House of Prayer

Chad Eberly, Director
Phone: (610) 373-9900   Email: ChadE@rhop.net www.rhop.net

Uniting leaders together in strategic Kingdom relationships for the purpose of transformation in the Reading region. Our priorities include advancing the Kingdom of God in the Reading region through relationship, the unity of the body of Christ, the house of prayer, and strategic initiatives that will produce transformation.

Life Transforming Ministries: Coatesville Regional

Bill Shaw, Executive Director
643 East Lincoln Highway, P.O. Box 29, Coatesville, PA 19320
Phone: (610) 384-5393   www.QuietRevolution.org

A catalyst in the movement for church unity and community transformation. Generated out of humility and united prayer the mission of LTM is to feature the Lordship of Jesus Christ by being a conduit for the development of trusting cross cultural relationships and incubator of collaborative ministry initiatives.

Lebanon Valley Prayer Network

Stephen J. Sabol, Executive Director
825 North Seventh Street, Lebanon, PA 17046
Phone: (717) 273-9258

The Lebanon Valley Prayer Network exists to lay a foundation of worship and intercessory prayer for the purpose of birthing transformation in the Lebanon Valley.

Lebanon 222

Jay McCumber, Director
515 Cumberland Street, Lebanon, PA 17042
Phone: (717) 279-5683

The Lebanon 222 Team exists to discern and implement God's heart for the Lebanon Valley.

Capital Region Pastors' Network

Dave Hess, President
Jo Wright, Ministry Assistant
P. O. Box 9, Camp Hill, PA 17001-0009
Phone: 717.909.1906   Email: c.reg.pastors@pa.net

We are a network of pastors in the Capital Region of Pennsylvania committed to Christ and to developing relationships among pastors, rooted in prayer, which lead to partnerships in ministry bearing the fruit of revival.

York Prays

Jim Herbert, Pastor of Emmanuel Christian Fellowship
2309 East Philadelphia Street, York, PA 17402
Phone: 717-840-0840   Email: jimherbert@ecfyork.com
www.yorkprays.com

The York Coalition for Transformation is a collaboration of men and women of God who are committed to *sustained Godly transformation* in York City and County.